Security. Cooperation. Governance.

SECURITY.
COOPERATION.
GOVERNANCE.

*The Canada-United States
Open Border Paradox*

Christian Leuprecht
and
Todd Hataley
Editors

University of Michigan Press
Ann Arbor

Published in the United States of America by the
University of Michigan Press
Printed and bound by CPI Group (UK) Ltd, Croydon, CR0 4YY

First published October 2023

A CIP catalog record for this book is available from the British Library.

Library of Congress Cataloging-in-Publication Data

Names: Leuprecht, Christian, 1973– editor
https://orcid.org/0000-0001-9498-4749 | Hataley, Todd S. (Todd Steven), 1963– editor. |
    Michigan Publishing (University of Michigan), publisher.
Title: Security. Cooperation. Governance. : The Canada-United States open border paradox
    / Christian Leuprecht and Todd Hataley, editors.
Description: Ann Arbor : University of Michigan Press, 2023. | Includes bibliographical
    references and index.
Identifiers: LCCN 2023018051 (print) | LCCN 2023018052 (ebook) |
    ISBN 9780472075713 (hardcover : acid-free paper) | ISBN 9780472055715 (paper :
    acid-free paper) | ISBN 9780472903054 (OA ebook)
Subjects: LCSH: Border security—Canadian-American Border Region. | Border security—
    United States. | Border security—Canada. | Canadian-American Border Region—
    Security measures. | Canadian-American Border Region—Politics and government.
    | United States—Relations—Canada. | Canada—Relations—United States. | United
    States—Commerce—Security measures—Canada. | Canada—Commerce—Security
    measures—United States.
Classification: LCC JV6483.S45 2023 print) | LCC JV6483 (ebook) | DDC 327.73071—
    dc23/eng/20230705
LC record available at https://lccn.loc.gov/2023018051
LC ebook record available at https://lccn.loc.gov/2023018052

DOI: https://doi.org/10.3998/mpub.12393633

Library of Congress Control Number: 2023018051

An electronic version of this book is freely available, thanks in part to the support of libraries
working with Knowledge Unlatched (KU). KU is a collaborative initiative designed to make
high quality books Open Access for the public good. More information about the initiative
and links to the Open Access version can be found at www.knowledgeunlatched.org.

The University of Michigan Press's open access publishing program is made possible
thanks to additional funding from the University of Michigan Office of the Provost and the
generous support of contributing libraries.

Contents

Digital materials related to this title can be found on the Fulcrum platform via the following citable URL: https://doi.org/10.3998/mpub.12393633

Illustrations

Figures

Table

Acronyms

BIG	Borders in Globalization
BPRI	Border Policy Research Institute
BTB	Beyond the Border
CANPASS	Canadian Passenger Accelerated Service System
CBP/OBP	US Customs and Border Protection/Office of Border Patrol
CBSA	Canada Border Services Agency
CSG West	Council of State Governments—West
EDL	Enhanced Drivers License
EMBC	Emergency Management BC
FAST	Free and Secure Trade
IBET	Integrated Border Enforcement Team
ICE	US Immigration and Customs Enforcement
IMTC	International Mobility & Trade Corridor
MOU	Memorandum of Understanding
NAFTA	North American Free Trade Agreement
NEXUS	*Program name; not an acronym*
NGO	Nongovernmental Organization
OR	Oregon
PACE	Pacific Corridor Enterprise Council (see also below)
PACE	Peace Arch Crossing Entry (see also above)
PCC	Pacific Coast Collaborative
PNEMA	Pacific Northwest Emergency Management Agreement
PNWBHA	Pacific Northwest Border Health Alliance
PNWER	Pacific Northwest Economic Region

RCMP   Royal Canadian Mounted Police
SBD   Smart Border Declaration
WA   Washington State
WHTI   Western Hemisphere Travel Initiative

Acknowledgments

This book has been a long time coming. The project turned out to be far more complex and involved than we could have anticipated. No one had ever tried to study an entire international border from the bottom up, from the perspective of substate jurisdictions, let through a security lens. While there is plenty of literature using a top-down approach of methodological nationalism, as this volume shows, given the confluence of dynamics of twenty-first-century bordering processes, this conventional approach to studying borders in general, and border security in particular, is highly problematic. It yields selective, distorted and misleading results that, in the end, perpetuate suboptimal border policy choices by central governments.

Since this had never been attempted before anywhere, we first had to develop a suitable method, and then we had to find the right expertise. On both counts we underestimated just how ambitious that would prove. That is partly the reason why every chapter in this volume was written by a team of scholars, some of whom are also former border practitioners, who often brought different yet complementary perspectives to help achieve our aim. This turned out to be a bit of a flying-the-plane-while-building-it exercise. To achieve the robust, systematic, and parallel approach to the chapters that you are about to enjoy, we prodded authors through multiple rounds of revisions. We applaud and appreciate their patience in supporting us in seeing this project through. We are exceptionally proud of them and their culmination.

The project would not have materialized without the leadership in border studies provided by Emmanuel Brunet-Jailly at the University of Victoria. Funding from his Social Sciences and Humanities Research Council of Canada Partnership Grant #895 2012 1022 on Borders in Globalization (BIG) was instrumental to realizing the project, as was proficient administrative support by his team, especially Nicole Beates-Eamer. On the Ontario chapter we want to acknowledge research assistance by Hayley McNorton. We should also acknowledge the Institute of Intergovernmental Relations at Queen's University, whose endowment provided for the funds that make this book open access.

The result is so unique and different, and makes so important a contribution, that the book was picked up by the first and only press we approached. That speaks volumes for a manuscript whose primary source of data is Canada. We are grateful to Elizabeth Demers, who believed in this manuscript from the outset, and to Haley Winkle for helping to connect the many loose ends. Mary Hashman ensured the manuscript's layout and delivery, and Daniel Otis did an very proficient job at a final set of copy edits. We tried their patience as we struggled quite a bit with how best to realize a reviewer's proposal to add a conclusion to the manuscript. That delayed delivery of the volume to the publisher for several months, but once the conclusion came together and we recalibrated the introduction, we thought the book was much better, and we thank both anonymous reviewers for their valuable expertise. We are also grateful to the many people who took time to provide feedback on different chapters and different stages of the manuscript as a whole; the quality of the chapters reflects their extensive input along the way. We also want to acknowledge Anne Holley-Hime, who yet again worked her magic on copyediting.

In the end, we hope that this book prods decision-makers and practitioners to approach policy concerning the Canada–US border in a more nuanced fashion, but also that it drives a more differentiated method to the study of borders and bordering processes. The global community of exceptional scholars in border studies from across the disciplines has been a real inspiration to us, as people and as scholars, and our dialogue with that community was a major impetus for this book.

Christian Leuprecht and Todd Hataley
Kingston, Canada
March 2023

Foreword

Passing Through the United States–Canada Border

Christopher Sands

Borders have long been key to regulating the interactions among political communities in general, and in and across North America in particular. Borders are the front line of state-to-state interaction, the point where differences and similarities either cause friction or are managed and resolved. How borders manage or resolve friction is at the heart of this book. As a living laboratory, the Canada–United States border has emerged as an example for the global community of a complex twenty-first-century border that is both multilayered and collaborative. Borders are dynamic, they evolve and mature, all as part of the ongoing bordering process. The authors of this book observe, document, and theorize about the nature of the Canada–United States border, giving readers insight into a living-borders laboratory of multilevel and cross-jurisdictional policymaking.

Readers of this book will come to appreciate the tension inherent to border policy, and how international relations theory sharpens our understanding of borders as points of connection and disconnection between people and peoples. Historically, borders—disputes and cooperation, fortifications, and liberalization—are central to understanding the dynamics of US–Canada relations. The US–Canada border is a critical case study whose lessons, so well documented in this volume, are relevant to borders and neighbors beyond North America.

Contributions to this book illustrate the extent to which local geography, economic linkages, and political engagement on border policy shape outcomes and opportunities. But local input does not weigh heavily in national decision-making about the border, and federal officials do not have the capacity to micromanage local affairs. Under the aegis of bilateral relations there is considerable variation, experimentation, and adaptation across the length of the US–Canada border, despite efforts to standardize regulatory and inspection regimes by both countries.

Border disputes were the predominant concerns of the United States and British North America from 1776 until 1867, when Britain amalgamated most of its North American colonies and territories to form the Dominion of Canada, and they continued into the interwar period of the first half of the twentieth century. Unregulated cross-border activities, such as illegal migration, trade in alcohol, and even the cross-border smuggling of clothing and precious gems led to the creation of the US Border Patrol (formed in 1924 and initially called the Mounted Patrol), the building of immigration services at the border (starting in 1905), and the establishment and deployment to western Canada of the Royal Canadian Mounted Police (formed in 1873 and initially called the North-West Mounted Police).

After World War II, the two countries looked at the integration of military production in wartime as a model, which allowed for specialization and comparative advantages that could provide mutual benefits. A series of bilateral agreements soon followed, from the US–Canada Defense Production Sharing Agreement (1956) and North American Aerospace Defense Command (NORAD) (1958), to the Automotive Products Trade Agreement (also known as the Auto Pact, 1965), culminating in the Canada–United States Free Trade Agreement (CUSFTA 1988). The CUSFTA explicitly eliminated "national content" as a designation to prevent either country from adopting domestic preferences and introduced a rule-of-origin system that calculated "North American content" by an agreed formula. The North American Free Trade Agreement (NAFTA 1992) and eventually the United States–Mexico-Canada Agreement (USMCA 2020) also based tariff-free market access on a rule of origin that determined what qualified as "North American" content.

Recalling the relative openness of this period is not just an exercise in nostalgia. It helps to explain the context of the chapters in this book. In the early 1990s when the CUSFTA was being implemented, I ran a trade and investment office for the State of Michigan in Port Huron. A city of 35,000 people, Port Huron is at one end of the Blue Water Bridge that connects to Sarnia, Ontario. It was common for people in these communities to cross the border to meet a friend for lunch, go shopping, or visit family. There was also illicit transit of the border that took advantage of the relative ease of crossing to traffic in drugs, weapons, counterfeit goods, and even people.

The CUSFTA built on this relative ease of crossing by individuals to facilitate commercial traffic. In the automotive industry, "just-in-time" logistics capitalized on the ease of crossing the border to deliver parts to assembly plants as they were needed, saving costs by eliminating the need to maintain an inventory. Slowly, the ease of crossing the border transformed border communities like Port Huron. When the border took longer to cross, and the paperwork for customs became more onerous, truck drivers planned to stop for gas, a meal, or even an overnight stay. Warehouses stored goods until they were ordered from across the border. Mechanics specializing in trucks were ready for repairs and safety checks in border communities. Near Port Huron, there was a Canadian National (CN) rail tunnel, and Great Lakes shipping passed by all day and night. A marine services economy, like the one supporting truck and rail, was available, too. After the free trade agreement, this commerce grew in volume, but increasingly, it was just passing through the community. When the trucks, trains, and ships no longer stopped, the businesses that had grown up to support this commerce began to disappear.

The September 11, 2001, terrorist attacks on the United States prompted new security measures and inspection requirements at the border between the United States and Canada. Then came pandemics. In 2003 an outbreak of Sudden Acute Respiratory Syndrome (SARS) in Toronto and Vancouver tested the coordination between public health systems in Canada, where the outbreak emerged, and in the United States, which sought to stop the spread. In 2008, the United States, Canada, and Mexico developed the first North American Plant and Animal Pandemic Influenza plan to capture the lessons learned from SARS for future coordination in a pandemic. These plans saw the border as a tool for slowing the spread of a highly contagious virus and provided a blueprint that governments would follow when COVID-19 emerged in 2020.

The takeaway for readers of this book is that the United States and Canada have developed a dynamic, collaborative process for managing their border, from which strategic benefits have accrued across the continent and in local communities. For almost a century, the United States and Canada have managed their border relationship with local, regional, national, and international initiatives and solutions, keeping the border "working" for both states. With globalization, even people who live far from the border in the United States and Canada cannot escape its effects on their security, prosperity, and health. Borders matter not just to those who live in the borderlands, but to those who live well beyond the border as well.

ONE

Introduction

Christian Leuprecht, Todd Hataley, and Emmanuel Brunet-Jailly

This book is about security along the Canada–United States border. At and beyond the border, how security is constructed is commonly portrayed as a rational process, largely driven by policies made by central governments. The findings from the chapters in this volume challenge both propositions: the rational nature of border security, and the dominant role of central governments in making border security policy. To the contrary, the findings suggest that local and sectoral input into the bordering process often outweighs that of central governments and mediates it substantially. Far from rational, border security policy emerges as multilevel governance involving power relationships that are dispersed across vertical and horizontal axes and public-private partnerships. Institutional state-to-state relationships still matter, but an institutionalist approach alone cannot fully explain the transformation of the security relationship between two neighboring states over recent decades: it fails to account for the way local dynamics intervene in bordering processes.

The aim of this book, then, is to change how people think about Canada's border with the United States. It is also meant to change the way people think about borders in North America. And it intends to change how people think about borders in general. Specifically, this book makes four novel contributions:

To begin, it is the first systematic empirical study of a country's entire border to challenge a monolithic construction of state borders. Commonly we refer to the Canada–US border as a singular entity. However, this book suggests there are actually several Canada–US borders that are informed by logics of cooperation, coordination, and collaboration. Differences among these Canada–US borderlands have led to different forms of governance, which are informed by different scales and border practices that are specialized by sector. In other words, this book shows the extent to which Canada–US borderlands are characterized by borders that are "nested" and "multiscalar" in terms of their quintessentially distinguishing features. Instead of a single international border dyad, it turns out that this dyad, like all international borders, is characterized by extensive variation along and across the border. Yet decisions on managing the peripheries along the border tend to be centralized in national capitals, even more so since the turn of the millennium. This increasingly centralized and uniform approach to border policy is not fit for the purposes of highly variegated borders and the specialized requirements of regional cross-border communities.

Second, this book makes the case for a more nuanced approach to state borders. Those differences are inherent in the many different transborder links at the substate level that are so important to regional and local communities but often get lost in the conventional realist perspective. So the book can also be read as a critique of the methodological nationalism that pervades the study of "international borders," and of the shift away from traditional border functions such as state-level security and the maintenance of territorial integrity.

Third, by documenting these transborder, regional community links, the book shows how the border has been moving away from the actual boundary line. Ergo, the third objective of this book is to reframe our traditional thinking about borders as geographic limits on state power or territoriality, to that of a border regime, where power and politics are geographically and functionally dispersed and a common set of interests, institutions, ideology, and ideas shapes the trajectory of border change.

Fourth, the book posits the open-border paradox: borders depend on extensive cross-border cooperation for their effectiveness and legitimacy (Brunet-Jailly 2007, 351–57). At a minimum, the bordering process, be it cooperative or otherwise, is dialectical, driven by actors and contingent on structural frameworks. Open borders are well managed and multiscalar, reliant on extensive cross-border cooperation at multiple governmental and nongovernmental levels that cluster across borderlands.

In sum, the book challenges a long- and well-established functionalist and statist literature on center-periphery relations regarding the formation of Western states and their territorial dominance—i.e., their territoriality and the exercise of sovereignty and control over their peripheries, which is particularly salient in economic, social, and cultural matters but also in security and border security. In this book each chapter documents how, despite the clear presence of federal agencies and officials, local and regional organizations (public, private, nonprofit) play a fundamental role in the bordering process and concurrent bordering policy. The chapters also detail how the intricate roles of culture and socioeconomic forces factor into policy implementation across the borderlands and straddle the boundary line.

However intuitive it may seem, there is relatively little methodical empirical research to support these propositions. So this book is not merely a study of Canada's border with the United States. Rather, it treats the Canada–US border as a laboratory of experimentation—seven laboratories of experimentation to be exact, that cover the length of the land border. To the best of our knowledge, no other study has hitherto taken such a systematic approach to comparing two adjacent countries' entire land border dyad.[1] By virtue of its length, Canada's border with the United States lends itself well to this task precisely because it is so diverse. At the same time, it is limited to two countries, which makes it easier to compare differences across regions than if multiple countries were involved; it is a most-similar-systems design to facilitate within-case comparison. It is also a peaceful and well-established border, which makes it relatively easy to study. Fieldwork along many of the most contentious borders that stand to benefit from the approach of this book is notoriously difficult and treacherous, so Canada's border with the United States offers a natural experiment for research into cross-border cooperation with implications beyond North America. To be clear, the purpose is not to study Canada–US cross-border relations, or the state of the border between the two countries. Instead, the book studies this border as a "living laboratory" that gives the contributors to this volume an in-depth look at the mechanics of a modern/global border. As a living laboratory of borderlands, the Canada–US borderland challenges the established literature of center-periphery relationships in which social science has established the primacy of governments' centers over their peripheries; i.e., our collective works points to changing patterns in territorial politics and the general understanding that states' policies delineate effective boundary lines across borderland regions and design and implement border policies. In this book the evidence underscores that in our era of globalization, central state border policies mediate a multitude of partnerships where substate governments, nonpublic actors, and the private sector also play critical roles, which results in varied, nested, and multiscalar border regimes.

Governing Borderlands

The relationship between territory and power is commonly understood as territorial politics and territoriality (Elden 2013; Sassen 2006; Gottmann 2007)—that is, how the center organizes peripheral spaces, and the role of borders and boundaries in delineating the extent of power relations across a given territory. However, the evidence in this book suggests that this conventional state-centric and territorialist logic fails to account for the variable geometries of spatialities and functionalities of current bordering processes.

Initially, the tension between center and periphery was understood as rooted in a territory and its *Leitkultur* (Lipset and Rokkan 1967). The center leverages the institutions of the state to oppress communities at the periphery: Uighurs at the periphery of China, Jammu and Kashmiris at the peripheries of India and Pakistan, or Basques straddling the border of France and Spain. As the center extends its dominant form of nationalism to the legal limits of the peripheral culture, tensions between the center and its peripheries tend to be analyzed through the lens of the peripheral ethnic cultures. Rokkan and Urwin (1982) suggested that the center develops from a specific culture of privilege that encompasses both economic and political powers, expanding into areas of policy such as military and administrative domination and uniformization. Shils (1975) posited the center as a dominating core where a preponderance of economic, political, and institutional networks converge. This proposition holds that greater power emerges out of a plurality of diversity in a progressive process of unity. This approach informs the common perspective on the Canada–US border, which the findings in this book challenge. It is also invoked to explain the processes of expansion and of submission of peripheral regions. For instance, Lipset and Rokkan (1967) propose that territory and culture are related. French political scientist Duverger described the ethnonationalist center's domination over peripheral minority nationalisms (Seiler 1989); he contrasted the democratic and bottom-up forms of periphery nationalisms against the autocratic and top-down forms of dominant ethno-nationalism, which he saw in many imperialistic and nondemocratic countries. For Seiler (1989) forms of peripheral nationalism were manifestations of resistance to a domineering center attempting to extend its national and cultural domination to all aspects of the state onto the peripheries. Thus, for Seiler, peripheries were places of resistance.

In the early twenty-first century those views have adopted a modernist paradigm—that function should be the new domineering organizing principle of social and political organizations. For Keating (2008), however, this paradigm reached its pinnacle long ago, and it is increasingly obsolete. Instead, scholars have been rediscovering the relevance of territorial politics to state transformation and transnational integration. In other words, the politics of peripheries actually matter. According to Keating, the modernist approach originates with Durkheim, who wrote "we can almost say that a people is as much advanced as territorial divisions are superficial" (1964, 187). Keating (2008, 60) cites Karl Deutsch (1966, 80) and the politics of submission: that state territories formed around centers as they expanded their economic, cultural, political, and institutional influence into peripheries. Deutsch's modernist argument was rooted in the view that regional, peripheral, or community cleavages were not found in sovereign governments (Keating 2008, 61). For Deutsch, political communities made governments, and state-building processes either brought cultural communities together or gave rise to secessions and independent states. Similar views are echoed by historians of the construction of modern states such as France, Italy, and Germany, which were the result of nationalistic processes the center used to integrate peripheries. The resulting formation of borders was considered perfectly "natural" (Keating 2008, 61). In reality, this bordering process reflects relations of power of the center over the periphery.

To account for the resurgence of various forms of nationalisms in the regional and other political peripheries of many European states (Belgium, France, Spain, the United Kingdom), Keating proposes "Bringing Territory Back In" (2008, 62). Of note is the emergence of new vocabularies to describe these rediscovered phenomena of antithesis to the center: multilevel governance (Hooghe and Marks 2001), spatial rescaling (Brenner 2004), post-Westphalian order (Blair 1999), postnationalism, the end of territory (Badie 1995), and the borderless world (Ohmae 1995). The vast literature on the regional and the local is an implicit critique of the view that territorial politics is only about the construction of the state, depoliticization, and the search for efficiencies in local and regional administration.

With the advent of globalization, borderland scholars documented increasing tensions between centers and peripheries, focused largely on economic-integration tensions. For instance, Ohmae (1995) and Chen (2005) documented how integrated borderlands are being pulled together across boundary lines to form international economic hubs or economic cross-border regions. Their work focuses on the role of market forces in integrating economic regions; both authors document how market forces pull borderland areas together into global economic regions. Ohmae (1990) suggests that progressive state decentralization leads to the emergence of economic regions that span international boundaries. For instance, one such region spans the Mekong watershed, bringing together seven states (Cambodia, China, India, Laos, Myanmar, Thailand, and Vietnam); another is the maritime regions of the Bohai Sea and the Yellow Sea that connect China, both Koreas, and Japan (Chen 2005). The borders that run across large urban regions in Europe need not impose *barriers* but can actually be *resources* for the economic actors (Sohn 2020). Trade across the borderland is a distinct competitive advantage and can act as a catalyst to mobilize the whole borderland region as a growth strategy. Although Sohn (2020) is unable to identify specific drivers, he suggests that specific "resources" are activated because "above all [they are] social and historically contingent constructions" (2020, 308).

One novel contribution of this book is the finding that, in support of economic incentives, nationalist and security concerns may leverage similar resources across borderlands, such as the need to cooperate, coordinate, or collaborate across borders (Leuprecht et al. 2021). The need to leverage resources on both sides of the border integrates the borderlands across the boundary line. Harnessing such cross-border synergies changes the nature of the border. Cross-border cooperation is necessary to enhance economic interactions, economic integration, and economic growth (Brunet-Jailly 2022b). On the one hand, cross-border regions, such as the Southeast Asian Greater Mekong Subregion and the European Union versions (called Euroregions), are sites of surprising economic growth and outstanding economic cooperation and integration. On the other hand, they are sites of intense local and regional politics, along with concurrent functional, financial, and infrastructure planning that spans boundary lines.

In North America, by contrast, economic integration is less impressive because its primary locus is the Great Lakes region and the adjoining sub-state jurisdictions on either side of the international border. Although this may seem counterintuitive, the evidence in this book shows that integration does not actually extend across all of the Canada–US borderlands, or of the US–Mexico borderlands for that matter. That outcome is a function of a boundary distinguished by differences. In Latin America and Africa cross-border regions are much smaller, and in these regions, cross-border synergies may be constrained by tensions between states, regions, and communities, and also by corruption and uncontrolled criminality. The African Union and Latin American organizations such as MERCOSUR (Spanish for The Southern Common Market) note that economic integration across the Common Market of the South or the Latin American Free

Trade Association is impeded by a lack of continental economic integration (Brunet-Jailly 2022b, 10).

Yet literature on cross-border integration neglects the security implications of political or functional relationships for borderlands. The literature does not account for the fact that international relations theory explicitly flags the role of specific rules, such as the exclusive exercise of violence within a sovereign territory, or the basic idea of territorial integrity as fundamental to relations between members of the international community. How to theorize the changing nature of borders in a globalizing world is an open debate, one characterized by concepts such as the vacillating border (Balibar 2002), mobile border (Amilhat-Szary and Giraut 2015), and borders in motion (Konrad 2015). However, these discussions remain fundamentally state-centric. Although they engage Agnew's notion of "the territorial trap" (1994), they fail to transcend a territorialist logic, let alone reconcile it with the prevailing security imperative.

In stressing the concepts of "border-zone" (La Pradelle 1928), "bending border" (Chen 2005), "borderlands" (Brunet-Jailly 2007), "border regions" (Sohn 2020), "states' border realism" (Iwashita 2016), "borderities" (Amilhat-Szary and Giraut 2015), or "borderscapes" (Rajaram & Grundy Warr 2007, Brambilla 2015) to understand the nature of borders and border regions, the literature on cross-border integration posits states as central to border questions. Innovative approaches such as "borderscaping" (Brambilla 2015) underscore the importance of hegemonic and counterhegemonic imaginaries in their "territorialist imperatives," but offer only inchoate glimpses into the changing logic of borders because they remain conceptually anchored in statist/territorialist views of borders (Agnew 1994; Brenner 1999; Stark 2016).

By contrast, this book expands beyond Sassen's notion of "borderings and bordering capabilities" (2015, 45). It draws on Laine's (2016) ideas that bordering operates at different scales depending on multiple and heterogeneous agents. Burkner (2019) observes that cooperation across borders gives rise to "complexity of agent scaling" (Burkner 2016, 84); that is, forms of social practices lead to continual adjustment of social relations across scales that span borders. The book's findings, however, suggest that various forms of local or regional agency may not always exist, or that they can develop alongside policy developments and implementation through *coordination, cooperation, and collaboration* (Leuprecht et al. 2021; Castaner and Olivera 2020). Indeed, at a stage of coordination cross-border relationships may take the form of policy parallelism, in which partners share their respective goals. The partnership is marked by collaboration when partner countries' help each other implement both their respective and their common goals on both sides of the boundary line. Country partners may also choose to extend mutual collaboration beyond particular objectives. So, this book asks: What happens to security when it depends on issues that span international boundaries? Does it manifest in forms of coordination, cooperation, or collaboration? What forms of governance are at work? At what scales and in which social practices do they show up?

Nesting Canada's Borderlands at North American Scale

Katzenstein (1996) has referred to Canada as "arguably the first postmodern state par excellence" because its past reflects the foundation of much global political, social, and economic transformation: Canada is a federal state with a colonial history, and an increasingly diverse settler population composed of waves of immigrants over nearly two centuries. At a time when free trade was being discussed and the North American Free Trade Agreement was being implemented across North America, Canada seemed to be ahead of globalization, and, in Stephen Clarkson's words, "ahead of the borderless world in which governments play a lesser role while markets are liberated to operate for the greater good of the greater (global) community" (2001, 502).

In the grand scheme of the global economy, Canada is relatively small, with a relatively small government that is adapting from a "multilevel state" into the higher levels of "global governance" (Clarkson 2001, 503). Although it is the smallest among the G7 economies, its disproportionate levels of connectivity make it a key player in the globalizing world. During the latter decades of the twentieth century, Canada underwent a strategic transformation that was domestically consequential: in regionalizing its economic policy, Canada jettisoned previous national policies (Courchene and Telmer 1998), and Canadian public policy underwent a general internationalization (Doern, Pal, and Tomlin 1996). Contra the nationalist impetus of yesteryear, part of this great transformation was the rediscovery of the Canadian province as the appropriate scale for enhancing innovation in the post-Fordist, nascent information-communication economy (Clarkson 2001, 516). The regionalization of public policy was complemented by major cities, some significantly larger than some provinces, pressing their leading role in policy debates. Canada's urban regions underwent major democratic reorganization to position them as leaders in this new economic paradigm, through the emergence of a multilevel "nested" state in which multiple administrative, economic, and international borders organize the workings of regional knowledge economies that are embedded in the global economy (Brunet-Jailly 2022a).

Canada's "provincial particularisms" are at the core of Clarkson's argument. As this book suggests, those regional/provincial economic and cultural particularisms and the security implications that follow now straddle the boundary line with the United States. As postulated by Stephenson (1974), the prior pan-Canadian west-east economy has been shifting to a north-south relationship between Canadian provinces and American states, with an arrangement in the form of the Pacific NorthWest Economic Region (PNWER), which consists of five US states and five Canadian provinces and their twenty policy working groups (PNWER, 2022).

While this may be intuitive for US states that border Canada, and indeed the thirty-eight US states that have Canada as their primary trading partner, it is not true for the United States as a whole. For most of Canada's existence, initially as a colony and then as a country, Canada's vantage point has been to look south. The same does not hold for Americans who, by and large, tend not to look north (or south, for that matter, the Monroe doctrine notwithstanding), at least not in a similar fashion; since the end of the World War II, America's interests have been global, with a particular focus on Europe. As northern Canada becomes more accessible, borders in the north have been figuring more prominently. Canada's north actually borders seven countries physically: seven circumpolar countries complement its land border with the United States (Denmark, including Greenland and the Faroe Islands, Finland, Iceland, Norway, Sweden, and Russia).

However, Canada's place on the map is only a small part of the border story. In a globalized world especially, borders transcend the physical demarcations between sovereign states. The contemporary understanding of borders extends to institutional practices that locate the border away from the physical borderline. This perspective also offers greater appreciation for the differences among regional borders, including those between the Cascadia Pacific Northwest, the Great Lakes region, the Maritimes, and the North. These regions have distinctive local cultural, economic, and historical attributes, which are articulated by local border stakeholders. Individually, these regions are characterized by unique regional practices. As a whole, they are peripheries nested within and subject to hegemonic sovereign state-level policy and a national border narrative that gives expression to a dominant historical, economic, and cultural legacy that does not necessarily scale with regional practices.

Early studies described the Canada–US border as a static geographic phenomenon, but today the border is viewed as dynamic and variable. Scholars such as Boggs (1940), Whittlesey (1944), Jones (1945), and Fischer (1957) maintained a state-centric view of borders as rigid lines of defense, created by humans and subject to change through human interaction. These initial studies, although acknowledging the human impact on the border, were remiss in exploring the border per se and its underlying bordering processes as an object of analysis. A revival in border scholarship in the early 1980s produced new approaches to understanding borders, beyond the border as merely a static line (e.g., Strassoldo and Delli Zotti 1982; Sack 1986; Paasi 1996, 1999; Brunet-Jailly 2005). Yet scholarship on the Canada–US border remained firmly focused on the border merely as a component of larger issues of federal politics, such as immigration, security, and trade.

Charles Doran (1984) laid the foundations of international relations research on the diverse dynamics of cross-border relationships within international politics by conceptually specifying the "psychological-cultural," "trade-commercial," and "political-strategic" dimensions of the Canada–US relationship. This approach has inspired decades of scholarship on Canada–US relations (e.g., Hale 2012; Gattinger and Hale 2010). His book *Forgotten Partnership* differs from this volume insofar as it stressed the "borderless" character of Canada–US relations, and not the regional character of cross-border relations discussed in this volume. Doran emphasized "Canada in the world" in the context of NAFTA and NATO. This volume differs markedly in approach from the methodological nationalism that has been the dominant paradigm in analyzing the binational and bilateral relationship. Doran's perspective examined international security on the assumption that Canada and the United States were closely aligned, such that the border virtually disappeared. That perspective purposely downplayed the border in the context of international trade. It was as though the border had disappeared so that goods, services, and people could move unimpeded, that is, "efficiently."

By contrast, in this book Canada's borders are considered a function of regionally differentiated practices and processes shaped by complex connections and regional relationships with the United States and other global entities and actors. We analyze how bordering practices vary with regional histories, geographies, and interests. Although a similar situation exists in states across the globe, the novelty of this book is that it conveys an alternative method for maximizing the self-interest of Canada, and the dual interest in North America of Canada and the United States. Canada's borders are regional in character, dispersed among trade corridors, sup-

ply chains, seaports, food-producing communities, and international organizations, among other factors. This dispersal of border functions makes
border management, and especially security functions, more difficult and
highlights the importance of nonconventional border-management activities to achieve coherent policy. The book discusses how traditional notions
of border security ("defend the line") no longer reflect the reality of bordering processes.

Canada's borders exist in the context of the larger, shared North American borderlands (e.g., Kilroy, Rodriguez Sumano, and Hataley 2013;
Andreas and Snyder 2000). The September 11, 2001, terrorist attacks on
New York City and Washington, DC, marked a turning point in the study
not only of the Canada–US border, but borders in a continental context.
While some scholars expressed concerns about globalization and economic
liberalization eroding the function of the US borders, Andreas (2003)
argued that territoriality continued to matter: US borders were not eroding, but rather their function was shifting to address challenges from global
economic liberalism and the absence of war as a tool for territorial gain.
Although Andreas acknowledged the fluidity of borders and the fact that
border functions moved beyond the geographic boundary line, he had little
to say about the underlying process that produced this shift. Moreover, an
underlying assumption in much of the literature at the time was that borders were homogenous and responded to a stimulus in a like manner. Flynn
(2003) echoed Andreas insofar as he maintained that borders were critical
to maintaining territorial integrity, and that the best way to accomplish
this was to move some of the tradition functions of the border away from
the physical line. The re-entrenchment of borders in North America post-
9/11 led some scholars to suggest that changing border strategies meant
the Canada–US border was becoming "Mexicanized" (Andreas 2005). This
comparison, between the Canada–US border and the US–Mexico border, grew out of changing trends along the Canada–US border, including
the politicization of the border and its receiving more attention from law
enforcement and the military.

In contrast to the conventional statist-based, realist response to the
9/11 terrorist attacks, regional security emerged as an alternative paradigm
to jointly secure the perimeter of North America, protecting the continent
from outside threats such as terrorism and transnational organized crime.
To this end, the Security and Prosperity Partnership (SPP) was launched
in March of 2005. The SPP was to be built on five main policy initiatives, including the creation of smart, secure borders (Kilroy, Rodriguez,
and Hataley 2013). It shifted the conception of North American borders

away from maintaining the integrity of the state, toward building capacity for shared border management and the movement of North American borders away from their traditional geographic locations. For example, North American cross-border regions resulted from the competitive advantage they provided to local and regional actors as instruments of public management (Brunet-Jailly 2008, 2012). Although Canada and the United States were looking for strategies to improve the legitimate border movement of people and cargo, the SPP's overarching goal remained territorial integrity, particularly that of the United States. The Western Hemisphere Travel Initiative and the requirement that enhanced documentation was needed to enter the United States, and subsequently Canada, made it clear that compartmentalization of the Westphalian world remains the ordering principle of territorial integrity (Newman 2001).

Since 9/11, the US–Canada relationship has morphed into a continental security community whose hallmark is the extent to which mutual cooperation has led to an intentional shift of the joint border away from the actual borderline. That shift had to reconcile an inherent tension between the imperatives of "economic globalization" and "territorial security" at the US–Canada border (Alper and Loucky 2017). Kent (2011) frames US–Canadian border cooperation as a compromise between disparate national interests in which Canada is primarily concerned about trade while the United States is more concerned about terrorism and irregular migration. However, the outcome of this bilateral cross-border cooperation reflects a compromise of ideals, sovereignty, and pragmatism, one that is frequently managed from a position of indifference. Instead of focusing on security at the joint border, the United States and Canada have taken a continental approach to building a comprehensive security system around common interests related to the border, as manifest in policing, counterterrorism, intelligence, and defense to detect, disrupt, and deter threats (Hataley and Leuprecht 2019).

Ultimately, borders form part of larger borderland regions, not just physically between neighboring countries, but also at international airports, seaports, customs warehouses, and embassies, which are considered part of the borderland region because they perform quintessential border practices. These include such tasks as preclearance and issuing visas, in complex policy and governance systems that weave together both border functions and politics. This book thus problematizes borders beyond their mere geographic position at the edge of one state and the beginning of another. Canadian borders, particularly those located at the perimeter or beyond the continent, are access points to a larger shared North American and global space. The context of Canada's relationship with the United States provides for a shared yet bounded space and imagery. Canadian borders are an inextricable part of the North American region, and this informs Canadian border policy.

In sum, the chapters in this volume raise three major themes:

1. Reconceiving Canada's borders. The Mercator projection world maps that were once commonplace in classrooms suggest that Canada only borders the United States. This worldview is reinforced by the fact that the vast majority of Canadians live near the US border. That view is bolstered by the premise that Canada and the United States share the "longest undefended border in the world." Historically, culturally, and economically, Canada's southern border with the United States has been paradigmatic. Especially in the north, but also along the southern Canada–US border, technology, globalization, indigenous rights, and climate change are precipitating a more pluralistic and nuanced understanding of Canada's borders.

2. Distinctive geographies and nested bordering practices characterize regional variation across Canada's international boundary with the United States. Bordering practices have long been shown to be regionally contingent. However, this is the first study to examine the extent of regional bordering practices across an entire international border. The chapters in this volume detail and compare the unique local border practices that distinguish Canada's regional borders. The chapters explore the conditions that give rise to regional bordering practices and explain why such practices persist. Economic, cultural, and historical variables emerge as characteristics that shape—and as resources that are leveraged to shape—relationships across the border. Across Canada's peripheral borderlands, these variables share commonalities, giving rise to a bordering dialectic with a dominant singular national Canadian border.

3. Canadian borders form edges that connect a network of continental and increasingly global border nodes that are multiscalar and thus require a multilevel approach to governing Canada–US borderlands. In the age of globalization, Canada and North America are no longer the "fire proof house, far from inflammable materials" that Senator Raoul Dandurand famously posited in his 1924 speech to the League of Nations. Still, to move goods or people

into the North American space requires a significant commitment. Except for products and people moving overland through South and Latin America, getting to North America requires air and/or sea transport, which is a commitment in both time and resources that requires planning and thought. In the aftermath of the terrorist attacks in the United States on September 11, 2001, President George W. Bush's commitment to step up continental perimeter security accelerated the systematic comanagement of the joint border with Canada. The chapters in this volume thus reinforce that open borders correlate with cross-border coordination, cooperation, and collaboration in terms of effectiveness and legitimacy.

These observations raise key questions. First, why do regional borders even exist? There are plenty of studies on regional borders, usually on cross-border cooperation and governance (cf. Hataley and Leuprecht 2018; Pipkin 2018; Lange 2018). However, there is little work on the conditions that cause regional borders to persist. Second, what conditions explain the emergence of regional borders, and are these conditions the same or different from those that explain their continuity? This volume explores economics, culture, history, and institutional development as explanatory variables. Finally, how can variation in nested peripheral borders and bordering processes be reconciled with a common denominator in the form of a dominant national border? Answering this question requires us to control for differences and commonalities, for periphery and core, along the entire border, which is among the central empirical and methodological innovations of this volume. To this end, the study disentangles two opposite dynamics based on particular and common needs, values, and expectations: centripetal forces that transcend regional differences and pull commonalities toward a single national border policy, and countervailing centrifugal forces that give rise to or reinforce local or regional borders. Cross-border coordination, cooperation, and collaboration, then, generate a dialectic that reifies and reinforces regional bordering processes.

As a theme, regional borders harken not only to the regions that characterize the border, but also to the broader continental context of borders within North America as a region. These borders are local and fluid, yet by virtue of cross-border coordination, cooperation, and collaboration they reflect multilateral characteristics of the whole continent, enabling distinctive border cultures and social practices. These bordering practices include strategies such as relocating borders away from the actual borderline, developing cross-border structures and partnerships that address specific local needs, and developing a nuanced appreciation of border challenges in a local context.

Socioeconomic Factors of Regional Bordering Processes

Borders, border policy, and the bordering process are commonly associated with activities of the state because the state traditionally allocates resources along state borders for purposes such as security, revenue collection, and demarcation. This reductionist state-centric approach has restricted the conventional analysis of borders and border policies to central state-based actors who make and implement policy in a uniform and consistent manner. Yet that approach reflects an inchoate understanding of the stakeholders involved in bordering practices, which are equally shaped by nonstate actors and organizations (Parker and Adler-Nissen 2012). These stakeholders participate in the bordering process in meaningful and tangible ways as organizations and individuals (Cooper and Perkins 2012). The same border thus has different meanings, depending on the stakeholder (Balibar 2002). The regional borders observed in this volume reflect the diverse ideas, interests, and ideologies of local stakeholders. Border stakeholders are not geographically confined, nor is the actual border. The concept of border regions recognizes that border stakeholders are dispersed, but cluster by regional interests, as manifested in the myriad regional border organizations and institutions mentioned in this book. The analysis shows how these regional ideas and voices are aggregated and reflected in the bordering process. To this effect, it intentionally disaggregates the actors and the processes by which borders are produced and reproduced.

Bordering practices can produce and re-produce the status quo, but they also change how the border functions (Parker and Adler-Nissen 2012). Any descriptive analysis of the border produces a snapshot in time that illustrates functions that maintain a border and rules that govern the border regime. The studies in this book identify different functional logics across different border regions. The bordering process is most frequently shaped by social practices derived from pre-existing institutional structures, but other forces are also influential. Institutional structures that characterize national borders exhibit and assert some consistency with regard to rules and norms. At the same time, this book demonstrates the extent to which these institutional structures interact with and are interpretated by regional border stakeholders who generate locally nuanced conversations, ideas, and outcomes.

The Approach of This Study

In the spirit of qualitative comparative methods, all chapters have the same structure. Initially, the authors set the scene by contextualizing their regional border. The first section describes the principal actors for the border region: security organizations, state actors, nonstate actors (such as NGOs), associations, and interest groups. This section also operationalizes the core concepts to be used: How are safety and security understood in that regional context? That is, what are the local needs, values, and expectations? For instance, Québec refers to "public security," whereas the rest of Canada tends to refer to "public safety." The distinction is not just semantic. Security is commonly provided by a third party, which, in return for ceding certain rights, provides "freedom from" the actual occurrence of danger, injury, fear, loss, anxiety, crime, attack, and other threats. By contrast, safety is the general condition that gives rise to feeling secure. Public safety, then, is the welfare of the general public. Public security, by contrast, entails concrete measures of protection: law enforcement activities aimed at protecting goods and people. Public security covers both public and private actors, and has the strategic capacity to fulfil law enforcement functions with the objectives of maintaining order and public safety over a defined territory, and of applying the rule of law (cf. Leuprecht, Kölling, and Hataley 2019, 6).

Although security commonly pertains to threats to territorial integrity and sovereignty, Québec's conception is more expansive, in part because it has a different, more dirigiste understanding of the state and its obligation toward citizens. This section also explores the social dimension of transborder security to identify different conceptions and approaches, including the societal context that informs decision-makers and policymakers and the laws and policies that are enacted. Part of the aim in this section is to leverage societal issues and debates about border security to illustrate how representations of security differ by region.

The second section offers an environmental scan of current and persistent anthropogenic and naturogenic security issues across the region from a transboundary perspective. This scan also covers threat-mitigation strategies, with particular emphasis on efforts that transcend physical, digital, or imaginary borders.

The third section complements the second with a review of future trends and the emerging threat environment. It surveys the security challenges the border region faces, along with current and prospective trends in coordination, cooperation, and collaboration to avert these threats.

The fourth section inventories formal and informal transboundary coordination, cooperation, and collaboration agreements at the regional level, and also at the federal level when they have a bearing on that region. Informal agreements have been proliferating, so they are intentionally included. The section briefly outlines the agreement, contextualizes it, and explains the nature of the benefit(s).

The fifth section details two types of governance models. The first is concerned with the way that nested borders give rise to and manifest in multilevel governance: the nature and mechanisms of vertical arrangements currently in place between local and provincial governments, Aboriginal and provincial or local governments, provincial governments and the federal government, and so on. The second is concerned with intergovernmental affairs, notably horizontal cross-border collaborations, such as the annual meeting between the Atlantic premiers and the governors of New England.

For illustrative purpose the penultimate section takes up a policy case study to illustrate how the earlier observations manifest in practice. These case studies challenge Agnew's "territorial trap"—the conventional conception that restricts the border to the geographic borderline. These case studies demonstrate that efficient and effective management of an open border entails bordering practices that are shifting away from the actual boundary line. These case studies also reveal how territorial institutions and border arrangements are often poorly aligned to achieve economies of scale and have a synergistic effect on policy issues that span the border. In the following section we present each of our seven case studies starting on the western side of the continent with British Columbia, Cascadia, and the Pacific, and then moving eastward to Alberta and the Northwest, the Prairies and Midwest, Ontario and the Great Lakes, Québec and the Eastern Seaboard, the Atlantic and New England, and the Territorial North.

The Seven Case Studies

British Columbia, Cascadia and the Pacific. Because of its geography as a corridor along the Pacific Ring of Fire, and its history as a late arrival in the Canadian Confederation, British Columbia's security remains distinct. It has a strong presence of the Royal Canadian Mounted Police (RCMP) and also a strong and persistent presence of multiple local, regional, and provincial law enforcement agencies (and concurrent agreements) working together across border-straddling networks with their US peers. Emergency management dominates a shared understanding of public safety, including emergency and natural disaster preparations that, under the coordination of organizations such as the Pacific Northwest Economic Region, form the foundation of a pan-regional culture of coordination, cooperation, and collaboration and policy alignments, and also a culture of innovation in matters of security. Examples abound, with, for instance, PACE/CANPASS/NEXUS, Enhanced Drivers Licenses, Integrated Border Enforcement Teams, Shiprider, marine cargo, border wait time measurement, and Advanced Traveler Information Systems. In sum, the form of cross-border security governance that emerges in British Columbia leads to policy parallelism whereby multiple agencies work together to implement similar policy goals on both sides of the boundary line; the Beyond the Border Initiative of 2012 is an outstanding example of interaction and partnership between national and subnational agencies in the region.

Alberta and the Northwest. This region is landlocked, and its major urban centers are isolated and far from both provincial and international boundaries. Its economy is fossil-fuel dependent. Its security, and border security in particular, depends largely on multiple interjurisdictional arrangements, at the core of which are the Canadian Border Services Agency, the RCMP, and the Alberta Law Enforcement Response Team (ALERT). Due to the geographical isolation, the border is a lower priority. Among the 231 agreements managed by the provincial office of intergovernmental affairs, only a handful focus on the border, one focuses on intelligence (with CSIS), another one on vehicle registration (Justice Canada), and a few are about the funding of First Nations police services. A number of other agreements implement a regional approach to border and provincial security. Examples include partnerships with PNWER, the Council of State Governments West, and fire and other emergency-management organizations that bring US and Canadian regional bodies together. Interestingly, security organizations (municipal police forces, RCMP, the Canadian Border Services Agency) coordinate their operations when necessary but do not rely on formal agreements.

The Prairies and the Midwest. Because of the level of expertise necessary to assess risks in Prairie provinces, experts are required for the review of meat or wheat shipments across the international boundary line. Risk assessments have evolved with the type of threat, which may affect seeds, meat, or other agricultural exports. Each type of assessment requires expertise that is not available at the boundary line or at border gates, so the practice of preclearance, or clearing goods in advance of arriving at the border, was adopted. In the Prairie provinces it is the provincial government that reviews and implements programs with the appropriate expertise in partnerships with networks of professionals, including farms and loading and transit warehouses, all of which may be hundreds of miles from the border.

Ontario and the Great Lakes. Distinct from other Canadian provinces, Ontario's borderlands reflect the high level of trade crossing the border with the US in Ontario, and the resulting economic integration of the Great Lakes economic region. This is the second-largest urban region of eastern North America, with nearly 15 million inhabitants (Brunet-Jailly 2022a). Its geography is organized around the Great Lakes and connecting waterways, which span nearly 1,200 kilometers from Québec City to Detroit, linking the St. Lawrence River with Lake Ontario, Lake Erie, and Lake Huron. This is the largest such cross-border region in North America in terms of trade and economic size, and also in terms of integration of its industries, in particular its manufacturing automotive industries and related economic networks, which rely on just-in-time production across the boundary line. These industries now benefit from particularly sophisticated border security technologies and trusted trader programs that rely on X-ray and gamma-ray imaging and biometrics that are well adapted to road and truck transportation across this vast border region.

Québec and the Eastern Seaboard. Driven by an ambitious provincial international agenda, border security in Québec and the eastern seaboard is primarily understood as resulting from trade security interests, which are in part complemented by more traditional concerns about terrorism, violent extremism, organized crime, and irregular migration. Early in the new century the province of Québec signed agreements with adjacent US states on security cooperation and information sharing. It joined in large transboundary partnerships; in matters of immigration, for instance, all levels of government cooperate, including municipalities. However, far from being institutionalized, policing rests on personal relationships and results from nonformalized contexts.

Atlantic Canada and New England. Along the Atlantic coasts of Canada and the United States, "trade moves on saltwater" (chapter 2, 14), so border and security issues emerge along coasts and harbors. Yet the layering of security resulting from security agencies does not translate effectively to the private sector's shipping and harbor corporations. In part, this is because private harbor authorities struggle to implement security constraints that would increase costs and reduce the attraction of harbors on the continent, and also because, among the multiplicity of operators, there is a particular a lack of cooperation among private and public operators and agencies, which continues to frustrate the container-screening goals set by the Canadian Senate in 2007. In sum, security infrastructures are neglected.

The Territorial North. In the Canadian Arctic, controlling borders has long been about maritime and air monitoring of a few harbors and land crossings. It is predominantly the role of the Canadian and US military in partnership, and primarily focused on search and rescue missions in regions spanning thousands of square miles. Climate change, however, has been progressively transforming the North into a shipping destination, thus increasing security threats. These take the form of increased migration, smuggling, and criminal activities that benefit from remoteness and the generally inadequate capacity to respond in communities across the North.

These seven studies of regional transborder governance illustrate the extent to which borders are nested and the multiscalar nature of cooperation and bordering practices. The chapters are presented west to east, starting with British Columbia on the Pacific coast, followed by Alberta, the Prairies, Ontario, Québec, the Atlantic provinces, and the Territorial North. Each contribution documents the spatial complexity of cooperative transborder security arrangements.

NOTE

1. The small literature on the Canada–United States border is largely historic and/or regional in nature; e.g., *Drawing Lines in the Sand and the Snow: Border Security and North American Economic Integration*; *Borders Matter: Homeland Security and the Search for North America*; *How Much do National Borders Matter?*; *Permeable Border: The Great Lakes Basin as Transnational Region, 1650–1990*; *Arc of the Medicine Line: Mapping the World's Longest Undefended Border across the Western Plains*; *The Border: Canada, the U.S.*; *A Good and Wise Measure: The Search for the Canadian-American Boundary, 1783–1842*; and *Dispatches from the 49th Parallel*.

REFERENCES

Agnew, John. 1994. "The Territorial Trap: The Geographical Assumptions of International Relations Theory." *Review of International Political Economy* 1, no. 1: 53–80.

Alper, Don K., and James Loucky. 2017. "Canada–US Border Securitization: Implications for Binational Cooperation." *Canadian-American Public Policy* 72.

Amilhat-Szary, Anne-Laure, and Frederic Giraut. 2015. "Borderites: The Politics of Contemporary Borders." In *Borderites and the Politics of Contemporary Mobile Borders*, edited by Anne-Laure Amilhat-Szary, and Frederic Giraut. London: Palgrave Macmillan.

Andreas, Peter. 2003. "A Tale of Two Borders: The US-Mexico and U.S.-Canada

Lines After 9–11." *Center for Comparative Immigration Studies* 77: 1–14. https://escholarship.org/uc/item/63r8f039

Andreas, Peter. 2005. "The Mexicanization of the US-Canada Border: Asymmetric Independence in a Changing Security Context." *International Journal* 60, no. 2: 449–62.

Andreas, Peter, and Timothy Snyder. 2000. *The Wall Around the West: State Borders and Immigration Control in North America and Europe*. Lanham, MD: Rowman & Littlefield.

Badie, Bertrand. 1995. *La Fin des Territoires: Essai Desordre Internat*. Paris : Fayard.

Balibar, Etienne. 2002. *Politics and the Other Scene*. London: Verso.

Blair, Anthony (Tony). 1999. "Doctrine of the International Community." *BritishPoliticalSpeech*. http://www.britishpoliticalspeech.org/speech-archive.htm?speech=279

Boggs, S. Whitmore. 1940. *International Boundaries: A Study of Boundary Functions and Problems*. New York: Columbia University Press.

Brambilla, Chiara. 2015. "Exploring the Critical Potential of the Borderscapes Concept." *Geopolitics* 20, no. 1: 14–34.

Brenner, Neil. 1999. "Globalisation as Reterritorialisation: The Re-scaling of Urban Governance in the European Union." *Urban Studies* 36, no. 3: 431–51.

Brenner, Neil. 2004. *New State Spaces: Urban Governance and the Rescaling of Statehood*. Oxford: Oxford University Press.

Brunet-Jailly, Emmanuel. 2005. "Theorizing Borders: An Interdisciplinary Perspective." *Geopolitics* 10, no. 4.

Brunet-Jailly, Emmanuel. 2007. *Borderlands, Comparing Border Security in North America and Europe*. Ottawa, Canada: University of Ottawa Press.

Brunet-Jailly, Emmanuel. 2008. "Cascadia in Comparative Perspectives: Canada–US Relations and the Emergence of Cross-Border Regions." *Canadian Political Science Review* 2, no. 2.

Brunet-Jailly, Emmanuel. 2012. "In the Increasingly Global Economy, Are Borderland Regions Public Management Instruments?" *International Journal of Public Sector Management* 25, no. 6/7: 483–491. https://doi.org/10.1108/09513551211260685

Brunet-Jailly, Emmanuel. 2022a. "US-Canada Border Cities and Territorial Development Trends." In *Border Cities and Territorial Development*, edited by Eduardo Medeiros, 209–27. London: Routledge–Taylor and Francis.

Brunet-Jailly, Emmanuel. 2022b. "Cross-Border Cooperation: A Global Overview." *Alternatives, Global, Local, Political, Sage Journals* 47, no. 1: 3–17. https://doi.org/10.1177/03043754211073463

Burkner, Hans-Joachim. 2019. "Scaling and Bordering: An Elusive Relationship?" *Journal of Borderlands Studies* 34, no. 1: 71–87.

Carroll, Francis M. 2001. *A Good and Wise Measure: The Search for the Canadian-American Boundary, 1783–1842*. Toronto: University of Toronto Press.

Castaner, X., and N. Olivera. 2020. "Collaboration, Coordination and Cooperation Among Organisations: Establishing the Distinctive Meanings of These Terms Through a Systematic Literature Review." *Journal of Management* 46, no. 6: 965–1001.

Chen, Xiangming. 2005. *As Borders Bend: Transnational Spaces on the Pacific Rim*. Lanham, MD: Rowman & Littlefield.

Clarkson, Stephen. 2001. "The Multilevel State: Canada in the Semi-Periphery of Both Continentalism and Globalization." *Review of International Political Economy* 8, no. 3: 501–27. https://doi.org/10.1080/09692290110055858

Cooper, Anthony, and Chris Perkins. 2012. "Borders and Status-Functions: An Institutional Approach to the Study of Borders." *European Journal of Social Theory* 15, no. 1: 55–71.

Courchene, Thomas J., and Colin Telmer. 1998. *From Heartland to North American Region State: The Social, Fiscal and Federal Evolution of Ontario*. Toronto: Faculty of Management, University of Toronto.

Deutsch, Karl F. 1957. *Political Community and the North Atlantic Area: International Organization in the Light of Historical Experience*. Princeton: Princeton University Press.

Doern, G. Bruce, Leslie A. Pal, and Brian W. Tomlin. 1996. *Border Crossings: The Internationalization of Canadian Public Policy*. Toronto: Oxford University Press.

Doran, Charles F. 1984. *Forgotten Partnership: US-Canada Relations Today*. Baltimore: Johns Hopkins University Press.

Durkheim, Emile. 1964. *The Division of Labour in Society*. New York: Free Press.

Elden, Stuart. 2013. *The Birth of Territory*. Chicago: University of Chicago Press.

Fischer, Eric. 1957. "The Spatial Factor in Political Geography." In *Principles of Political Geography*, edited by Hans W. Weigert et al. New York: Appleton-Century-Crofts.

Flynn, Stephen E. 2003. "The False Conundrum: Continental Integration vs. Homeland Security." In *The Re-bordering North America? Integration and Exclusion in a New Security Environment*, edited by Peter Andreas and Thomas J. Biersteker, 110–27. Routledge.

Gattinger, Monica, and Geoffrey Hale. 2010. *Borders and Bridges: Canada's Policy Relations in North America*. Oxford: Oxford University Press.

Gottmann, Jean. 2007. *La Politique des États et leur Géographie* (1951) Paris: CTHS.

Hale, Geoffrey. 2012. *So Near Yet So Far: The Public and Hidden Worlds of Canada-US Relations*. Vancouver: UBC Press.

Hataley, Todd, and Christian Leuprecht. 2018. "Determinants of Cross-Border Cooperation." *Journal of Borderland Studies* 33, no. 3: 317–18.

Hataley, Todd, and Christian Leuprecht. 2019. "Bilateral Coordination of Border Security, Intelligence Sharing, Counter-Terrorism, and Counter-Radicalization." In *Canada-US Relations: Sovereignty or Shared Institutions? Canada Among Nations series*, edited by David Carment and Christopher Sands, 87–104. Basingstoke, UK: Palgrave Macmillan.

Hooghe, Liesbet, and Gary Marks. 2001. *Multi-level Governance and European Integration*. Lanham, MD: Rowman and Littlefield.

Iwashita, Akihiro. 2016. *Japan's Border Issues—Pitfalls and Prospects*. Philadelphia: Routledge.

Jones, Stephen B. 1945. *Boundary-Making: A Handbook for Statesmen, Treaty Editors and Boundary Commissioners*. Washington, DC: Carnegie Endowment for International Peace.

Katzenstein, Peter J., ed. 1996. *The Culture of National Security: Norms and Identity in World Politics*. New York: Columbia University Press.

Keating, Michael. 2008. "Thirty Years of Territorial Politics." *West European Politics* 31, no. 1–2: 60–81. https://doi.org/10.1080/01402380701833723

Kent, Jonathan D. 2011. "Border Bargains and the 'New' Sovereignty: Canada-US border Policies from 2001 to 2005 in Perspective." *Geopolitics* 16, no. 4: 793–818.

Kilroy, Richard J., Abelardo Rodriguez Sumano, and Todd Hataley. 2013. *North American Regional Security: A Trilateral Framework?* Boulder, CO: Lynne Rienner Publishers.

Konrad, Victor. 2015. "Toward a Theory of Borders in Motion." *Journal of Borderland Studies* 30, no. 1: 1–17.

Laine, Jussi P. 2016. "The Multiscalar Production of Borders." *Geopolitics* 21, no. 3: 465–82.

Lange, Emily. 2018. "Cross-Border Cooperation in Action: Taking a Closer Look at the Galicia-North of Portugal European Grouping of Territorial Cooperation." *Journal of Borderland Studies* 33, no. 3: 415–32.

La Pradelle, Paul. 1928. *La Frontiere: Etude de Droit International.* Paris: Les Editions Internationales.

Laxer, James. 2003. *The Border: Canada, the U.S. and Dispatches from the 49th Parallel.* Toronto: Doubleday Canada.

Leuprecht, Christian, Emmanuel Brunet-Jailly, Todd Hataley, and Tim Legrand. 2021. "Patterns in Nascent, Ascendant and Mature Border Security: Regional Comparisons in Transgovernmental Cooperation, Coordination and Collaboration," *Commonwealth and Comparative Politics* 59, no. 4: 349–75. Special Issue on Patterns in Border Security: Regional Comparisons.

Leuprecht, Christian, Mario Kölling, and Todd Hataley. 2019. *Public Security in Federal Polities.* Toronto: University of Toronto Press.

Lipset, S. M., and S. Rokkan. 1967. "Cleavage Structures, Party Systems and Voter Alignments: An Introduction." In *Party Systems and Voter Alignments: Cross National Perspectives*, edited by S. M. Lipset and S. Rokkan. New York: Free Press.

Newman, David. 2001. "Boundaries, Borders and Barriers: A Geographic Perspective on Territorial Lines." In *Identities, Borders, Orders: New Directions in International Relations Theory*, edited by Davide Newman. Minneapolis: University of Minnesota Press.

Ohmae, Kenichi. 1990. *The Borderless World.* New York: Harper Collins.

Ohmae, Kenichi. 1995. *The End of the Nation State: The Rise of Regional Economies.* New York: Free Press.

Paasi, Anssi. 1996. *Territories, Boundaries and Consciousness: The Changing Geographies of the Finnish-Russian Border.* New York: John Wiley and Sons.

Paasi, Anssi. 1999. "Boundaries as Social Practice and Discourse: The Finnish-Russian Border." *Regional Studies* 33, no. 7: 669–81.

Pacific NorthWest Economic Region (PNWER). 2022. "Working Groups." https://www.pnwer.org/working-groups.html

Parker, Noel, and Rebecca Adler-Nissen. 2012. "Picking and Choosing the Sovereign Border: A Theory of Changing State Border Practices." *Geopolitics* 17, no. 4: 773–96.

Pipkin, Seth. 2018. "Cashable Value: Social Capital and Practical Habits in the

Analysis of Collaborative Cross-Border Economic Development." *Journal of Borderland Studies* 33, no. 3: 329–50.

Rajaram, P. K., and Carl Grundy-Warr, eds. 2007. *Borderscapes: Hidden Geographies and Politics at Territory's Edge*. Minneapolis: University of Minnesota Press.

Rees, Tony. 2007. *Arc of the Medicine Line: Mapping the World's Longest Undefended Border across the Western Plains*. Lincoln: University of Nebraska Press.

Rokkan, S., and D. W. Urwin. 1982. *The Politics of Territorial Identity: Studies in European Regionalism*. London: Sage Publications.

Sack, Robert David. 1986. *Human Territoriality: Its Theory and History*. Cambridge: Cambridge University Press.

Sassen, Saskia. 2006. *Territory, Authority, Rights—From Medieval to Global Assemblages*. Princeton: Princeton University Press.

Sassen, Saskia. 2015. "At the Systemic Edge." *Cultural Dynamics* 27, no. 1: 173–81.

Seiler, Daniel Louis. 1989. *International Political Science Review* 10, no. 3: 191 207.

Shils, Edward. 1975. *Center and Periphery: Essays in Macrosociology*. Chicago: University of Chicago Press.

Sohn, Christophe. 2020. "Border Regions." In *Handbook on the Geographies of Regions and Territories 2020*, edited by Anssi Paasi, 298–310. Cheltenham, UK: Edward Elgar.

Stark, Heidi Kiiwetinepinesiik. 2016. "Criminal Empire: The Making of the Savage and Lawless Land." *Theory and Event*. 19, no. 4.

Stevenson, Garth. 1974. "Continental Integration and Canadian Unity." In *Continental Community?* edited by Thomas Axline. Toronto: McClelland and Stewart.

Strassoldo, Raimondo, and Giovanni Delli Zotti, editors. 1982. *Cooperation and Conflict in Border Areas*. Milano: Franco Angeli Editore.

Whittlesey, Derwent. 1944. *The Earth and the State: A Study of Political Geography*. New York: Henry Holt and Company.

TWO

British Columbia
and the Pacific Northwest

Benjamin Muller, Laurie Trautman, and Nicole Bates-Eamer

Introduction

British Columbia's cross-border characteristics are distinctly regional. While this is the case in all Canadian provinces, British Columbia (BC) has unique dimensions related to the population's close proximity to the border, the high mobility of people across the border, and the ports and marinas that process international travel and trade. Furthermore, a shared culture and history and a strong connection to the environment transcends the Canada–United States border in this region and influences how its residents perceive security. The region stands apart because of the extent of cooperative relations across the Pacific Northwest. Cross-border multilevel governance characterizes this region; this includes a broad array of cross-border arrangements, public-private partnerships, and bottom-up innovations in border security collaboration. The region also provides a good example of attempts to reconcile regional priorities with national frameworks for border security across a broad range of actors and stakeholders.

British Columbia enjoys close economic, social, and cultural ties with its stateside neighbors in the Cascadia region, particularly with Washington State. Alignment of culture and values across the border is closer in Cascadia than in any other region along the Canada–US border (Brunet-Jailly 2008; Konrad and Nicol 2011). Even the governor of Washington

25

was comfortable commenting that the border with British Columbia was a "fiction" (Canada–United States Inter-Parliamentary Group 2009); in a joint letter to their national governments, together with the premier of British Columbia (2008), the governor acknowledged that citizens viewed the border as "little more than a formality." Of BC's 4.6 million people, 3.1 million live in the Lower Mainland or greater Victoria area (Statistics Canada 2016), and these regions lie either along or near the border. The population in this region is growing rapidly, its economy is evolving, and the Lower Mainland is the most densely populated region in Canada (Statistics Canada 2017).

British Columbia shares domestic borders with the Yukon Territory, Northwest Territories, and Alberta, and international borders with four American states: Alaska to the northwest, Washington, Idaho, and Montana to the south. An international marine boundary runs along the west coast of the province and facilitates a trade gateway to Asia. The southern border with the state of Washington is the most active and contains some of Canada's busiest air, land, and sea ports (Government of Canada, CBSA 2019). The four busiest border crossings are between BC and Washington, which form the "Cascade Gateway" (Peace Arch–Blaine, Pacific Highway–Blaine, Aldergrove-Lynden, and Abbotsford-Sumas). Additional land crossing points are located at Point Roberts (a peninsula disconnected geographically from Washington State) plus nine more across the BC interior. Prior to the 2020 COVID-19 pandemic, Amtrak Cascades provided twice-daily passenger rail service between Vancouver, BC, and Eugene, OR. BC shares maritime borders with the US states of Washington and Alaska, as well as maritime borders that extend into international waters. The border with Washington in the Salish Sea runs equidistant from the two shores through the Juan de Fuca Strait south of Vancouver Island and divides the Canadian Southern Gulf Islands from the American San Juan Islands in the Haro Strait and Strait of Georgia. Three different operators provide daily ferry service between Vancouver Island and Washington State, including the government-owned Washington State Ferries. The Alaskan Marine Highway operated by the government of Alaska also runs a ferry service from the Port of Prince Rupert in northern BC to several destinations along the Alaskan coast. However, compared with busy commercial and leisure traffic along the Cascade Gateway land crossings, all other borders in BC are relatively quiet. In total, BC (and the Yukon) have forty-three land, air, and marine ports of entry. These ports process a diverse range of passenger and commercial traffic from all over the world and through all travel modes (Government of Canada, CBSA 2019). Comparatively little border research has been done on BC's southeast borders with Idaho and Montana, the northwest border with Alaska, or its maritime border with international waters.

This chapter discusses several dimensions of security related to BC's borders: regional concepts of security, main actors, existing and emerging security threats, and cooperation agreements; it concludes with a case study on fentanyl. BC's security concerns related to the border demonstrate the tension between federally conceived notions of national security and regional understandings of security, which in this region are buttressed with extensive cross-border collaboration with a focus on securing the flows of people and goods, as well as securing the ecological diversity of the region.

Operationalizing Concepts

Regional Concepts of Security

In our understanding of security, we accept the principle premise of critical security studies: security is a contested concept. In other words, there is no objective notion of security; rather, it is subjectively defined by different actors in different situations. As some of the earliest work in critical security studies suggests, not only is security a contested and subjective concept, one can see a broad range of "sectors" of security, well beyond the traditional notions of government executives, militaries, and the like. There is also ecological security, economic security, health security, and deeply held connections with regional and national identity (Buzan, Waever, and de Wilde 1997). Accordingly, when speaking of security in borderlands, central concerns are collaboration across law enforcement and security agencies and related developments in surveillance and risk assessment. However, specifically in a border region such as the Pacific Northwest, it is equally germane to consider the roles of nonstate stakeholders who effectively foster collaboration to enhance cross-border travel, commerce, and trade and who support a broader range of security.

In borderlands as robust as those of the Pacific Northwest, border security has much to do with openness and commerce, and the extent to which border security is synonymous with securing the free flow of goods, services, and tourists. Superimposed on this notion of security are the state-centric definitions of border security and the agencies that represent such conceptions of security. The terrain for what is more traditionally referred to as border security is motivated by the respective federal governments' preoccupations with international threats and dangers, divergent national legislation on controlled substances, and differential immigration and asylum policies. For many nonstate stakeholder groups, to be discussed later, a secure border does not necessarily exclude such considerations, but the emphasis is on strategies that facilitate and support transborder trade, commerce, and travel. In sharp contrast, Republicans of the Trumpian flavor (and many others from the past four decades or longer) are persuaded of the utility of walls, unmanned aerial vehicles or drones, and a broad range of surveillance security devices, facilitated by bilateral law enforcement cooperation, as essential elements of contemporary border security. Making trusted traveler schemes such as NEXUS more robust and accessible *is* security for many local stakeholders in the Pacific Northwest, but this is not necessarily contrary to the enhanced surveillance, inspection, and detention focus of the federal governments. The notions of security that underlie these strategies and approaches are very different. As in other regions, but perhaps more robustly in the Pacific Northwest, there is significant binational cooperation across law enforcement and border security agencies, and more notably, among nonstate stakeholder groups throughout the borderlands, which often possess richer, more nuanced notions of what it means to make the border secure.

Social Dimension of Security

From 1991 until its termination in the wake of the terrorist attacks on September 11, 2001 (9/11), residents of the Pacific Northwest enjoyed one of the "thinnest" urban borders in North America under the PACE (Peace Arch Crossing Entry) program. This BC program, the only one of its kind along the Canada–US border, allowed precleared vehicles displaying the PACE decal to drive through the Peace Arch crossing without stopping for a security check. Before the program was scrapped and replaced with the more security-intensive NEXUS card, nearly 30 percent of southbound vehicle traffic at the Peace Arch entered through the PACE lane (Whatcom Council of Governments 2015). Even now, BC and Washington have the highest uptake of NEXUS membership and Enhanced Driver's License participation (EDLs) along the Canada–US border (BPRI 2012b, 2012c).

In the context of such a vibrant border culture, it is no surprise that border stakeholders in the Pacific Northwest region, despite acknowledging the role of the border in national security, overwhelmingly reject the dominant state-centric paradigm of "security primacy" in border management. The assertion that "security trumps trade" or other similarly legitimate flows is viewed with suspicion by many in the Pacific Northwest borderlands, who express concern about the increasing militarization of their borders, are uncomfortable under the scrutiny of cameras and questions at the border, and feel no safer with these new security measures in place (Konrad 2010). As in many other borderlands, the synthetic national line used to reify the imagined community struggles to challenge the daily lived experiences of the borderlands' inhabitants who in many cases regularly traverse borders for relatively mundane activities such as purchasing fuel for their cars or milk at the local shops.

This social attitude toward border security finds expression in regional political actors and institutions. BC and Washington State have historically worked together to lobby their respective national governments in favor of their regional security interests. In 2006 and 2008, the governor of Washington State and premier of British Columbia wrote joint letters to their national governments expressing concern over the United States's Western Hemisphere Travel Initiative (WHTI).[1] While acknowledging the importance of a secure border, they argued for security priorities to be balanced against "the free flow of goods and people" (Office of the Premier and Office of the Governor 2006; Premier Gordon Campbell and Governor Chris Gregoire 2008).

The following section provides detailed information about the main actors—mainly from the Canadian or British Columbian perspectives—whose work intersects with security or border issues.

Main Actors

Border security in the Pacific Northwest is a multilevel endeavor that includes diverse actors drawn from federal, provincial, state, and municipal governments, law enforcement, private industry, and community organizations. As discussed above, securing the border is as much about facilitating the high volume of flows of people and products as it is about securing flows or spaces. Furthermore, the shared culture of the Pacific Northwest results in extensive networks of nonstate actors working together to promote the security and prosperity of the region's ecosystem and economy.

State Actors

As in all provinces, in BC, the Canada Border Services Agency (CBSA) and the Royal Canadian Mounted Police (RCMP) are the two main federal actors in Canada that patrol, monitor, enforce, and regulate the border.

This occurs both at and between ports of entry, including land, air, rail, and marine ports. In 2018–2019, the CBSA employed more than 1,800 officers in the region, who worked at ports of entry, including cruise-ship terminals and marinas, international airports and rail stations, and highway crossings, and at container-exam facilities, immigration holding centers, and trade and regional offices. They partner with airport, port, and harbor authorities to coordinate border enforcement at these ports.

The BC RCMP employs 6,800 police officers (but 10,480 employees), which is one-third of the entire force, making it the largest division in the RCMP in Canada (Government of Canada, Royal Canadian Mounted Police, 2021a). The history of the province and its later entrance into confederation as the westernmost frontier of Canada, resulted in a disproportionate federal footprint on law enforcement; only eleven municipalities have their own police force and there are no provincial police, unlike in more populous provinces such as Ontario. This large federal stamp on local and provincial law enforcement allows for greater interoperability and capacity for cooperation at borders, since borders are federally governed in both Canada and the US. The RCMP also work with the Canadian Coast Guard who provide patrol vessels, helicopters, and personnel to ensure maritime and national security in the Pacific.

The BC RCMP's Border Enforcement Team (BET) plays several roles in securing the border. They police the border at and between ports in partnership with provincial, national, and international agencies and communities. They collect and develop intelligence for national security investigations and combat organized crime. In particular, the Federal Serious and Organized Crime unit in BC is focused on drug trafficking, human smuggling, investment frauds and scams, and counterfeit currency and goods (Government of Canada, Royal Canadian Mounted Police, 2021b). Finally, the BET also intercepts individuals who enter the country in violation of regular entry processes and procedures.

Key actors at the provincial level whose work relates to border governance include the ministries of Public Safety and Emergency Services, Transportation and Infrastructure, Health, and other ministries related to securing biodiversity and the Salish Sea ecosystem. The ministries of Public Safety and Emergency Services oversee policing services and emergency management. As discussed above, the RCMP carry out the majority of policing services in BC, although one municipality along the US border, Abbotsford, has its own municipal police. Emergency Management BC (EMBC) coordinates emergency and disaster response—a key public safety concern in BC, which covers provincial preparations for catastrophic earthquakes and planning for disruptions in or damage to critical infrastructure. The BC Ministry of Environment and Climate Change and the BC Ministry of Health are responsible for environmental and health security in the province, and both have formal and informal agreements in place with their counterparts in Washington State in order to share information and respond to crises (see below). The Ministry of Transportation and Infrastructure regulates the roads, vehicles, and critical infrastructure that crisscross the border.

Formal intergovernmental arrangements—including those with Canada and with other provinces, such as Alberta—are coordinated by the Intergovernmental Relations Secretariat of British Columbia. BC and Washington have also established several bilateral sector-specific forums, task forces, or councils (notably in areas of environmental governance) in addition to participating in larger intergovernmental organizations with other actors in the Pacific Northwest.

Indigenous Actors

As reconciliation and recognition of Indigenous sovereignty and self-determination advance in Canada, First Nations are emerging as key actors on issues regarding the territoriality of states. There are 203 First Nations in BC (British Columbia Assembly of First Nations 2021), more than in any other province. Relationships among Indigenous nations transcend borders, and self-determining nations and peoples are reimagining economic, social, and political connections across the world (Corntassel 2021). For example, the Coast Salish Nation covers both the traditional territories of Coast Salish nations in BC and western Washington tribes who have lived in relationship with the shorelines, mountains, and watersheds of the Salish Sea since time immemorial. These nations, divided by the colonial border, share family connections and a common culture, politics, and language. While in effect composed of many groups of Coast Salish peoples living throughout British Columbia and Washington (and not one "actor" per se), to realize a nation-to-nation relationship with Indigenous peoples, as the federal government purports to do, requires recognizing the role of these actors regarding questions of territorial jurisdiction.

Given that the colonial Canadian–US border straddles traditional Indigenous territories, there are several Indigenous organizations working to minimize the impact of the border on Indigenous peoples. The BC Assembly of First Nations works with the federal government to explore secure options for Indigenous peoples crossing the border. The Coast Salish Gathering is a policy forum for Indigenous peoples to identify shared environmental concerns across their traditional territories. They bring these issues to the attention of government officials to secure and protect the resources and ecosystems of their ancestral territories. First Nations in Canada claim that the Jay Treaty of 1794 (signed by the United States and Great Britain) gives them the right to freely cross the Canada–US border, but for legal and historical reasons it is no longer valid. Indeed, the Western Hemisphere Travel Initiative (WHTI) that came into effect in 2008 was deemed by many Indigenous peoples to directly violate the Jay Treaty. The identification card and passport requirements of the WHTI for border crossings resulted in changes to the First Nations "status cards" that allow Indigenous peoples access to a bundle of treaty rights, including full access to residency on reservations and recognition from the Government of Canada. This change, in the name of alleged post-9/11 security imperatives, is a powerful example of state-centric security concerns that undermine and challenge the complexities of the borderland's identities, cultures, socioeconomics, and other factors that thrive in spaces such as the Pacific Northwest. As a result, there is an urgent need for measures to facilitate the mobility of Indigenous peoples within their traditional territory, which is transgressed by the colonial Canada–US border.

Nonstate Actors

The Pacific Northwest stands out among Canada–US border regions for the number and diversity of intergovernmental organizations working to address a wide range of cross-boundary policy issues, including security (Abgrall and Policy Research Initiative 2005; Alper 2004; Brunet-Jailly 2008; Konrad and Nicol 2011; Ranger et al. 2004). Many of these organizations are formed as public/private partnerships with representatives from major regional industries active in policy working groups and decision-making bodies. They may be multisectoral or focus on a specific sector such as the environment, the economy, or transportation. While the region is lauded for the degree of cross-border cooperation and extensive communities of practice, recent studies have shown that much of this cooperation is ad hoc and informal (Border Policy Research Institute 2018), and rarely jointly funded (Sarë 2020).

The largest and most influential regional organization is the Pacific Northwest Economic Region ([PNWER]; Pacific Northwest Economic Region 2015), a public/private organization that brings together executive-level government and industry officials from British Columbia, Alberta, and the Yukon Territory in Canada, and Washington, Oregon, Idaho, Montana, and Alaska in the United States. PNWER is organized into four deliberative and decision-making bodies comprising public- and private-sector stakeholders, plus a dedicated Secretariat with elected officers from the member states. PNWER coordinates more than a dozen policy working groups, including one dedicated to border issues. The Border Issues Working Group actively participated in the development and implementation of the Canada–United States Beyond the Border Action Plan. Other PNWER working groups also intersect with security-related concerns, including the Cross-Border Livestock Health Working Group, the Ocean Policy Working Group, the Transportation Working Group, and three separate Energy Working Groups looking at sustainability and cross-border energy networks. Of particular note in the Pacific Northwest is the extent to which PNWER and similar nonstate stakeholder collaborative groups often treat security in a much richer, more nuanced fashion than federal border and law enforcement agencies, which highlights the different conceptions of security operating in the borderlands. Furthermore, the *absence* of working groups or issue areas within PNWER related to irregular migration, international terrorism, or national crime issues, and the focus instead on threats to the natural environment and to collaborative economic activity, could be interpreted as a reflection of the regional security concerns vis-à-vis the border.

The Center for Regional Disaster Resilience (2014) created out of PNWER also houses several projects across sectors focused on regional protection of critical infrastructure, health security, cyber security, maritime resilience, and other essential security areas. The Center for Regional Disaster Resilience regularly conducts studies, tabletop exercises, and workshops with other public and private sector actors in the region.

In the transportation and infrastructure field, the International Mobility and Trade Corridor Program (IMTC) was created by the Whatcom Council of Governments in 1997 to improve mobility and security at the border crossings between BC and Washington in the Cascade Gateway. It remains one of the largest regional actors in border infrastructure. Over fifty private and public organizations at all levels of government on both sides of the border—federal, provincial/state, and municipal—are represented in its main decision-making body, the Core Group. The IMTC lobbies for regional border and transportation interests, collects data on border crossings, and acts as a conduit for local partners to jointly fund construction and research projects at the border. Of similar note, the Future Borders Coalition (2021) draws on a rich history of binational collaboration in the

Pacific Northwest and speaks to a broad conception of security with robust protections for trade, commerce, travel, and services, despite differential notions of risk and danger across the border and the unique challenges of the COVID-19 pandemic. Also interested in facilitating cross-border trade, the Pacific Northwest Innovation Corridor, launched in 2018, links Vancouver, Seattle, and Portland to "create opportunity and prosperity beyond what they and their surrounding regions could achieve independently" (Cascadia Innovation Corridor 2021). While not directly linked to security, its mandate reflects the spirit of the region in terms of cooperation; it also has implications for the increased mobility of people and products across the border.

In the area of health security, the Pacific Northwest Border Health Alliance ([PNWBHA] 2009) was another cross-border intergovernmental organization with a structure similar to that of PNWER. It was formed to address health security issues in the region. Beginning as a bilateral initiative between BC and Washington, its signatories grew to include the governments of Alberta, Saskatchewan, the Yukon Territory, Oregon, Idaho, Montana, and Alaska. It connected public health officials in the relevant jurisdictions, released guidelines on regional health cooperation, and hosted workshops on cross-border responses to public health emergencies. PNWBHA targets all levels of government, including municipal and Aboriginal governments. The PNWBHA no longer appears to be operational.

British Columbia and Alberta also participate as associate members in the Council of State Governments West (CSG West), which is composed of legislators and legislative staff from the thirteen westernmost American states. CSG West includes policy committees dedicated to cross-border cooperation on security and health.

In the academic field, the Border Policy Research Institute (BPRI) at Western Washington University in Bellingham promotes policy-oriented research on the Canada–United States border and border policy in general, with a focus on issues in the Pacific Northwest. The BPRI is actively involved in regional cross-border organizations, including PNWER and the IMTC. The institute produces border- policy briefs, reports, and research/working papers on border issues, and also hosts events that bring regional actors together to discuss issues related to regional security, economic integration, and environmental protection (among others).

Taken together, the above-named actors work to promote and secure an integrated regional economy and the people it serves, based on values of collaboration and cooperation over competition, particularly in innovative sectors such as technology and health. There are, however, several other regional NGOs whose work intersects more indirectly with border concerns, in that they are interested in securing the integrity and health of the shared environment. Notably, the Cascadia Center for Regional Development at Seattle's Discovery Institute researches and advocates on cross-border transportation in the region, and People for Puget Sound and the Georgia Strait Alliance work on cross-border environmental policy. For an overview of environmental NGOs working in the Salish Sea, see Sarë (2020) and regional agreements below. Furthermore, organizations working to secure migrants and Indigenous rights are also active in this region.

Environmental Scan

Contemporary discourses related to the war on terror influence activities at the BC border, but such concerns have rarely taken a firm foothold in these borderlands. According the CBSA's website, the Pacific region is a high-risk environment for contraband, immigration fraud, and illegal activities such as use as a drug corridor and for gang-related activities, money laundering, and irregular arrivals (Government of Canada, Canada Border Services Agency 2019). Despite incidents such as the so-called "Millennium Bomber," a perennial preoccupation with trade, contraband, and migration has animated the politics of this borderland. While regionally unique, discourses and practices prevalent at the BC border, particularly in terms of management of the "other" vis-à-vis immigration policy, indicate that it is far from immune to the long-standing reliance on detention and deportation in Canada (see Pratt 2005). The reaction to the announced arrival of boats with undocumented migrants in both 1999 and 2011 along the BC coast provides convincing testimony to the federal government's ongoing commitment to deportation and detention, and securitization of migration has remained constant both before and after 9/11 (Mountz 2010; Pratt 2005; Rygiel 2012; Walters 2015). The securitization of migration is not necessarily supported by residents of the region.

Both Vancouver and Seattle (as well as other cities and counties in Washington state) adhere to the spirit of sanctuary cities. Sanctuary cities ensure that newcomers are provided with safe access to municipal services regardless of their immigration status, and often support a "don't ask, don't tell" (about immigration status) policy to build stronger relationships with immigrant and refugee communities. In effect, local officials in sanctuary cities do *not* assist federal immigration enforcement officials by detaining individuals or getting involved in federal immigration enforcement. Research shows that compared to nonsanctuary jurisdictions, sanctuary jurisdictions are safer and economies are stronger (Wong 2017). In a similar spirit, No One Is Illegal in Vancouver–Coast Salish Territories is also an immigrant and/or racialized persons group with a vision "that challenges the ideology of immigration controls; and combats racial profiling, detention and deportation, the national security apparatus, law enforcement brutality, and exploitative working conditions of migrants" (No One Is Illegal 2021).

Undocumented migration has also been defined as a security issue for law enforcement at the Canada–US border, and it takes on a unique regional concern considering BC's open maritime border with international waters. Despite the vast distance, undocumented migrants have departed from Asia for BC ports. In 1999, a ship carrying 186 undocumented migrants from China was intercepted off the coast of Vancouver Island (Alphonso 2001); in 2010, nearly 500 Tamil migrants from Sri Lanka arrived in BC on a ship that departed from Thailand (Carlson and Hansen 2010). However, unauthorized entry in the BC region, particularly through the maritime border, has not attracted significant academic attention (see Mountz 2010), and the data and statistics are notoriously unreliable due to the clandestine nature of the movement. Human trafficking, however, is an issue that current cross-border mechanisms fail to address (Norfolk and Hallgrimsdottir 2019); in terms of protecting human rights, it is perhaps of greater concern than unauthorized entry.

Organized crime is a persistent concern for federal law enforcement along the entire Canada–US border, but especially in the BC–Washington nexus, where cross-border criminal networks are well established and well connected. An Integrated Border Enforcement Team threat assessment published by the RCMP in 2010 indicated that the most ubiquitous concerns tended to fall into the categories of smuggling/organized crime and illegal immigration. Drug smuggling is a particular concern in the region due to the proximity of major ports in Vancouver and Seattle, but currency and firearms are also frequently seized by border officials (Government of Canada, RCMP 2010b).

As discussed earlier, natural disasters—notably their potential impact on critical infrastructure—are a particular regional concern. Wildfires, landslides, floods, and other severe weather events are common in the Pacific Northwest; earthquakes and tsunamis are a less immediate but much more devastating possibility (EMBC 2014). Emergency planning for natural disasters is already well advanced through the work of PNWER, and the region benefits from emergency management agreements signed between state and provincial governments as well as at the federal level.

Another concern specific to the region relates to environmental security: the preservation of shared natural resources in the Pacific Northwest biosphere. Environmental issues have historically been a high priority in the Pacific Northwest, with residents drawing notions of regional identity and culture from the physical environment (Abel et al. 2011; Alper 2004). Among the many environmental concerns, oil spills are high on the agenda, considering the amount of crude oil shipped through the region from farther inland. The Pacific States/British Columbia Oil Spill Task Force was formed in response to two high-profile oil tanker accidents in 1988 and 1989 (including the infamous *Exxon Valdez* spill in Alaska) that affected the coast on both sides of the international border (Pacific States/British Columbia Oil Spill Task Force 2015). Residents in the Pacific Northwest welcomed the Canadian government's commitment of $1.5 billion in 2016 for the Ocean's Protection Plan, which includes funding for oil spill response, environmental and ecological restoration, and partnerships with Indigenous communities to protect the coast (Government of Canada 2021).

British Columbians have also demonstrated their concern for environmental security in their response to proposed pipelines that would transport crude oil from Alberta to tankers at BC ports bound for China and other trading partners in Asia and the Pacific. Public opinion polls have shown that British Columbians oppose the construction of the pipelines, citing the risk of oil spills and the presence of foreign tankers on their northern coast as concerns (Angus Reid Institute 2012, 2014a). In early 2020, Wet'suwet'en hereditary chiefs, opposing a natural gas pipeline through their territory in northern BC, sparked nationwide protests in Canada regarding jurisdiction over resource development on traditional Indigenous territories; BC's urban residents were overwhelmingly sympathetic to these protests. Tensions over pipeline construction have flared to the point that leaked memos showed the RCMP expressing concern that "violent anti-petroleum extremists" posed a security threat to Canada's national critical infrastructure (McCarthy 2015). The RCMP suggested that the anti-petroleum movement was international in scope and that Canadian activists were being financed by American charities (Government of Canada, RCMP 2014). The debate over pipelines thus manifests competing domestic and transnational conceptions of security.

Given the volume of people and goods crossing the border, the spread of infectious diseases and other public health threats is always a concern.

Shortly after the COVID-19 pandemic began, PNWER facilitated calls with elected officials to address the pandemic as a region. This included sharing best practices, information, and lessons learned across jurisdictions.

Horizon Scan

Many of the current security issues in the region—natural disaster planning, oil spills and other environmental concerns, Indigenous governance, pandemics, and the threat of terrorism—are naturally forward-looking in orientation. Security collaboration in these areas often comprises network building and strategic planning to increase regional resiliency in response to uncertain (but probable) future incidents.

Cybersecurity is a growing concern in cross-border management. It was noted as one of the four priority areas for collaboration under the Beyond the Border Action Plan (Government of Canada 2011), which led to the creation of a Joint Cybersecurity Action Plan and Joint Statement of Privacy Principles in 2012. The Action Plan set out three goals: improved cyber incident management collaboration, joint engagement and information sharing with the private sector, and cooperation on public awareness efforts. Canada has also committed to ratify the Council of Europe Convention on Cybercrime under the Beyond the Border initiative (Government of Canada 2015). In response to the transnational challenges, BC's Privacy and Information Commissioner has been particularly proactive, with ground-breaking investigations into the role of AggregateIQ Data Services in Cambridge Analytica as well as Facebook with the federal Privacy Commissioner (Office of the Privacy Commissioner for BC 2019; Office of the Privacy Commissioner of Canada 2019).

New security technologies are being deployed along the border that themselves need securing to protect the integrity of the system and the personal information collected from border crossers (Muller 2008, 2009), and these will only proliferate as vaccination passports emerge in response to the COVID-19 pandemic. Concerns about the Radio Frequency Identification technology in Enhanced Drivers Licenses and NEXUS cards may have hindered take-up of the programs (BPRI 2012b). Concerns are more prevalent on the Canadian side of the border, where residents are wary of exposing their digital information to less-stringent American privacy laws (McPhail et al. 2009). Indeed, Konrad's (2010) survey of stakeholders in the Pacific Northwest showed that roughly half of respondents were either neutral or disagreed that technology enhancements improved the border crossing at the Cascade Gateway.

Transboundary Cooperation Agreements

The Pacific Northwest benefits from a highly developed network of regional and federal agreements, both formal and informal. Regional and federal security or defense agreements from which the region benefits number in the thousands at the federal level alone (Brunet-Jailly 2012). This section, however, only summarize some of the most important cross-border arrangements applicable in this border region.

Federal Agreements

Canada and the United States are federal states subject to a division (or separation) of powers between national and subnational governments. BC handles its relationship with Canada on an issue-specific basis through connections between individual provincial and federal ministries, and more formally on a general basis through its Intergovernmental Affairs office. Outside these formal institutions of vertical governance within the Canadian federal system, horizontal linkages at the subnational level begin to play a bigger role in influencing federal policy toward borders and border regions.

Regional border security takes place within the framework of broader federal agreements. Since 2011, Beyond the Border has expanded preclearance programs for people and goods. At the regional level, the Canada–U.S. Preclearance Agreement signed under the Beyond the Border framework in 2014 allowed for immigration preinspections at cruise, ferry, and rail terminals in British Columbia, and a marine cargo preclearance pilot was launched in Prince Rupert, BC. Indeed, a main concern of the Customs and Border Protection staff in BC was ensuring that new facilities, such as a marine terminal in Victoria, enabled preclearance procedures. Trusted Trade/Trusted Traveller programs, such as NEXUS and FAST, were also expanded and received new dedicated lanes at BC border crossings (Government of Canada 2015). The Canada–US Free Trade Agreement in 1988, followed by the North American Free Trade Agreement (NAFTA) in 1993 and, most recently, the Canada–United States-Mexico Agreement (CUSMA) in 2020, removed many of the barriers to trade between the two countries. NAFTA was intended to speed up the process of economic integration in the region and set the course for future cooperation in managing flows at the border (Brunet-Jailly 2012). Since 9/11, however, the push for further economic integration has been tempered by the demands of the security primacy paradigm, as reflected by the fact that the number of people crossing the border has not increased. The difficult negotiations during CUSMA represent a low point for cross-border collaboration in the Pacific Northwest, but the new administration seems to have returned to a commitment to collaborating on cross-border initiatives.

Many of the most innovative and successful federal border security practices emerged out of experimentation in the Pacific Northwest—either as purely regional initiatives, or as a testing ground for federal pilots. The following programs have roots in the Pacific Northwest (BPRI 2011, 2012a, 2012b, 2012c, 2012d):

- PACE/CANPASS and NEXUS
- Enhanced Driver's License
- Integrated Border Enforcement Teams
- Shiprider
- Marine cargo preclearance
- Border wait-time measurement (Advanced Traveler Information Systems)

Regional Agreements

Cross-border organizations play a critical role in regional governance and regional agreements. More than simple intergovernmental organizations, these institutions include stakeholders at multiple levels of government, from municipalities abutting the border and smaller public agencies to relevant ministries of the federal governments. The private sector is also highly incorporated into the governance structure of the PNWER, comprising its Board of Directors and a Private Sector Council, and participating in policy working groups (Abgrall and Policy Research Initiative 2005).

As Brunet-Jailly demonstrates (2008), these institutions can be usefully contrasted with governance models within the EU to show the uniquely North American approach to horizontal governance deemed "policy parallelism." In contrast to an EU-like model that relies on state-like supranational institutions to dictate policy, the Pacific Northwest border region has constructed regional institutions at multiple subnational levels to align their own policies across the border and lobby their federal governments to do likewise. Concessions in federal border policy can then, in turn, shape the culture and policies of the borderlands, as regional actors adapt, for example, to the Beyond the Border initiative (BPRI 2012c, 2012d). In other words, horizontal interactions between regional actors alter vertical interactions between national and subnational governments, and vice versa.

As neighbors sharing many of the same values, priorities, and policy issues, the governments of BC and Washington enjoy a particularly close informal relationship. BC–Washington joint cabinet meetings are held almost annually. It was out of these meetings that the two decided to work together on developing the Enhanced Driver's License program. When it was introduced in response to the WHTI in 2008, this program allowed residents of BC and Washington to cross the border by presenting a special WHTI-compliant license rather than having to apply for and carry a passport. It was the first program of its type in North America (Government of BC Intergovernmental Affairs Secretariat 2015; Government of BC and Government of the State of Washington 2006; Ranger et al. 2004).

In the environmental realm, BC has several formal multilateral and bilateral agreements with its neighbors. BC, Alaska, Washington, Oregon, and California established the Pacific Coast Collaborative in 2008 to facilitate regional best practices in environmental and clean energy policies. These five governments plus the state of Hawaii also comprise the Pacific States/BC Oil Spills Task Force. At the bilateral level, BC and Washington signed an Environmental Cooperation Agreement in 1992 and established the BC/Washington Environmental Cooperation Council, which oversaw the work of various cross-border environmental task forces prior to the creation of the Pacific Coast Collaborative. BC also has Environmental Cooperation Arrangements and memorandums of understanding in place with bordering Idaho and Montana (Alper 2004; Government of BC and State of Montana 2010; Government of BC Intergovernmental Affairs Secretariat 2015; Ranger et al. 2004). BC and Washington also occasionally participate in each other's policy and training exercises, especially in emergency management (EMBC 2014).

Many of the region's formal and informal cross-border agreements have come out of its intergovernmental organizations, which provide local actors with a venue and framework in which to build these partnerships. PNWER in particular has been instrumental in forging formal cross-border agreements and informal procedures, action plans, best practices, and commitments between state and provincial governments. The IMTC also brings together provincial/state governments, municipalities, and other public- and private-sector actors to determine a joint list of regional border infrastructure priorities, explore potential partnerships, and identify sources of funding for border projects (Whatcom Council of Governments 2015). As early as 1996, the provincial, territorial, and state governments of BC, the Yukon Territory, Washington, Oregon, Idaho, and Alaska had formal arrangements for cross-border assistance in disaster response in place in the form of the Pacific Northwest Emergency Management Agreement, which was expanded in 2006 to include new procedures for implementation.

Policy Case Study

Fentanyl Crisis—Cross-Border Flow of Supply?

The movement of illegal drugs across the Canada–US border is neither novel nor compelling. Illicit drugs of all sorts have long been trafficked for profit across international borders and boundaries to satisfy demand, and in the Canadian case, BC has often had a preeminent place in this relationship (Grayson 2008). However, the contemporary crisis with the trafficking and use of fentanyl or carfentanyl is qualitatively different, not only in its impact on individuals and the community, but also in methods of trafficking. This controlled substance moves illegally across the border, in the BC border in particular through the postal system. The bulk of the mail containing the ingredients for the drug comes from the Asia-Pacific region and enters through Canada Post's Pacific Processing Facility.

The Government of Canada is advancing bilateral and trilateral efforts to interdict the importation of illegal opioids. Bilateral work is underway with the United States Drug Enforcement Administration from an intelligence and strategic perspective to understand how best to engage in a trilateral cooperative manner with China, where much of the opioids originate. Although the RCMP and CBSA have been focusing collective operational efforts with their law enforcement counterparts in China, just about all Western countries report that Chinese law enforcement is notoriously uncooperative and exceedingly cumbersome to deal with. Still, a memorandum of understanding between the RCMP and municipal police agencies was renewed in September 2016 to enhance cooperation on combating crime. Both parties committed to work together to combat the flow of illegal fentanyl and other opioids into Canada. The RCMP and the Chinese Ministry of Public Security continue to discuss how to advance investigations against such shared threats. Canada has engaged in trilateral discussions on the opioid crisis with the United States and Mexico through the new North American Drug Policy Dialogue. In October 2016, the three partner nations met to discuss the current opioid crisis, and agreed, among other measures, to explore an aligned approach by the three countries, as well as countries outside of the continent that are influential in producing and trafficking opioids (House of Commons 2017).

Significant movement has been made on cross-border coordination and collaboration on this issue and on policy and legal changes in terms of the definition and law enforcement related to managing these opioids. In 2017 Parliament passed Bill C-37, an act to amend the Controlled Drugs and Substances Act and to make related amendments to other acts. Those related amendments were intended to prevent the uncontrolled import into Canada of devices that can be used to manufacture illicit drugs, such as pill presses and encapsulators, and to provide authority to officers at the border to open packages weighing thirty grams or less. CBSA agents and employees of Canada Post now have greater discretion to inspect suspicious international mail, should there be reasonable grounds for search and seizure.

In the summer of 2017, the fentanyl and opioid crises began to reach epidemic levels. As the number of deaths mounted, particularly on the streets of Vancouver, BC, it became a public health epidemic. This case shows that divergent values within political culture are often more relevant to the way issues related to border security are dealt with than any lack of cooperation, coordination, or goodwill among the government agencies in BC and Washington who are charged with managing the border. From the cross-border perspective, interagency cooperation in managing this issue is a success, but this perception of success underscores the extent to which such analyses are beholden to state-centric notions of security. Families who have lost loved ones to fentanyl and opioids would see this as anything but a success.

Conclusion

Security in the context of British Columbia has a distinctly regional character. This is not to suggest that British Columbians reject federal security concerns; the polls, articles, and reports cited above indicate that BC residents do appreciate national security issues, though perhaps not as strongly as their counterparts in other regions of Canada. Rather, regional actors are concerned with broader security priorities of their own, including preparations for a catastrophic earthquake, preventing oil spills on their coastlines, and preserving the wealth of natural resources for which the region is known. Federal policymakers have always acknowledged that security at the Canada–US border must be balanced with the free flow of people and goods, but this chapter suggests that Cascadians, who have a strong border culture and recent memory of a much more porous border, tend to place greater emphasis on the latter issues. In fact, the Cascadian experience questions the representation of security as at odds with or on the opposing side of a continuum with liberty. Instead, securing these borderlands is about securing a confluence of interests, actors, sectors, and stakeholders' concerns; managing and protecting resources; maintaining a place at the table for local Indigenous peoples; and helping commerce to thrive. These considerations are as necessary to border security as effective law enforcement and control of contraband. Ultimately, collaboration takes place across all tier levels of governments and within public-private and nonstate actors in partnerships concerned with environmental and health issues and trade.

Future research could pursue this line of inquiry further, investigating the extent to which perceptions of "security" and of specific threats diverge vertically among federal actors, regional actors, and regional residents within the BC context, and also horizontally across other border regions in Canada. Future research may also attempt to identify potential "points of vulnerability" in BC's borders, notably in places where the "border" is extraterritorial and defined by flows rather than a traditional "line in the sand." This might include, for example, the preclearance borders at Vancouver's international airport, the Amtrak Cascades rail terminal, and the ferries that run between Vancouver Island and Washington State. Given the rapidly evolving nature of modern borders under the forces of globalization, it is becoming increasingly important to understand how these extraterritorial borders might differ from traditional "line" borders from a security perspective.

Note

1. The WHTI, introduced by the US government in 2004 and fully implemented at all ports of entry by 2009, required all border crossers into the United States to present a passport or other "WHTI-compliant" identity document. Prior to the WHTI, Canadian and American citizens could cross the border by presenting a valid driver's license (Office of the Premier and Office of the Governor 2006).

REFERENCES

Abel, Troy D., Jenni Pelc, Lauren Miller, Jacqueline Quarre, and Kathryn Mork. 2011. "Borders, Barriers, and Breakthroughs in the Cascadia Corridor." Research Report 15. Border Policy Research Institute. http://www.wwu.edu/de pts/bpri/files/2011_AbelT_ResReport_No_15.pdf

Abgrall, Jean-François, and Policy Research Initiative (Canada). 2005. "A Survey of Major Cross-Border Organizations between Canada and the United States." Policy Research Initiative. https://www.bibliotheque.assnat.qc.ca/DepotNume rique_v2/AffichageFichier.aspx?idf=102035

Alper, Donald K. 2004. "Emerging Collaborative Frameworks for Environmental Governance in the Georgia Basin-Puget Sound Ecosystem." *Journal of Borderlands Studies* 19, no. 1: 79–98.

Alphonso, Caroline. 2001. "Three Men Found Guilty of Aiding Illegal Migrants." *Globe and Mail*, February 26, sec. National News.

Angus Reid Institute. 2012. "Opposition to Northern Gateway Remains High in British Columbia." Angus Reid Institute. http://angusreid.org/opposition-to -northern-gateway-remains-high-in-british-columbia/

Border Policy Research Institute (BPRI). 2011. "Perimeter Security and the Beyond the Border Dialogue: Perspectives from the PNW–Western Canada Region." Seminar Proceedings. Seattle, WA: Border Policy Research Institute. http:// www.wwu.edu/bpri/files/2011_Jul_BBWG_Seminar_Proceedings.pdf

Border Policy Research Institute (BPRI). 2012a. "Federal Initiatives Can Be at Odds with Regional Ones." Policy Brief. Border Policy Brief. Border Policy Research Institute. http://www.wwu.edu/bpri/files/2012_Spring_Border_Brief .pdf

Border Policy Research Institute (BPRI). 2012b. "Is RFID the Answer to Resurgent Border Traffic?" Policy Brief. Border Policy Brief. Border Policy Research Institute. http://www.wwu.edu/bpri/files/2012_Winter_Border_Brief.pdf

Border Policy Research Institute (BPRI). 2012c. "The 'Beyond the Border' Dialogue at Age One: Policy and Political Implications for the Pacific Northwest." Seminar Proceedings. Seattle, WA: Border Policy Research Institute. http:// www.wwu.edu/bpri/files/2012_BTB_Proceedings_Master.pdf

Border Policy Research Institute (BPRI). 2012d. "Beyond the Border: Making the Action Plan Work for You." Forum Proceedings. Vancouver, BC: Border Policy Research Institute. http://www.wwu.edu/bpri/files/2012_Nov_VBOT_Procee dings.pdf

Border Policy Research Institute (BPRI). 2018. "Regional Cross-Border Collaboration Between the U.S. & Canada." Border Policy Brief vol. 13 (Fall 2018). https://cedar.wwu.edu/cgi/viewcontent.cgi?article=1112&context=bpri_public ations

British Columbia Assembly of First Nations. 2021. "Vision and Mission." https:// www.bcafn.ca/about-bcafn/vision-mission

Brunet-Jailly, Emmanuel. 2004. "NAFTA, Economic Integration, and the Canadian-American Security Regime in the Post-September 11, 2001 Era: Multi-Level Governance and Transparent Border?" *Journal of Borderlands Studies* 19, no. 1: 123–42. https://doi.org/10.1080/08865655.2004.9695620

Brunet-Jailly, Emmanuel. 2007. *Borderlands: Comparing Border Security in North America and Europe.* Ottawa: University of Ottawa Press.

Brunet-Jailly, Emmanuel. 2008. "Cascadia in Comparative Perspectives: Canada–– U.S. Relations and the Emergence of Cross-Border Regions." *Canadian Political Science Review* 2, no. 2: 104–24.

Brunet-Jailly, Emmanuel. 2012. "A New Border? A Canadian Perspective of the Canada–US Border Post-9/11." *International Journal* 67, no. 4: 963–74.

Buzan, Barry, Ole Waever, and Jaap de Wilde. 1997. *Security: A New Framework for Analysis.* London: Lynne Rienner Publishers.

Canada–United States Inter-Parliamentary Group: Canadian Section. 2009. "Report of the Canadian Parliamentary Delegation to the Pacific NorthWest Economic Region—Border Challenges and Regional Solutions: 2010 Olympics and the Pacific Northwest Experience." Washington DC: Parliament of Canada. https://www.parl.ca/diplomacy/en/Publication?sbdid=b225e754-7575 -4997-b904-59cc0c1e72b2&sbpidx=1&Language=E&Mode=1&sbpid=72090 8aa-f3c6-41d1-bcfa-4b80d0461a2c

Carlson, Kathryn Blaze, and Darah Hansen. 2010. "Harper 'Will Not Hesitate' to Change Laws; Tamil Migrant Ship; PM Says People-Smuggling 'Trend' a Threat to Canada's Borders, as Asylum-Seekers Continue to Be Detained." *Vancouver Sun,* August 18, sec. Westcoast News.

Cascadia Innovation Corridor. 2021. "About." www.connectcascadia.com/#about

Center for Regional Disaster Resilience. 2014. "Critical Infrastructure Regional Integrated Action Strategy." Seattle: Center for Regional Disaster Resilience, Pacific Northwest Economic Region. http://www.regionalresilience.org/uplo ads/2/3/2/9/23295822/puget_sound_critical_infrastructure_regional_integrat ed_action_strategy.pdf

Corntassel, Jeff. "Indigenous Internationalism and Expressions of Indigenous Rela- tionships." October 2020. Unpublished document. https://www.cigionline.org /static/documents/indigenous_rights_special_report_web_1.pdf

Emergency Management BC (EMBC). 2014. "Emergency Management BC Stra- tegic Plan 2014/2015–2016/2017." Government of British Columbia. http:// www.embc.gov.bc.ca/em/Emerg_Mgmt_BC/EMBC-Strategic-Plan.pdf

Future Borders Coalition. 2021. "Innovation in the U.S.–Canada Border Relation- ship." https://www.futureborderscoalition.org/

Government of British Columbia. Intergovernmental Relations Secretariat. 2015. "Intergovernmental Arrangements." http://www.gov.bc.ca/igrs/prgs/intergova gmts.html

Government of British Columbia, and Government of the State of Montana. 2010. "Memorandum of Understanding and Cooperation on Environmental Protec- tion, Climate Action and Energy." http://www.gov.bc.ca/igrs/attachments/en /MTEnvCoop.pdf

Government of British Columbia, and Government of the State of Washington. 2006. "Washington-British Columbia MOU with Respect to a Collaborative Approach to the Use of Available Public Health and Health Services Resources to Prepare For, Respond to and Recover from Public Health Emergencies." http://www.pnwbha.org/wp-content/uploads/2010/04/BC-WA-Public-Health -Collaboration-MOU-Signed.pdf

Government of Canada. 2011. "Beyond the Border: A Shared Vision for Perimeter Security and Economic Competitiveness (Action Plan)." Government of Canada. http://actionplan.gc.ca/en/page/bbg-tpf/beyond-border-action-plan

Government of Canada. 2015. "Beyond the Border Implementation Report—March 2015." Implementation Report. Ottawa, ON: Government of Canada. http://actionplan.gc.ca/en/content/beyond-border-implementation-report-march-2015

Government of Canada. 2021. "Ocean's Protection Plan." From Transport Canada. https://tc.canada.ca/en/initiatives/oceans-protection-plan

Government of Canada, Canada Border Services Agency. 2019. "Executive Vice-President's Transition Binder 2019." https://cbsa-asfc.gc.ca/pd-dp/tb-ct/evp-pvp/pacr-rpac-eng.html

Government of Canada, Foreign Affairs Trade and Development Canada. 2010. "Agreement Between the Government of Canada and the Government of the United States of America on Emergency Management Cooperation." http://www.treaty-accord.gc.ca/text-texte.aspx?id=105173

Government of Canada, Royal Canadian Mounted Police. 2008. "Canada–United States IBET Threat Assessment 2007." 27 May. http://www.rcmp-grc.gc.ca/ibet-eipf/reports-rapports/threat-menace-ass-eva-eng.htm#vii

Government of Canada, Royal Canadian Mounted Police. 2010a. "Canada-U.S. Shiprider." Canada-U.S. Shiprider. June 25. http://www.rcmp-grc.gc.ca/ibet-eipf/shiprider-eng.htm

Government of Canada, Royal Canadian Mounted Police. 2010b. "Canada-United States IBET Threat Assessment 2010 (Reporting on Year 2009)." Canada-United States IBET Threat Assessment 2010 (Reporting on Year 2009). http://www.rcmp-grc.gc.ca/ibet-eipf/reports-rapports/2010-threat-menace-eng.htm

Government of Canada, Royal Canadian Mounted Police. 2012. "Integrated Border Enforcement Teams (IBETs)." April 9. http://www.rcmp-grc.gc.ca/ibet-eipf/index-eng.htm

Government of Canada, Royal Canadian Mounted Police. 2014. "Critical Infrastructure Intelligence Assessment: Criminal Threats to the Canadian Petroleum Industry." Leaked document. http://www.desmog.ca/sites/beta.desmogblog.com/files/RCMP%20-%20Criminal%20Threats%20to%20Canadian%20Petroleum%20Industry.pdf

Government of Canada, Royal Canadian Mounted Police.2021a. "About the RCMP in B.C." https://bc-cb.rcmp-grc.gc.ca/ViewPage.action?siteNodeId=2094&languageId=1&contentId=108

Government of Canada, Royal Canadian Mounted Police. 2021b. "Federal Serious and Organized Crime (FSOC)." https://bc-cb.rcmp-grc.gc.ca/ViewPage.action?siteNodeId=23&languageId=1&contentId=10275

Grayson, Kyle. 2008. *Chasing Dragons: Security, Identity and Illicit Drugs in Canada.* Toronto: University of Toronto Press.

House of Commons. 2017. "Report and Recommendations on the Opioid Crisis in Canada, Report of the Standing Committee on Health." Ottawa: Government of Canada, Standing Committee on Health. https://www.ourcommons.ca/DocumentViewer/en/42-1/HESA/report-6; "Government Response to the Report of the Standing Committee on Health." https://www.ourcommons.ca/DocumentViewer/en/42-1/HESA/report-6/response-8512-421-134

Konrad, Victor. 2010. "'Breaking Points,' but No 'Broken' Border: Stakeholders Evaluate Border Issues in the Pacific Northwest Region." Research Report. Border Policy Research Institute. http://www.wwu.edu/bpri/files/2010_Jul_Report_No_10_Breaking_Points.pdf

Konrad, Victor, and Heather N. Nicol. 2011. "Border Culture, the Boundary Between Canada and the United States of America, and the Advancement of Borderlands Theory." *Geopolitics* 16, no. 1: 70–90. https://doi.org/10.1080/146 50045.2010.493773

McCarthy, Shawn. 2015. "RCMP Express Alarm over 'Anti-Petroleum' Ideologists." *Globe and Mail*, February 17. News.

McPhail, B., K. Boa, J. Ferenbok, K. L. Smith, and A. Clement. 2009. "Identity, Privacy and Security Challenges with Ontario's Enhanced Driver's Licence." In *Science and Technology for Humanity (TIC-STH), 2009 IEEE Toronto International Conference*, 742–47. https://doi.org/10.1109/TIC-STH.2009.5444399

Mountz, Alison. 2010. *Seeking Asylum: Human Smuggling and Bureaucracy at the Border*. Minneapolis: University of Minnesota Press.

Muller, Benjamin J. 2008. "Governing through Risk at the Canada/US Border: Liberty, Security, Technology." Working Paper No. 2. Border Policy Research Institute. http://www.wwu.edu/bpri/files/2008_Sep_WPNo2.pdf

Muller, Benjamin J. 2009. *Security, Risk and the Biometric State: Governing Borders and Bodies*. London: Routledge.

No One Is Illegal. 2021. "About Us." https://noii-van.resist.ca/about-us/

Norfolk, Alexander, and Helga Hallgrimsdottir, 2019. "Sex Trafficking at the Border: An Exploration of Anti-Trafficking Efforts in the Pacific Northwest." *Social Sciences*, MDPI, 8, no. 5 (May): 1–18. https://ideas.repec.org/a/gam/jscscx/v8y2 019i5p155-d232172.html

Office of the Premier, and Office of the Governor. 2006. "Backgrounder: Agreements Signed by BC and Washington." *Backgrounder: Agreements Signed by BC and Washington*. June 20. http://www2.news.gov.bc.ca/news_releases_2005-20 09/2006OTP0107-000829-Attachment1.htm

Office of the Privacy Commissioner for British Columbia. 2019. *Investigation Report*. P19–03. PIPEDA-035913. https://www.oipc.bc.ca/investigation-reports/2363

Pacific Northwest Border Health Alliance (PNWBHA) (Governments of British Columbia, Alberta, Yukon Territory, Saskatchewan, Alaska, Idaho, Montana, Oregon, and Washington). 2009. "Pacific Northwest Border Health Alliance Memorandum of Understanding." http://www.pbphpc.org/wp-content/uploa ds/2011/02/MOU-Complete-with-MT1.pdf

Pacific Northwest Economic Region. 2015. "Center for Regional Disaster Resilience." *Center for Regional Disaster Resilience*. http://www.regionalresilience.org/

Pacific States–British Columbia Oil Spill Task Force. 2015. "Oil Spill Task Force | The Pacific States—British Columbia." http://oilspilltaskforce.org/

Pratt, Anna. 2005. *Securing Borders: Detention and Deportation in Canada*. Vancouver: UBC Press.

Premier Gordon Campbell, and Governor Chris Gregoire. 2008. "The British Columbia/Washington State Partnership on Extended Driver's Licences."

Canadian Parliamentary Review 31, no. 1. http://www.revparl.ca/english/issue .asp?param=188&art=1269

Privacy Commissioner of Canada. 2019. *Joint Investigation of Facebook, Inc.* https:// www.priv.gc.ca/en/opc-actions-and-decisions/investigations/investigations-in to-businesses/2019/pipeda-2019-002/

Ranger, Louis, Dieudonné Mouafo, Jeff Heynen, and Nadia Ponce Morales. 2004. *Building Cross-Border Links: A Compendium of Canada–US Government Collaboration.* Ottawa: Canada School of Public Service Action-Research Roundtable on Managing Canada-U.S. Relations.

Rygiel, Kim. 2012. "Governing Mobility and Rights to Movement Post 9/11: Managing Irregular and Refugee Migration through Detention." *Review of Constitutional Studies* 16, no. 2: 211–41.

Sarë, Margit. 2020. "Non-Governmental Organizations and Cross-Border Environmental Cooperation: Salish Sea and Balti Sea Regions." Research report. Bellingham, WA: Border Policy Research Institute. https://cedar.wwu.edu/bp ri_publications/118/

Statistics Canada. 2016. "Census Profile, 2016 Census. British Columbia." https:// www12.statcan.gc.ca/census-recensement/2016/dp-pd/prof/index.cfm?Lan g=E

Statistics Canada. 2017. "B.C.'s Lower Mainland." https://www150.statcan.gc.ca /n1/pub/11-402-x/2011000/chap/geo/geo02-eng.htm

Walters, William. 2015. "Migration, Vehicles, and Politics: Three theses on Viapolitics." *European Journal of Social Theory* 18, no. 4: 469–88.

Whatcom Council of Governments. 2015. "IMTC." *The International Mobility and Trade Corridor Program.* http://theimtc.com/

Wong, Tom K. 2017. "The Effects of Sanctuary Policies on Crime and the Economy." *Center for American Progress.* (January 26). https://www.americanprogress .org/issues/immigration/reports/2017/01/26/297366/the-effects-of-sanctuary -policies-on-crime-and-the-economy/

THREE

Alberta and the Northwest

Jamie Ferrill, Geoffrey Hale, and Kelly Sundberg

Introduction

Alberta's borders and borderlands are distinctive among Canadian provinces. Although Alberta ranks third in the country by GDP (Statistics
Canada 2020a) and fourth in population, it differs from Ontario, Québec,
and British Columbia (BC) in at least three important ways. First, it is landlocked, so it depends on far-flung transportation corridors to reach North
American or transoceanic markets. Second, it generates a disproportionate amount of its prosperity from fossil fuels and related upstream and
downstream economic activity, so its economy is heavily export-driven and
dependent on politically and legally contested trade corridors that extend
far beyond its physical borders inside and beyond Canada. Third, it has few
population centers close to interprovincial or international borders, or to
major urban areas in neighboring regions.

Due to its distinctive geography and socioeconomic, political, and societal characteristics, border security issues in Alberta thus extend beyond
conventional issues of national security, border management, law enforcement, and (im)migration. In contrast to the robust social and political
dialogue on borders and borderlands in provinces such as British Columbia, Ontario, and Québec, Alberta's sparsely populated borderlands have
reduced the political salience of physical borders. However, its dependence
on broadly dispersed trade corridors for its commodity exports has made

Alberta increasingly sensitive to the fragmentation of bordering processes and to limits on effective reciprocity within and beyond North America. Border issues specific to Alberta are typically examined through trade and supply-chain-based lenses involving a mix of economic, public safety, and related regulatory systems (Anderson and Hale 2018). This chapter necessarily interrogates these issues in the context of the open borders paradox and considers the weaknesses and strengths in the alignment of territorial institutions and border arrangements. Transcending traditional concepts of border security, regionally diverse perspectives and challenges help to illustrate Alberta's nuanced border and the conditions that cause its regional borders to persist.

Key Drivers Behind Security in Alberta: Geography and Socioeconomics

The context for border and borderlands security and related public safety issues in Alberta is primarily a function of geography and socioeconomics. Situated east of the Rocky Mountains, Alberta's major urban centers are hundreds of kilometers apart. Calgary and Edmonton are the fourth- and fifth-largest metropolitan centers in Canada, with populations of 1.4 million and 1.2 million respectively; they have different municipal government structures (unicity vs. minimally coordinated regions with multiple governments) and social profiles. Five smaller cities provide regional manufacturing and service centers for Alberta's central and outlying regions. The closest major Canadian and United States cities are located a day's drive or more from most major Alberta cities.

These spatial factors dilute conventional border security threats common to areas such as the Lower Mainland of British Columbia, Ontario's cross-border urban regions bordering Michigan and upstate New York, and heavily traveled border regions in Québec and New Brunswick (Anderson and Hale 2018; Winterdyk and Sundberg 2010). Moreover, heavy dependence on air travel gives extra significance to major international airports in Calgary and Edmonton, Canada's fourth- and fifth-largest airports, respectively (Statistics Canada 2020b). These issues gained higher salience during the 2020 COVID-19 pandemic, when inadequate airport screening of international travelers became a significant challenge for provincial public health officials in Alberta (Selley 2020; Potter 2020; Staples 2020; Palmer 2020).

The key drivers affecting Alberta's border security and public safety are heavily influenced by broader socioeconomic forces, including but not limited to responses to changing climates, rather than those specific to border regions. Nonpharmaceutical opioid abuse has been the largest persistent threat to public safety in recent years—reflecting broader trends across North America. Alberta's proportional rate of opioid deaths and hospitalizations has been second highest among Canadian provinces in recent years, after British Columbia (Canadian Institute for Health Information 2018). Cross-border gun trafficking, sometimes including "straw purchases" of weapons for resale on illegal markets, remains a significant issue fueling gang violence in major cities (King 2016; St. Onge 2018). The internet-fueled spread of political extremism, which transcends national borders, has also become a growing concern in recent years (McCoy, Jones, and Hastings 2019).

Despite extensive inward migration since 1990, Alberta's resource-oriented economy contributes to economic and political attitudes more comparable to those of other Prairie provinces and of US Plains and Mountain states than to central Canada or to the BC Lower Mainland—notwithstanding some overlap of libertarian social attitudes with those of Pacific Coast states (Policy Research Initiative 2008, 6–7). Agencies such as the Canada Border Services Agency (CBSA), Royal Canadian Mounted Police (RCMP), and Canadian Security Intelligence Service (CSIS) are key border security actors, as in other provinces (Winterdyk and Sundberg 2010). However, the border security mandate issues are somewhat muted by other public security priorities within Alberta compared to other provinces that border the United States—especially relative to British Columbia, Manitoba, Ontario, and Québec.

Geography

Alberta is situated between 60° and 49° latitude north of the Canada–US border, with British Columbia and the Rocky Mountains to the west, Saskatchewan and the Great Plains to the east, Northwest Territories to the north, and Montana to the south. At 255,200 mi^2 (661,185 km^2), Alberta covers about 7 percent of Canada's total land mass. Its two largest cities, Edmonton and Calgary, are the largest major Canadian metropolitan regions not within 60 miles (100 km) of the US border.[1] Except for Saskatchewan, distances between Alberta's major cities and its land border crossings are greater than in any other Canadian province (Anderson and Hale 2018), as noted in figure 3.1 below. The nearest major Canadian city—Greater Vancouver—is located about 600 miles from Calgary, and

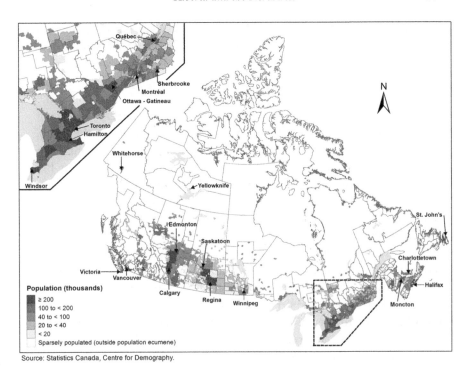

Source: Statistics Canada, Centre for Demography.

Figure 3.1. Alberta's population distribution in Canadian context. Source: *Statistics Canada. Population Distribution Map, as of July 1, 2020.*

700 miles from Edmonton. To the east in Saskatchewan, Saskatoon is 320 miles from Edmonton, and Regina is 470 miles from Calgary. The nearest large American metropolitan regions—Seattle (680 miles from Calgary) and Salt Lake City (790 miles)—have limited economic relations with Alberta, although historic migration patterns have linked the latter to communities in Southern Alberta.

Montana, the closest American state, is sparsely populated, with most of its major population centers in the southern part of the state. Kalispell and Great Falls are the closest cities to the international border in Montana (about 80 and 120 miles, respectively) and 200 miles from Lethbridge, Alberta's largest borderlands city (2019 population: 101,000). As a result, irregular cross-border migration has not been a major issue in recent memory, with international contraband smuggling coming in through the Calgary and Edmonton International Airports and Coutts and Carway land ports of entry.

Seven highways (but only one divided highway) connect Alberta to

British Columbia along the roughly 800-mile western border, mainly in remote northwestern Alberta. Twenty (two divided) connect Alberta with Saskatchewan along the roughly 750-mile eastern border; one connects Alberta and the Northwest Territories along the roughly 340-mile northern border; and six (one divided) connect Alberta and Montana along the 185-mile southern border (Alberta Motor Association 2019). Three rail corridors connect Alberta to the west, seven to the east, one to the north, and one to the south (Canadian National Railway 2019a)—although much Alberta-related traffic flows through regional gateways on the Idaho–BC and Saskatchewan–North Dakota borders. Even with two major international airports, Alberta is a vast and relatively isolated region whose lengthy trade and travel corridors are subject to disruption, at times due to extreme winter weather.

To increase Alberta's global reach and trade capacity, the international terminal at the Edmonton International Airport (YYG) was expanded in 2012, followed in 2016 by the expansion of the international terminal at Calgary International Airport (YYC). As a result, air passenger volumes for Alberta rose to over 25.6 million in 2018, 16 percent of Canada's total air passenger volume (Airports Council International 2019). Conversely, because most of Alberta's population is concentrated in the centrally located cities of Edmonton and Calgary, volumes of passenger traffic crossings by land from Alberta to the US are significantly lower than for British Columbia, Ontario, and Québec, most of whose populations live within 200 miles of the international land border, and often, major American urban centers. While Calgary is a major hub for transborder air travel, changes in the organization of Canadian air travel require many travelers to connect to international flights through Toronto and Vancouver.

Socioeconomics

Alberta accounts for 11 percent of Canada's population but generated 16.8 percent of Canada's total real GDP in 2018 (Statistics Canada 2020a). Alberta has an abundance of heavy crude and natural gas reserves. With the world's third-largest oil reserve, after Venezuela and Saudi Arabia, Alberta has the inherent potential to generate sizeable prosperity for many years, subject to continued demand for petrochemicals and the capacity to export its oil and gas to outside markets (US Energy Information Administration 2020; Government of Alberta 2017). Alberta's mining, oil, and gas sectors—most significantly, crude oil extraction—accounted for 26.4 percent of provincial GDP, dominating Alberta's interprovincial and international commerce (Government of Alberta 2017). However, its major refinery markets are primarily on the Pacific Coast, southern Illinois, or the US Gulf Coast. Associated long, increasingly contested transportation corridors function as extended borderlands subject to overlapping and competing interests.

Major agri-food sectors account for a significant but smaller share of Alberta's exports. Alberta accounts for about 42 percent of Canada's cattle herd; three major beef-processing plants account for 85 percent of domestic capacity (Statistics Canada 2017; Edmiston 2020). Animal health and food safety issues remain high-profile priorities, as cattle and processing supply chains are closely integrated with those in the western United States, despite persistent efforts by the United States to thicken borders by expanding protectionist "Country-of-Origin Labeling" regulations (Moens and Vivanco-Leon 2012; Wipf 2019). Crop exports are highly diversified by commodity and external markets. This interdependence creates broader food-security issues. Alberta's exports are dependent (with other provinces) on seasonal agricultural guest workers for planting and harvesting. Periodic disruptions for major processors—most recently during the COVID-19 pandemic—can have a nationwide impact on the proverbial "farm to fork" process (Baum, Tait, and Grant 2020; Ivison 2020).

Alberta is also home to Canada's venture stock exchange (TSX Venture Exchange), Canada's second-largest airline (WestJet), along with robust professional services, diversified agri-food, and forestry sectors. Still, oil sands production remains the central economic driver for the province and has a major impact on most other economic sectors (Government of Alberta 2017). Extensive natural gas reserves provide potential feedstock for hydrogen production to support an anticipated energy transition in response to climate change.

Geology has bestowed immense oil and gas reserves on Alberta. However, the interaction of politics and geography over competing visions of land use, energy, and place-based and climate-related environmental policies has undercut the revenue potential from Alberta's oil sands (Ramsey 2018), and with it, many Albertans' economic security as the multiple subnational (provincial, state, and Indigenous) borders that intersect its extended trade corridors are thickened. The resource sector has served as a "bulwark against wage stagnation and working-class dislocation in Canada, and thus a key element in economic security" until the prolonged post-2015 downturn (Speer 2018, 5; Milligan 2018). However, this prosperity is heavily dependent on updating and expanding both domestic and export infrastructure, particularly pipelines crossing domestic, Indigenous, and international borders, to sustain the industry's continued growth, while mitigating the effects of greenhouse gas emissions.

From Alberta's vantage point, the greatest security risk facing its borders is the challenge of expanding pipeline capacity to export fossil fuels—with societal contestation relating to climate change and other issues (including Indigenous rights) occasioning systematic litigation along far-flung pipeline corridors in both countries. Four major and two midsize operational pipelines move crude oil from Alberta to British Columbia, Central Canada (for natural gas), and the United States (totaling 4.13 million barrels/day). Most oil exports to Central Canada currently follow Enbridge's mainline system through the United States, making them vulnerable to federal and state-level political and regulatory challenges, although Irving Oil received permission in 2020 to ship Alberta oil to its Atlantic Canada refineries through the Panama Canal (Morgan 2020). Due to this and other extraction-related issues, Alberta crude oil is sold at a significant discount, which ultimately shortchanges both the Albertan and Canadian economies and exacerbates political tensions.

In response to these developments, Alberta and other western Canadian provinces increasing steps to facilitate Indigenous participation in resource development and, prospectively, pipeline ownership. That effectively makes Indigenous populations, and other environmental actors, border stakeholders. However, the fragmented nature of Indigenous and environmental governance in both Canada and the US, the evolving context for legal and constitutional disputes—particularly government's "duty to consult" Indigenous communities (Newman 2014), and the periodic spillover of these debates into civil disobedience and the blockading of key infrastructure and/or pipeline rights of way illustrate the multiscalar nature of Alberta border politics, and the direct effect on large segments of Alberta's economy (Belanger and Lackenbauer 2015; Hanna and Alsup 2020). Given the complexity of pipeline development and its significance in Alberta's socioeconomic context, the concept is worthy of a more thorough exploration. What's more, is it is an illustrative example of the key tenet of this volume: the open-border paradox.

Case Study: Securing Energy Transmission
Amid Competing Imperatives

Cross-border energy transmission in North America and its varied security aspects are classic expressions of the open-border paradox, as discussed in the introductory chapter: the idea that "borders depend on extensive cross-border cooperation for their effectiveness and legitimacy." Leuprecht and Hataley note in general terms that "bordering process(es), cooperative or otherwise, are driven by actors and contingent on structural frameworks." These frameworks, and their evolution, are frequently driven by the interaction of institutions (both structural and rules- or process-based), ideas, and interests.

The paradoxical aspect of the open-border paradox pertaining to its energy dimension and related environmental and other concerns is that it depends on shared interests and perspectives of public interest both across national borders (broadly speaking) and along extensive corridors linking energy producers often located thousands of kilometers from energy consumers (Doern and Gattinger 2003). It also depends on the complementarity or compatibility of market and regulatory regimes (and their roles in mediating interest groups and ideological competition) that structure various forms of energy production, distribution, and related provisions for environmental protection. Changing power relationships, both among diverse jurisdictions and between multiple states and competing societal interests, have contributed to border thickening and contingency. These debates may reflect competing hegemonic power-seeking or power-maintaining discourses (e.g., Levant 2011; Kraushaar-Friesen and Busch 2020), and those that place greater emphasis on reconciling competing goals and cultivating shared interests and mutual accommodation at multiple levels to maintain social acceptance and cohesion (Gattinger 2012; Hale and Belanger 2015).

Bordering: External and Internal

Bordering may be defined as "processes that define, structure, and regulate the rights and responsibilities of states toward one another, and their respective citizens and residents (including businesses), across national and sometimes sub-national boundaries" (Hale and Anderson 2021, 4). Such policies generally function in the context of broader policy regimes or systems. For energy infrastructure and related environmental issues, such policies help to determine the terms and conditions for approval and continuing operation of particular projects across national or subnational boundaries and, more rarely, cumulative effects in pursuit of evolving greenhouse gas emissions targets.

"Bordering" policies for energy, as Alberta's—and Canada's—largest export sector (68 percent and 21 percent respectively in 2019), take multiple forms. Canada, the United States, and Mexico have different regimes for producing and distributing different forms of energy—electricity (and varied fuel sources for power generation), oil, natural gas, and related inputs. The interaction and integration of energy and environmental goals and policies vary across jurisdictions and time periods, reflecting both government priorities and ideological and interest group competition. These variations are reinforced by differences in allocating responsibilities across the multiple jurisdictions of their respective federal systems (Hale 2019)—although they may also be buffered by provisions for reciprocal market access and nondiscrimination, including the 1977 Agreement . . . Concerning Transit Pipelines (Governments of Canada and the United States 1977).

Other forms of bordering include discrete provincial, state, and tribal (or First Nations) government rules governing land use and environmental regulation for energy production and transmission, and the use of systematic litigation to challenge the interpretation or application of existing and proposed rules. For example, Alberta's largest export pipeline cluster, the Enbridge mainline system,[2] passes through five states and multiple Native American territories via Superior, Wisconsin, in transit to Ontario (2,800 km) and southern Illinois's refinery hub (2,860 km; Enbridge 2021). TC Energy's Keystone[3] pipeline system transits six states (4,324 km) enroute to hubs in Oklahoma and Texas (*Oil Sands Magazine* 2021).

In Canada, federal and provincial regulatory outcomes, if not the underlying legislation, are increasingly conditional on the constitutional "duty to consult" First Nations and other Indigenous peoples over proposed energy, infrastructure, and other projects that may affect their use of traditional lands (Bergner 2016; Brideau 2019). Similar obligations apply under various US statutes to consultations with tribal governments, although their application is more uneven (Enbridge 2018; Sedisivam 2020). Both countries have signed the United Nations Declaration on the Rights of Indigenous Peoples, with its provisions for free, prior, and informed consent of indigenous peoples for resources and other projects that could affect their rights. The practical, legal, and other implications of these commitments are uncertain, vary across jurisdictions, and are likely to evolve over time.

Canada's cross-border energy infrastructure incorporates separate pipeline systems for oil and natural gas, along with electricity transmission lines and supplementary rail capacity. Alberta accounts for about 80 percent of Canada's oil production, with an additional 10 percent from Saskatchewan. Exports, almost exclusively to the US, have accounted for growing shares of Canada's oil production since 2010—about 80 percent of 4.6 million barrels/day (mmbd) total production in 2019. Imports, reflecting Canada's regionalized refining capacity, accounted for 0.9 mmbd (Natural Resources Canada 2020a; Canadian Energy Regulator 2021).

Canada's natural gas production is centered in Alberta (71 percent in 2019) and British Columbia (27 percent), averaging 16.6 billion cubic feet per day (bcf/d). However, shifting production patterns within North America have reduced relative export volumes and surpluses (45 percent, 7.4 bcf/d), with natural gas progressively replacing coal in baseload power generation in Western Canada, and growing US imports (2.9 bcf/d in 2019) to Central Canada (Natural Resources Canada 2020b).

Increased US environmental and political contestation since 2009, paradoxically, has led Canada to pursue both diversification of its export markets (and related pipeline capacity) to maintain its access to US markets and import displacement under favorable market conditions, but not without significant domestic opposition. Following the flow reversal of Enbridge's Line 9B between Sarnia, Ontario, and Montréal in the mid-2010s, transit pipelines crossing the US upper Midwest account for 53 percent of Ontario's and 66 percent of Québec's crude oil supply (Coletta 2021).

Export diversification has been constrained by multiple factors, not least the thickening of Canada's internal borders, particularly requirements to negotiate detailed agreements with dozens of First Nations in BC and elsewhere. Agreements on land use and environmental and economic benefits, sometimes including equity ownership, are effective preconditions for building pipelines and liquid natural gas (LNG) terminals to enable LNG exports to Asia. The latter also require federal *and* provincial (primarily BC) environmental assessments and permits (Natural Resources Canada 2020c). Both domestic and international environmental groups have sought to landlock Alberta oil and limit pipeline expansion as part of broader campaigns to reduce fossil fuel production and consumption. Similar pressures have given priority to the expansion of existing oil pipelines such as Trans Mountain from Edmonton to Vancouver over new construction, along with withdrawal or regulatory vetoes of several other projects in both Canada and the United States since 2015 (Hale 2019). One response of Canadian governments and industries has been to expand opportunities for Indigenous acquisition of ownership stakes in major resource projects, which illuminates competing perspectives in the Alberta context.

Both Canada and the United States are more self-sufficient in electricity production, although US regulatory reforms since the 1990s have encouraged more cross-border trade. With these patterns in mind, this case study focuses on bordering and competing security priorities in the context of Alberta's oil export and transit pipelines crossing the United States between points in Canada.

Security

Security takes multiple forms, depending on context. Energy security—the reliability of energy supplies and systems—has long been a strategic consideration for major industrial countries (Weintraub 2007; Yergin 2011). The integration of North American energy markets after 1985 was premised partly on Canada's contribution to US energy security following the OPEC oil shocks of the 1970s. Given regional conflicts within Canada and historical price volatility, market integration has helped to stabilize the economies of Alberta and other energy-producing provinces (Doern 2005). This integration—and the shared or complementary interests and policy priorities that have driven it—are central to the open-border paradox. However, while traditional security policies tend to be hierarchical or centrally coordinated, the responsibilities for technical reliability and public safety on which they depend are generally more decentralized, broadly distributed, and increasingly subject to more localized forms of contestation. Regulatory responsibility for security and for environmental and public safety policies governing energy infrastructure is widely diffused across energy subsectors and jurisdictions. However, operational responsibilities lie primarily with system owners (Hale and Bartlett 2019; Hale 2021).

Energy security is also premised on the reliability and resilience of production and distribution networks, which may be vulnerable to natural disasters, including hurricanes and forest fires, which have disrupted North American infrastructure in recent years (Hale 2011, 2019), earthquakes (prospectively, Thompson 2012), technical system failures, and human-induced disruptions. The last-mentioned may be a function of human error or criminal or foreign-state-sponsored interference, such as ongoing denial of service and ransomware attacks (Ivison 2021). Statistics Canada reports that 39 percent of energy- and utilities-sector respondents experienced cybersecurity incidents in 2019 (Sagan 2021). Disruptions of international energy markets arising from the Russia-Ukraine War have reinforced links between energy security and closer geopolitical cooperation, particularly between North American and European countries.

System failures may also contribute to significant environmental and public safety risks, and lead to the loss of public trust that has contributed to increased political conflicts over construction or renewal of energy infrastructure, along with the thickening of international and domestic borders noted above. For example, the 2010 Kalamazoo River pipeline spill, which required Enbridge to undertake a US$1.2 billion cleanup, has particularly polarized the politics of pipelines in Michigan, leading its governor to pursue the closure of another segment of the Enbridge mainline (Line 5) supplying both Michigan and Central Canada in 2020–2021, notwithstanding existing international agreements.

<h3 style="text-align:center">Integrating Markets, Security, Safety,
and Social Acceptance: The Energy "MESS"</h3>

Gattinger (2012, 2021) describes the evolving context for both cross-border and Canadian energy policies as a "MESS," requiring integration and balancing of *M*arket factors, *E*nvironmental protection, energy *S*ecurity, and *S*ocial acceptance. As noted above, political contestation, which is rooted in both place-based and climate-change concerns in both countries, has contributed to widespread conflicts over pipeline expansion. This section examines the integration of security and safety issues relating to two pipelines that link Alberta with both Ontario and midwestern US markets: Enbridge Line 3—part of a broader cluster of pipelines connecting Alberta with Superior, Wisconsin, at the head of Lake Superior, with links east and south; and Line 5, from Superior to Sarnia, Ontario, and points east.

The Enbridge mainline system dates to 1953, following major Alberta oil discoveries in 1947. Line 3 entered service in 1968. Most of Line 3's US route passes through Minnesota, whose northern lake districts are home to several self-governing Chippewa communities. Pipeline corrosion contributed to the failure of Line 6B through southern Michigan in 2010, heavily polluting the Kalamazoo River as noted above (Hale 2019). With similar risks along Line 3, Enbridge signed a consent order with the US Environmental Protection Agency (EPA, 2016) providing for both lines' reconstruction, subject to state regulatory approvals. Given growing environmental challenges to "greenfield" pipeline construction, Enbridge opted to expand Line 3 as part of a multipronged expansion of its main line following construction of the Alberta Clipper (Line 67) pipeline in 2010 to accommodate growing Canadian oil exports. Canada's National Energy Board issued a report recommending that the governor in council approve the Enbridge Line 3 Replacement Program, subject to 89 conditions. The governor in council subsequently issued Order in Council P.C. 2016–1048 directing the National Energy Board to issue a Certificate of Public Convenience and Necessity OC-63 to Enbridge Pipelines Inc. in respect of the proposed construction and operation of the Line 3 Replacement Program, subject to the terms and conditions set out in Appendix III of the National Energy Board Report of April 25, 2016. Concurrently, the National Energy Board was directed to dismiss Northern Gateway Pipelines Limited Partnership's application by Order in Council PC2016–1047. While Indigenous consultation was the subject of the Federal Court of Appeals decision in *Gitxaala Nation v. Canada*, 2016 FCA 187, quashing the Order in Council (P.C. 2014–809) issued by the previous government, the formal grounds for rejection were the governor in council's assessment (contrary to the Joint Review Panel's findings) that the project was "likely to cause significant adverse environmental impacts" that were "not justified in the circumstances" (Government of Canada 2016).

A key condition of state regulatory approvals of Line 3 was its relocation away from the original route across Minnesota's lake districts and several tribal territories. The support of some tribal governments was conditional on removal and cleanup of the original pipeline—giving Enbridge strong incentives to accommodate Native American interests within the regulatory process to avoid zero-sum outcomes. The legacy pipeline was limited to operating at 50 percent of capacity until project completion due to concerns over corrosion. Extended, systematic litigation in Minnesota over five years led to modest route changes but not the shutdown sought by pipeline opponents as part of broader, climate-change-related efforts to reduce Canadian oil imports. Minnesota and other upper Midwestern states remain heavily dependent on these imports for refinery feedstock and related energy security matters. The expanded Line 3 entered service on October 1, 2021, following extended regulatory scrutiny and litigation. The border has remained "open," but subject to the mutual accommodation, negotiated locally, of a much broader cluster of interests than in the past.

Line 5, built in 1953, is a 1,070 km pipeline between Superior, Wisconsin, and Sarnia, Ontario, which crosses Lake Michigan's Mackinac Strait (across its lakebed). The 2010 Kalamazoo oil spill noted above triggered strong support for the pipeline's removal among Michigan environmental groups. However, before leaving office Governor Rick Snyder obtained legislative approval in late 2018 for a utilities tunnel across the Strait to reduce future risks of oil spills—a conventional, if overdue, form of environmental mitigation. The tunnel would be built by Enbridge and owned by a newly created Mackinac Straits Corridor Authority (Government of Michigan 2021). The subsequent Democratic administration has challenged the law in court and sought to cancel the 1953 easement allowing for Line 5's continued operation, as promised before its election.

Given the substantial impact such actions would have on energy security in Central Canada, the Trudeau government has expressed concern over what it views as an infringement of the 1977 bilateral pipeline transit agreement. This treaty requires mitigation of regulatory actions that disrupt pipeline shipments across the US between points in Canada, with provisions for international arbitration between national governments—removing such issues from state jurisdiction. Alternative shipment options, whether by tanker or rail, also carry significant environmental risks. With the Biden administration (and its energy secretary, a former Michigan governor) deferring to state interests, Line 5's future remains subject to litigation and/or arbitration (Coletta 2021; Chase 2021).

Both pipeline cases help to illustrate the open-border paradox, with bordering processes dominated by state land use and regulatory policies, rather than cooperation among governments. In Minnesota, the EPA consent agreement and Enbridge's evolving willingness to accommodate tribal government priorities were key factors in negotiating conditions shaping the Line 3 renewal process despite intense political and legal contestation. In Michigan, Line 5 became a central issue in partisan political contestation, threatening to override the pragmatic "fix" of the Lake Michigan utilities tunnel, and placing much of Central Canada's crude oil supply at risk of a zero-sum outcome that shifts environmental risks (through use of lake tankers or railways to supply Canadian refineries), without eliminating them.

It remains to be seen whether existing legal and dispute-resolution processes, including those involving primacy of US federal or state laws, can resolve these conflicts without resorting to the compensation and/or arbitration processes provided for under the 1977 bilateral pipeline transit agreement. However, the primary assurance that the federal government will act on behalf of Alberta's interests presents a risk of major energy shortages and related price shocks to the federal government's constituents in Ontario and Québec—creating a shared interest within Canada that might not otherwise exist.

Societal Context for Trans-Border Security Issues

In addition to the significant issues of geography and socioeconomics, large-scale population growth, migration both interprovincial and international, and urbanization have affected the societal context for security and public safety attitudes in Alberta. The policy traction of these trends is shaped by the federal division of powers and the extent to which many Albertans feel their interests are accommodated by an often-distant federal government or through intergovernmental negotiations (Fair Deal Panel 2020). Canada's shift toward "economic class" or "skills-based" immigration policies since 1990, broadly supported by all major national parties, has kept immigration from being a polarizing issue in provincial politics (Perreaux 2018), although some employers' displacement of domestic workers (of varied backgrounds) by temporary foreign workers prompted a public backlash, leading to significant federal policy changes in 2013–2014 (Lilly 2021). However, growing provincial involvement in immigration through provincial nominee programs since 2000, combined with consistent economic growth until 2015, has typically reinforced legal and economic "pull" factors and public acceptance of immigration as a "positive sum." As in most of Canada, immigration is largely an urban phenomenon, although the hydrocarbon extraction and meat-packing industries have dispersed diverse immigrant communities to smaller, more remote cities such as Fort McMurray and Brooks to a greater extent than in some other provinces.

Attitudes toward climate-related security issues, which transcend national and regional borders but can have significant local and regional effects, reflect multiple factors. Albertans depend on energy resources for personal and collective prosperity, leading to their shouldering a disproportionate share of the costs of responding to climate issues. At the same time, Albertans make disproportionate fiscal contributions to subsidize public services in other provinces through federal tax revenues (Lafleur and Stedman 2018; Courchene and Courchene 2020). The province also faces a continuing need to adapt to repeated but unpredictable public safety risks arising from natural disasters, including major floods across southern Alberta in 2005 and 2013 and Fort McMurray in 2020, along with periodic major forest (and sometimes prairie) fires—discussed below. As with pipeline development, public contestation of specific proposals for protective infrastructure, regulatory delays, cross-cutting jurisdictions, and turnover in key provincial leadership positions have often delayed the design and implementation of remedial measures. These developments reflect widespread tendencies across communities and jurisdictions (within and beyond Alberta) to pursue the benefits of development while often attempting to shift and externalize related costs, which raises fundamental questions of governance.

Governance Models

The governance of security and related issues in Alberta reflects both the interaction of jurisdictional arrangements under Canada's federal system and the broader responsibilities for risk and emergency management involving public safety across multiple policy fields with inter-jurisdictional implications. In some cases, these arrangements interact with interprovincial and international trade agreements that govern market access for goods, services, capital, and business-related travel.

Law-enforcement dimensions of border security for Alberta are primarily addressed by the RCMP (executed primarily by federal policing resources within the RCMP's K Division) under the respective provincial police service agreements among the Government of Canada, Alberta, British Columbia, and other western provinces (and northern territories), together with the Alberta Law Enforcement Response Teams—ALERT (Government of Alberta 2019a; Government of British Columbia 2019), and, mostly peripherally, the Alberta Sheriffs Branch.

At ports of entry along the Alberta-Montana border, the CBSA works closely with US Customs and Border Protection officials, collocated at the Coutts-Sweetgrass Port of Entry and at the Calgary and Edmonton International Airports. However, it has few connections with provincial Alberta-based law enforcement beyond the Integrated Border Enforcement Team and the Integrated National Security Enforcement Teams. The former is a regional expression of a broader national, intelligence-driven process that brings together CBSA, RCMP, Customs and Border Protection, the US Border Patrol, and related agencies to manage cross-border law enforcement challenges. The Integrated National Security Enforcement Teams connect CBSA with representatives from the Edmonton Police Service, Calgary Police Service, and the Provincial Security and Intelligence Office.

As mentioned in the chapter on border security in British Columbia, there is value in Alberta expanding its relationship with the CBSA to address challenges such as the smuggling of fentanyl, other "street drugs," weapons, and dealing with organized crime activity (Theobald 2017). CBSA officials have begun to screen international packet mail to postal codes with above-average drug overdose statistics as a way to combat this trade. As a landlocked province, however, Alberta appears to be a lower priority for CBSA.

Access to Alberta's natural resources across both provincial and national borders, together with favorable interprovincial and international trade agreements, has never been more important for Alberta. Since 2006, Alberta has signed two significant trade agreements: the 2006 British Columbia–Alberta Trade, Investment, and Labour Mobility Agreement (TILMA), which includes British Columbia, Alberta, and Saskatchewan and the 2010 New West Partnership Trade Agreement (NWPTA), which includes British Columbia, Alberta, Saskatchewan, and Manitoba. . The original TILMA removed many of the barriers that had impeded trade and commerce between Alberta and British Columbia, including allowing provincially regulated and licensed professionals to work temporarily across the border in either province. The NWPTA (2018) furthers integration among the economies of the four western provinces. However, these agreements have been of minimal value in dealing with cross-border disputes (or contestation within the legal and regulatory systems of other provinces and states) over pipeline expansion.

Alberta's Office for Intergovernmental Relations manages 231 agreements between Alberta and the federation (Government of Alberta 2019b). Twenty-two of these intergovernmental agreements are specific to the Ministry of Justice and Solicitor General. Two agreements are specific to the Ministry of Health, coordinating assistance related to transborder health and infection matters. The Alberta-Canada agreement provides for federal RCMP officers to be seconded to assist with the victims in cases of missing and murdered indigenous women in Alberta. Another agreement provides for Alberta to contribute resources and expertise, assisting the Government of Canada in supporting foreign countries during pandemic outbreaks.

Few agreements are specific to law enforcement and security. Even fewer have a cross-border context: a 2017 agreement between the Alberta government and CSIS to access vital statistics data, a 2016 agreement between Alberta and Justice Canada to access vehicle registration data, and several agreements signed in 2017 between Alberta and Canada regarding the joint funding of First Nations police services in Alberta. Otherwise, the Alberta government has not actively sought assistance or support for cross-border law enforcement. While addressing crimes such as the smuggling and trafficking of drugs, weapons, and humans remains a top priority for Alberta law enforcement agencies, most transborder crime in western Canada occurs along the British Columbia–Washington state border, through the Vancouver International Airport, or via marine ports located in the Lower Mainland or Vancouver Island regions, beyond Alberta's border.

On other major public safety issues with transborder implications, the Canadian Food Inspection Agency oversees inspections of major meat-processing plants. It provides for periodic inspections by the US Department of Agriculture of plants exported to the United States. Occupational safety and health issues, such as those raised by the 2020 pandemic, are the responsibility of Occupational Health and Safety Services within Alberta Labour and Immigration.

Regulatory issues associated with interprovincial pipelines, including both permitting and environmental reviews, are consolidated within the Canadian Energy Regulator, a federal agency, formerly the National Energy Board. Rail-safety issues are overseen by Transport Canada, although a bilateral agreement signed in 2006 enables effective provincial responses to environmental incidents on national rail lines within the province, comparable to agreements for provincial enforcement of federal trucking regulations governing interprovincial carriers. All four Western provinces have harmonized truck configuration and related safety regulations to facilitate the seamless movement of goods across provincial borders.

Main Actors

National, Provincial, and Municipal Actors

A range of federal, provincial, and municipal actors oversee security-related portfolios in Alberta. While some have overlapping mandates, each has a distinct jurisdictional focus in terms of their power and role. The following section provides an overview of the primary actors in interprovincial and international collaboration and cooperation in the Alberta borderlands.

Economic

Along with the Calgary and Edmonton International airports, the northern and southern Trans-Canada Highway corridors serve as the primary transportation route for east-west Albertan commerce. Pipelines and railways also support major elements of Alberta's economic activity, facilitating exports of Alberta hydrocarbons.

Transport Canada regulates interprovincial trucking licenses and operations but has delegated many of its enforcement responsibilities to provincial ministries of transportation. Parks Canada and the RCMP also have enforcement roles as the Trans-Canada Highway passes through several national parks along the Alberta–British Columbia border. The 700-mile Mackenzie Highway that links Alberta with the Northwest Territories is a vital lifeline as the only highway that connects several of the nation's northern communities to resources and services in the south (Transport Canada 2011).

Alberta's international airports also serve as border facilitators, linking travelers from smaller centers to other Canadian cities and destinations abroad, and as air cargo hubs for high-value-added products. Transport

Canada regulates the safety framework for Canada's airports and air carriers, although locally governed airport authorities operate airports within
the province under federal law. CBSA and RCMP officers provide border
control and law enforcement at airports. Specific to the Calgary Airport,
Protective Policing Services are provided under contract by the Calgary
Police Service. In addition, US Customs and Border Protection (CBP) officers have been providing preclearance services to travelers flying directly
to US destinations from Calgary and Edmonton since the 1960s. Security
screening of travelers and their baggage is the responsibility of the Canadian Air Transport Security Agency, a federal crown corporation funded by
passenger user fees. Revisions to the Canada–US preclearance agreement
made in 2017 allow US CBP officials to function under US law (including refusing admission to travelers), but the location of screening facilities
places travelers under Canadian law until they pass through US Customs.

The governance of both Canadian National and Canadian Pacific Railways is another major dimension of Alberta's and Canada's borderlands
and their security. Both CP and CN Railways operate their own respective (private) police services, rather than having more usual public policing
arrangements. Long-standing federal laws in both countries enable both
railways' police services to operate on both sides of the Canada–US border (CN Rail 2019a, 2019b). Alberta also negotiated an agreement with
Ottawa in 2006 to take the lead in investigating and enforcing remedia-
tion of environmental damage resulting from train derailments, following
a major incident in rural Alberta in 2005.

As noted above, Alberta relies on transborder pipelines far more than
any other region in Canada. In 2018, the federal government purchased
the Trans Mountain Pipeline between Edmonton and Burnaby, BC, the
only major pipeline linking Alberta with the Pacific Coast, after the previous owner abandoned its efforts to expand the pipeline following extended
regulatory delays and legal challenges. Quantitatively and qualitatively, the
mining, oil, and gas sectors have an outsize influence on the bordering
policies affecting Alberta's security.

Regulatory

Formerly known as the National Energy Board, the Canada Energy Regulator (CER) has auspices over interprovincial and international oil, gas, and
electricity transmission. The CER and its cooperative agencies are especially important to the province given the energy sector's importance to
Alberta's economy. The CER works in cooperation with multiple agencies
to oversee energy regulation, including the US Federal Energy Regula-

tory Commission, through a memorandum of understanding (MOU) on enhanced interagency coordination. While the CER shapes strategies regarding interprovincial and international energy trade, regulation of energy production, transmission within provinces, and related environmental issues is mainly a provincial responsibility, overseen in Alberta by the Alberta Energy Regulator and Alberta Utilities Commission. Regulatory activities attempt to combine orderly economic processes, security, and, increasingly, mitigation of environmental and climate impacts. However, these objectives are intensely contested and difficult to balance.

Law Enforcement

The mandate for border security in Alberta, as in other provinces in Canada, is carried out by the RCMP and CBSA, which perform a broad range of federal policing and enforcement duties between and at ports of entry respectively. Other federal policing and law enforcement agencies, notably Parks Canada Rangers and CN and CP Police Services, at times also have a role in securing the international border.

Region-Wide Actors

A number of cross-border agreements and organizations address a regional approach to border security and provincial security: economic security, health (including agriculture), transportation, fire safety, and other forms of emergency management. They push the regional border beyond the borderline, while exemplifying transborder cooperation and collaboration. In particular, three agreements and organizations stand out.

Self-identified as the "gold standard of Canada–US relations," the Pacific Northwest Economic Region (PNWER) is a public/private non-profit that includes five US states, three Canadian provinces, and two Canadian territories. PNWER's regional networks enhance information-sharing on cross-border trade, livestock health, regional disaster resilience, invasive species control, and other regional health and security issues. With fifteen working groups (PNWER 2019), PNWER has four main decision-making groups with private- and public-sector stakeholders. The working groups range from those focused directly on border issues (including the engagement with Beyond the Border and Regulatory Cooperation Council processes) to a wide range of other economic and environmental issues (PNWER 2019).

Alberta also plays an active part in regional cooperation and information-sharing as an associate member of the Council of State Governments West

(CSG West), along with the thirteen western US states and three Pacific territories (CSG West 2016). CSG West is a nonpartisan NGO that facilitates discussions on agriculture, border crossings, economic competitiveness, energy, health, security, trade, and transportation among the western US states and the western Canadian provinces (CSG West 2016).

Fire and other forms of emergency management have become increasingly important security considerations for Alberta's borderlands and regional cooperation. Recent fire disasters, such as Slave Lake in 2011 and Horse River (Fort McMurray) in 2016, resulted in billions in insurance claims, suppression costs, recovery costs, and lost revenue—not to mention environmental impact—sometimes spilling over into (or from) British Columbia, Saskatchewan, or Montana. The 2016 Horse River fires, which involved firefighting crews from the US and elsewhere, were the costliest natural disaster in Canadian history (Tymstra et al. 2020) until freak storms in British Columbia destroyed several bridges along the main highway link between Alberta (and the British Columbia interior) and Vancouver in 2021. The Canadian Interagency Forest Fire Centre (CIFFC) in Winnipeg provides collaborative fire-management services that facilitate resource sharing, mutual aid, and information sharing. Through regional monitoring, the CIFFC can draw on national and international sources, and deploy and operationalize resources as needed to respond to forest fires across Canada, including Alberta.

Operationalizing Concepts

Horizontal Security Concepts

Municipal police services (apart from the RCMP) typically only communicate with their counterparts ad hoc during major crime or organized crime investigations. Horizontal collaboration and cooperation in criminal intelligence across Alberta's provincial borders generally falls to Criminal Intelligence Service Alberta (located in Alberta Law Enforcement Response Teams) within the wider Criminal Intelligence Services Canada network, and to a lesser extent, the RCMP. However, the principal municipal forces (i.e., Calgary Police Service, Edmonton Police Service) increasingly have active intelligence networks across Canada and into the United States. Though provinces often identify best practices in criminal justice policy, processes, and approaches, these duplications are not the result of formal interprovincial agreements or arrangements. Rather, they emerge organically at the agency level. The formal interplay among agencies in Alberta and those in adjoining border regions is more vertical (Alberta-Montana or Canada–United States) than the more informal horizontal relations (Alberta–British Columbia or Alberta-Saskatchewan).

Vertical Security Concepts

Although the RCMP has responsibility for border security between ports of entry (POEs) in Alberta, and Canadian Security Intelligence Service has primary responsibility for collecting and analyzing intelligence relating to foreign threats (specifically espionage, sabotage, foreign-influenced activities, the threat or use of acts of serious violence for political, religious, or ideological objectives, and covert subversion against the government), CBSA has primary responsibility for Alberta's international border security. As with most national border security services, CBSA operates at, beyond, and behind the border. At ports of entry, CBSA officers examine and process persons, goods, and agricultural products seeking entry to Canada. Alberta has six ports of entry. Most commercial traffic passes through the Coutts/Sweetgrass crossing that links Alberta with the US Interstate Highway system (I-15), referred to in an economic context as the CANAMEX/ North-South Highway System. Land border operations in Alberta (185 mi) and Saskatchewan (393 mi) are coordinated from Coutts. The capacity to assign certain administrative work (e.g., individual vehicle imports) electronically enables CBSA to maintain operations at low-traffic border crossings of mainly local relevance that otherwise might be uneconomical during times of relative fiscal constraint. Beyond the border, CBSA officers work out of high commissions, embassies, and other international locations to review and screen visa applications, coordinate efforts with foreign customs, immigration, and agricultural inspection services, and collect information on possible threats to Canada before they reach Canadian borders. Behind the border, officers work from "inland" offices located in Lethbridge, Calgary, and Edmonton, where they investigate incidents of persons or goods entering Canada despite being deemed inadmissible— ultimately arresting, detaining, and removing noncitizens present without legal authorization, or seizing contraband goods and agricultural products. The remoteness of border crossings across Alberta contributes to significant turnover among CBSA officers and related border delays, although the agency provides many officers with travel allowances so they can commute to work from Lethbridge and neighboring communities.

Alberta has six land POEs along the border with Montana, although only Coutts operates continuously. Of three air POEs, only YYC (Calgary) and YEG (Edmonton) offer regular international air travel and cargo services. Inland immigration enforcement, investigations, and intelligence units are also located in Calgary and Edmonton (CBSA 2022; Sundberg 2013). About 320 of the CBSA's roughly 6,500 border security officers work in Alberta: about 100 of them work at land POEs, about 110 at YYC, about 60 at YEG; the remainder work in inland immigration enforcement, investigations, or intelligence at either Calgary or Edmonton offices.

With under 5 percent of the total number of border security officers assigned to Alberta, CBSA does not feature prominently as a policing, law enforcement, or security organization within the province. Neither CBSA directors nor chiefs in Alberta regularly attend Alberta Association of Chiefs of Police meetings, or meet regularly with Alberta's municipal police services (AACP 2017). However, local interactions involving CBSA are increasing. CBSA inland immigration enforcement, investigations, or intelligence officers rarely participate in joint operations with a municipal police service or the RCMP. CBSA characteristically operates independently from other policing, security, and intelligence services in Alberta. CBSA processes about four million travelers each year, two-thirds of whom travel through YYC and YEG; officers conduct nearly 200,000 secondary examinations and take more than 5,000 customs-related enforcement actions (CBSA 2017a). CBSA's inland enforcement, investigations, and intelligence activities within Alberta constitute only a small fraction of the national total (CBSA 2017b; CBSA 2017c).

Horizon Scan

Along with cybersecurity and emerging technology, economic security and political influence have important implications in the context of Alberta's borders. The February 2020 shutdown of Canada's national rail service by protesters opposed to the Coastal GasLink pipeline in British Columbia demonstrates the capacity for disputes over pipelines, environmental issues, and Indigenous rights to spill over provincial borders (Hanna and Alsup 2020). As long as Alberta depends on moving hydrocarbons to global markets, it remains vulnerable to disruptions, protests, and political contest. While protests and disruptions are generally localized and transient, the political contest is a key vulnerability. Similarly, social-media-driven protests over Covid restrictions closed or disrupted Alberta's main north-south border crossing for three weeks in 2022, with disproportionate effects on agri-food trade, before the RCMP successfully de-escalated and peacefully dissipated the blockade. In essence, border security in Alberta reflects provincial interests as much as federal security priorities, and the perennial challenges of integrating regional interests within Canada's deeply fragmented political system.

Conclusion

Border and borderland security in Alberta has a complex and regionally distinctive geographic, socioeconomic, and political profile. It is shaped by a dynamic interplay and cooperation between government and civil society stakeholders, across multiple horizontal and vertical axes, and there is a notably strong presence across the oil and gas industries and air transportation. As a landlocked province, Alberta is heavily dependent on access to external markets, and thus on reciprocal accommodation of economic and security interests with other provinces and the United States. These factors will continue to influence how Alberta's borders are conceptualized politically and socially. Since Western provinces depend heavily on trade and contribute disproportionally to Canada's economic growth (Conference Board of Canada 2019), the security of trade and transportation (including pipeline) corridors will remain a major determinant for Alberta's national borders and border-security regime (Lafleur and Stedman 2018).

NOTES

1. Québec City is 110 mi. from Jackman, ME; Regina is 110 mi. from Raymond, MT; Saint John, NB is 110 mi. from Calais, ME. Halifax and St. John's are in provinces without US land borders.

2. The Enbridge mainline does not cross the Alberta/US border, but rather the Manitoba border. However its inclusion here is important among overall bordering issues for Alberta.

3. The Enbridge mainline does not cross the Alberta/US border, but rather the Manitoba border. However its inclusion here is important among overall bordering issues for Alberta.

REFERENCES

Airports Council International. 2019. *Annual World Airport Traffic Report, 2019.* Montréal: Airports Council International publication.

Alberta Association of Chiefs of Police (AACP). 2017. *Alberta Association of Chiefs of Police Active Membership.* https://aacp.ca/?page_id=182

Alberta Motor Association. 2019. *Interactive Road Reports and Maps*. https://roadre
ports.ama.ab.ca

Anderson, Greg, and Geoffrey Hale. 2018. "Borders in Globalization: Alberta in a
BiG Context." *Journal of Borderlands Studies* 34, no. 2: 149–56. https://www.ac
ademia.edu/72930426/Borders_in_Globalization_Alberta_in_a_BiG_Context

Baum, K. B., C. Tait, and T. Grant. 2020. "The Other Front Line." *Globe and Mail*,
May 2: A13–14.

Belanger, Yale D., and P. Whitney Lackenbauer, eds. 2015. *Blockades or Breakthroughs: Aboriginal Peoples Confront the Canadian State*. Montréal: McGill–
Queen's University Press.

Bergner, Keith B. 2016. "The Northern Gateway Project and the Federal Court
of Appeal: The Regulatory Process and the Crown's Duty to Consult." *Energy
Regulatory Quarterly* 4, no. 3. https://energyregulationquarterly.ca/case-comme
nts/the-northern-gateway-project-and-the-federal-court-of-appeal-the-regula
tory-process-and-the-crowns-duty-to-consult#sthash.cflekYmM.dpbs

Brideau, Isabelle. 2019. "The Duty to Consult Indigenous Peoples." # 2019–17-E.
Ottawa: Library of Parliament, June 12. https://lop.parl.ca/staticfiles/PublicW
ebsite/Home/ResearchPublications/BackgroundPapers/PDF/2019-17-e.pdf

Canada Border Services Agency (CBSA). 2016. *Audit of Immigration Enforcement*.
https://www.cbsa-asfc.gc.ca/agency-agence/reports-rapports/ae-ve/2016/ie
-emi-eng.html

Canada Border Services Agency (CBSA). 2017a. *Alberta POE Statistics*. Retrieved
directly from the CBSA via email.

Canada Border Services Agency (CBSA). 2017b. *Arrest, Detention, and Removal Statistics*. https://www.cbsa-asfc.gc.ca/security-securite/detent-stat-eng.html

Canada Border Services Agency (CBSA). 2017c. *Departments Results Report
2016/2017*. http://www.cbsa-asfc.gc.ca/agency-agence/reports-rapports/dpr
-rmr/2016-2017/report-rapport-eng.pdf

Canada Border Services Agency (CBSA). 2022. *Inland Office*. https://www.cbsa-asfc
.gc.ca/do-rb/services/inland-interieur-eng.html

Canadian Association of Petroleum Producers. 2019. "Canadian and U.S. Oil
Refineries and Pipelines." Calgary. https://static1.squarespace.com/static/52ab
b9b9e4b0cb06a591754d/t/5d02a07bea46fd00014b784d/1560453248200/2019
-CAPP-pipeline-refinery-map.pdf

Canadian Energy Regulator. 2021. "Canadian Crude Oil Exports: A 30-Year
Review." June 21. https://www.cer-rec.gc.ca/en/data-analysis/energy-commo
dities/crude-oil-petroleum-products/report/canadian-crude-oil-exports-30-ye
ar-review/index.html

Canadian Institute for Health Information. 2018. *Opioid Related Harms in Canada*.
Ottawa: December. https://www.cihi.ca/sites/default/files/document/opioid-re
lated-harms-report-2018-en-web.pdf

Canadian National Railway (CN Rail). 2019a. "Interactive Rail Network Map."
https://cnebusiness.geomapguide.ca

Canadian National Railway (CN Rail). 2019b. "CN Police Service." https://www
.cn.ca/en/safety/cn-police-service

Chase, Steven. 2021. "Canada Holding Biweekly Bilateral Meetings with U.S. on
Line 5 Shutdown." *Globe and Mail*, June 23.

Coletta, Amanda. 2021. "Looming Showdown as Michigan Governor Orders Canadian Pipeline Shut Down." *Washington Post*, May 2.

Conference Board of Canada. 2019. *Provincial Outlook Executive Summary: Autumn 2019*. https://www.conferenceboard.ca/e-library/abstract.aspx?did=10512

Courchene, Thomas J., and Teresa M. Courchene. 2020. *Fiscal Fairness: How Equalization Failed Alberta in Its Time of Need and How to Fix It*. Ottawa: Macdonald Laurier Institute. https://macdonaldlaurier.ca/files/pdf/20200408_MLI_AB _Equalization_Courchene_PAPER_FWeb.pdf

CSG West. 2016. "About CSG West." https://www.csgwest.org/about/AboutCSG West.aspx

Doern, G. Bruce, ed. 2005. *Canadian Energy Policy and the Struggle for Sustainable Development*. Toronto: University of Toronto Press.

Doern, G. Bruce, and Monica Gattinger. 2003. *Power Switch: Energy Regulatory Governance in North America*. Toronto: University of Toronto Press.

Edmiston, Jake. 2020. "Three Meat-Packing Plants Turn Out 85 Percent of Canada's Beef. How Did that Happen?" *Financial Post*, May 6. https://business.financ ialpost.com/commodities/agriculture/why-only-three-meat-packing-plants-pr ocess-the-vast-majority-of-canadas-beef

Enbridge, Inc. 2018. "The Case for Change." *Indigenous Rights and Relationships in North American Energy Infrastructure*. Calgary. https://www.enbridge.com/susta inability-reports/indigenous-discussion-paper/case-for-change

Enbridge, Inc. 2021. "Energy Infrastructure Assets." Updated August 4. https:// www.enbridge.com/~/media/Enb/Documents/Factsheets/FS_EnergyInfrastru ctureAssets.pdf?la=en

Fair Deal Panel. 2020. *Report to Government*. https://open.alberta.ca/dataset/d8933f 27-5f81-4cbb-97c1-f56b45b09a74/resource/d5836820-d81f-4042-b24e-b04e0 12f4cde/download/fair-deal-panel-report-to-government-may-2020.pdf

Gattinger, Monica. 2012. "Canada–U.S. Energy Relations: Making a MESS of Energy Policy." *American Review of Canadian Studies* 42, no. 4 (December): 460–73.

Gattinger, Monica. 2021. "Canadian Energy in North America and Beyond: Between an Economic Rock and a Progressive Hard Place." In *Navigating a Changing World: Canada's International Policies in an Age of Uncertainties*, edited by Geoffrey Hale and Greg Anderson, 399–428. Toronto: University of Toronto Press.

Government of Alberta. 2017. *Alberta's International Exports by Industry: A 10-Year Review*. https://www.albertacanada.com/files/albertacanada/SP-EH_AIME-10 -year-review.pdf

Government of Alberta. 2019a. *Policing in Alberta*. https://www.alberta.ca/policing -in-alberta.aspx

Government of Alberta. 2019b. "Inventory of International and Intergovernmental Agreements." https://open.alberta.ca/dataset/394ddff1-7a4f-479d-b8a4-9ce80 d67d6a5/resource/96b19def-98cb-41f2-a475-06fae697d2fc/download/cpe-inv entory-intl-intergovt-agreements-2018-2019.pdf

Government of British Columbia. 2019. "Provincial Policing." https://www2.gov .bc.ca/gov/content/justice/criminal-justice/policing-in-bc/the-structure-of-po lice-services-in-bc/provincial

Government of Canada. 2016. "Orders in Council 2016–1047." https://orders-in
-council.canada.ca/attachment.php?attach=32747&lang=en
Governments of Canada and the United States of America. 1977. "Agreement
between the Government of Canada and the Government of the United States
of America Concerning Transit Pipelines." *Canada Treaty Series: E101884—
CTS 1977 No. 29.* Ottawa: Global Affairs Canada.
Government of Michigan. 2021. "Line 5 in Michigan: Proposed Line 5/Great
Lakes Tunnel Project FAQs." https://www.michigan.gov/line5/0,9833,7-413
-100616-528646--,00.html
Hale, Geoffrey. 2011. "In the Pipeline or Over a Barrel? Assessing Canadian Efforts
to Manage U.S. Canadian Energy Interdependence." *Canadian-American Public
Policy* 76.
Hale, Geoffrey. 2019. "Cross-Border Energy Infrastructure: The Politics of Inter-
mesticity." In *Canada Among Nations: 2018—Canada-US Relations: Sovereignty
or Shared Institutions?*, edited by D. Carment and C. Sands, 163–92. Aldershot,
UK: Palgrave Macmillan.
Hale, Geoffrey. 2021. "National Security and Economic Security: Distributed vs.
Hierarchical Management of Domestic and Critical Infrastructure Security in
Canada and North America." In *Navigating a Changing World: Canada's Inter-
national Policies in an Age of Uncertainties*, edited by Geoffrey Hale and Greg
Anderson, 230–54. Toronto: University of Toronto Press.
Hale, Geoffrey, and Greg Anderson. 2021. "Multi-Level, Multi-Layer: Managing
Canada's Multiple Borders for Goods, Services, People, and Capital." In *Cana-
da's Fluid Borders: Trade, Investment, Travel, Migration*, 1–19. Ottawa: University
of Ottawa Press.
Hale, Geoffrey, and Cailin Bartlett. 2019. "Managing the Regulatory Tangle:
Critical Infrastructure Security and Distributed Governance in Alberta's Major
Traded Sectors." *Journal of Borderlands Studies* 34, no. 2: 257–79.
Hale, Geoffrey, and Yale D. Belanger. 2015. "From Social Licence to Social Part-
nership: Promoting Shared Interests for Resource and Infrastructure Develop-
ment." *Commentary #440.* Toronto: C. D. Howe Institute, December.
Hanna, Jason, and Dave Alsup. 2020. "A Protest Over a Pipeline Is Shutting Down
Train Service across Much of Canada." *CNN World*, February 15. https://www
.cnn.com/2020/02/14/americas/canada-rail-disruptions-pipeline-protests/?hpt
=ob_blogfooterold
Ivison, John. 2020. "Canada Avoids Predictions of Food Shortage." *National Post*,
May 23: A1.
Ivison, John. 2021. "Forget the Cold War. This Is Hot." *National Post*, April 7: A4.
King, Colbert I. 2016. "Guns Smuggled from the U.S. Fuel Bloodshed in Can-
ada." *Washington Post*, February 19. https://www.washingtonpost.com/opinions
/an-american-export-canadians-dont-want-illegal-guns/2016/02/19/b65d7b72
-d69a-11e5-be55-2cc3c1e4b76b_story.html?utm_term=.d07421c7734c
Kraushaar-Friesen, Naima, and Henner Busch. 2020. "Of Pipe Dreams and Fossil
Fools: Advancing Canadian Fossil Fuel Hegemony through the Trans Moun-
tain Pipeline." *Energy Research & Social Science*, 69, article 101695.
Lafleur, Steve, and Ashley Stedman. 2018. "Pipelines Aren't Just an Alberta Issue—
They Are Crucial to National Prosperity." *Macleans Magazine*, February 14.

http://www.macleans.ca/opinion/pipeline-arent-just-an-alberta-issue-they-are
-crucial-to-national-prosperity/

Levant, Ezra. 2011. *Ethical Oil: The Case for Canada's Oil Sands.* Toronto: McClelland and Stewart.

Lilly, Meredith B. 2021. "Reforming High-Skilled Temporary Foreign Worker Programs in Canada and the United States." In *Navigating a Changing World: Canada's International Policies in an Age of Uncertainties,* edited by Geoffrey Hale and Greg Anderson, 152–78. Toronto: University of Toronto Press.

McCoy, John, David Jones, and Zoe Hastings. 2019. "Building Awareness, Seeking Solutions: Extremism and Hate Motivated Violence in Alberta." *Organization for the Prevention of Violence,* June 18. https://preventviolence.ca/publication/building-awareness-seeking-solutions-2019-report/

Milligan, Kevin. 2018. "Resource Jobs Are Sustaining Canada's Middle Class. Period." *Globe and Mail,* April 16.

Moens, Alexander, and Amos Vivanco-Leon. 2012. *M-COOL and the Politics of Country-of-Origin Labeling.* Vancouver: Fraser Institute, June.

Morgan, G. 2020. "Oilsands' Unlikely New Route to the East." *Calgary Herald,* May 5: A1.

Natural Resources Canada. 2020a. Crude oil facts. Ottawa: October 6. https://www.nrcan.gc.ca/science-and-data/data-and-analysis/energy-data-and-analysis/energy-facts/natural-gas-facts/20067

Natural Resources Canada. 2020b. "Natural Gas Facts." Ottawa, October 6. https://www.nrcan.gc.ca/our-natural-resources/energy-sources-distribution/clean-fossil-fuels/natural-gas-facts/canadian-lng-projects/5683

Natural Resources Canada. 2020c. "Canadian LNG projects." Ottawa, August 6. https://www.nrcan.gc.ca/our-natural-resources/energy-sources-distribution/clean-fossil-fuels/natural-gas/canadian-lng-projects/5683

New West Partnership Trade Agreement (NWPTA). 2018. *Benefits of the Agreement.* http://www.newwestpartnershiptrade.ca/

Newman, Dwight G. 2014. *Revisiting the Duty to Consult Aboriginal Peoples.* Vancouver: UBC Press.

Oil Sands Magazine. 2021. "Oil Pipelines: Midstream." Updated July 7. https://www.oilsandsmagazine.com/projects/crude-oil-liquids-pipelines

Pacific Northwest Economic Region (PNWER). 2019. *Working Groups.* https://www.pnwer.org/working-groups.html

Palmer, Vaughn. 2020. "Feds Not Ready, but B.C. Will Go Ahead with Quarantine Plan on Friday." *Vancouver Sun,* April 10.

Perreaux, Les. 2018. "Canadian Attitudes toward Immigrants, Refugees Remain Positive: Study." *Globe and Mail,* March 22. https://www.theglobeandmail.com/canada/article-canadian-attitudes-toward-immigrants-refugees-remain-positive-study/

Policy Research Initiative. 2008. *The Emergence of Cross-Border Regions between Canada and the United States.* Ottawa, November. https://publications.gc.ca/collections/collection_2009/policyresearch/PH4-31-2-2008E.pdf

Potter, Andrew. 2020. "Federal Authority on the Ropes in Coronavirus Crisis." *National Post,* March 17: A10.

Ramsey, Caley. 2018. "Alberta Unveils 'Real-Time Loss-Revenue Counter' Amid

Pipeline Delays." *Global News Calgary*, November 15. https://globalnews.ca/ne
ws/4662706/alberta-lost-revenue-counter-pipeline-delays/

Sagan, Aleksandra. 2021. "Energy Companies Most at Risk of Cyber Attacks: Documents." *Calgary Herald*, June 22: B2.

Sedisivam, Naveena. 2020. "Federal Agencies Are Supposed to Consult with Tribes
about Pipelines. They Often Don't." *Grist*, January 2. https://grist.org/energy
/federal-agencies-are-required-to-consult-with-tribes-about-pipelines-they-of
ten-dont/

Selley, Chris. 2020. "Airport Chaos Does Little to Inspire Credibility." *National
Post*, March 17: A1.

Speer, Sean. 2018. "Working Class Opportunity and the Threat of Populism in
Canada." Ottawa: Macdonald Laurier Institute, December.

Staples, David. 2020. "The Road to Canada's COVID_19 Outbreak; Pt. 3: Timeline of Federal Government Failure at Border to Slow the Virus." *Edmonton
Journal*, March 31.

Statistics Canada. 2017. "Alberta Has the Most Beef Cattle in Canada and the Second Largest Total Farm Area." *The Daily*, Cat. 95–640-X, May 10. https://www
150.statcan.gc.ca/n1/pub/95-640-x/2016001/article/14808-eng.htm

Statistics Canada. 2020a. Table 36-10-0222-01. "Gross Domestic Product,
Expenditure-Based, Provincial and Territorial, Annual (x1,000,000)." https://
doi.org/10.25318/3610022201-eng

Statistics Canada. 2020b. Table 23-10-0253-01. "Air Passenger Traffic at Canadian
Airports, Annual." https://www150.statcan.gc.ca/t1/tbl1/en/tv.action?pid=2310
025301

St. Onge, Josée. 2018. "Straw Purchasing Puts More Legally Bought Guns in the
Hands of Alberta Criminals." *CBC News*, June 14. https://www.cbc.ca/news/ca
nada/edmonton/straw-purchasing-domestic-weapons-trafficking-increase-1.4
704987

Sundberg, Kelly W. 2013. "Internal Immigration Enforcement as a Key Feature in
National Security: A Review of Australia and Canada." *Journal of the Australian
Institute of Professional Intelligence Officers* 21, no. 1: 3–20.

Theobald, Claire. 2017. "Record Number of Organized Crime Networks Identified in Alberta." *Edmonton Journal*, July 16. https://edmontonjournal.com/news
/crime/record-number-of-organized-crime-networks-identified-in-alberta

Thompson, Jerry. 2012. *Cascadia's Fault: The Coming Earthquake and Tsunami that
Could Devastate North America*. Berkely, CA: Counterpoint Press.

Transport Canada. 2011. *National Highway System*. https://tc.canada.ca/en/corpora
te-services/policies/national-highway-system

Tymstra, Cordy, Brian J. Stocks, Xinli Cai, and Mike D. Flannigan. 2020. "Wildfire
Management in Canada: Review, Challenges and Opportunities." *Progress in
Disaster Science* 5, 100045: 1–10.

US Energy Information Administration. 2020. *International Energy Outlook*. https://
www.eia.gov/international/overview/world

US Environmental Protection Agency. 2016. "Enbridge Clean Water Act Settlement." July 20. https://www.epa.gov/enforcement/enbridge-clean-water-act-se
ttlement

Weintraub, Sidney, with Annette Hester and Veronica R. Prado, eds. 2007. *Energy*

Cooperation in the Western Hemisphere: Benefits and Obstacles. Washington, DC: Center for Strategic and International Studies.

Winterdyk, John A., and Kelly W. Sundberg. 2010. *Border Security in the Era of Al-Qaeda.* Boca Raton, FL: CRC Press.

Wipf, Kevin. 2019. "Shifting Figurative, Functional and Operational Borders: The Multiple Worlds of Agri-Food Trade and Border Regimes." *Journal of Borderlands Studies* 34, no. 2: 213–33.

Yergin, Daniel. 2011. *The Quest: Energy, Security and the Remaking of the Modern World.* New York: Penguin Random House Press.

FOUR

The Prairies and the Midwest

Todd Hataley, Christian Leuprecht, and Alexandra Green

Introduction

In the Prairies, the nature of cross-border movements makes security measures at the immediate, physical border, largely ineffective. Border crossings tend to be isolated, with limited mobility and infrastructure. Many of these crossings are seasonal and do not have the infrastructure to process large quantities of goods. Also, goods crossing the international border in this part of Canada are usually of agricultural origin and present different threats than those faced in other regions. Border officials have insufficient expertise to properly assess the risk associated with meat, wheat, or other biosecurity threats, so such threats are inspected by experts working at locations away from the border. The agricultural sector relies heavily on security processes for domestic shipping as well; as such, international processes are just part of doing business. In fact, these processes are favored because they assure the quality of the product and mitigate the risk of trading in spoiled or diseased product. Inspection processes protect all stakeholders, including the seller. Although preclearance in the Prairies is effective, some border crossings have had to adapt to biosecurity threats, such as mad cow disease. As the processes that contribute to a preclearance approach to security evolve, they are reinforced by transboundary agreements and practices such as those produced by North American Agriculture Marketing Officials and the Canada-US Consultative Committee on

Agriculture. These organizations are a small sample of cross-border initiatives that not only address potential biosecurity threats but reinforce the open-border paradox.

Infrastructure

Although the Prairie region includes the provinces of Alberta, Saskatchewan, and Manitoba, this chapter is focused on Saskatchewan and Manitoba, but the border biosecurity innovations detailed below apply equally to Alberta and across the rest of the border. This region also encompasses the land borders between these provinces as well as a portion of the international border between Canada and the United States. The international border in this region has thirty-two crossings, some busier and more advanced than others. The reliance on security practices away from the border in the Prairies differs from patterns elsewhere in Canada. The actual physical border lacks the infrastructure to process large items, and many of the border crossings are unusable during the colder months when there is more snow, and roads and ports of entry are frequently closed. Only three border crossings in the region are heavily used throughout the seasons. Furthermore, many of the border crossings in the Prairies are in isolated or sparsely populated areas.

North Dakota

North Dakota shares eighteen international border crossings with Manitoba and Saskatchewan. Pembina, Portal, Peace Garden, and Neche are favored by commercial carriers and used by most of the border traffic. By contrast, the Ambrose/Torquay port of entry (POE) is mainly used by local residents and vacationers, and annually, fewer than 100 trucks cross at the Hannah/Snowflake port of entry.

Only three crossings in North Dakota are open twenty-four hours a day, and one of the busiest ports is the North Portal/Portal POE. Here, US Customs and Border Protection processes approximately 100,000 cars going south annually. A Free and Secure Trade (FAST) lane, three additional car lanes, and three more passenger lanes were added in 2012 to accommodate the heavy flows of traffic (North Dakota, n.d.). While North Portal is exceptionally busy, the Pembina/Emerson crossing is by far the busiest. It is also open twenty-four hours and experiences more traffic than any other crossing in North Dakota—more traffic, in fact, than all the other North Dakota international border crossings combined. This crossing is also part of the Central North American Trade Corridor that connects to the United States at Interstate 75 (Montufar 1996). This corridor is significant because it "encompasses a 'Super Region' running from northern Mexico to Western Canada and on to Alaska—bound together by Highway 83" (Blank 2006, 6). This volume of southbound traffic often produces a delay, which is repeated when trucks travel northbound later in the week. There are three commercial lanes, a NEXUS lane, and the US portion of the border crossing has a loading dock and four cargo booths.

Montana

Montana and Saskatchewan face unusual coordination problems because Saskatchewan continuously observes Central Time throughout the year. By contrast, Montana adjusts for Daylight Savings Time (DST). Canadian hours of operation are listed as seasonal, and travelers are asked to call ahead to confirm. This can cause confusion about the hours of operation of POEs. The crossings in this region also experience some difficulty because of extreme weather and inadequate infrastructure. For example, the Chief Mountain crossing is closed during the winter months. Moreover, access to the road is sometimes restricted (usually in the spring) in terms of the weight and length of the vehicle (Montufar 1996). The Turner Road crossing is also seasonal, and the hours of operation vary according to DST and winter weather conditions. The Whitetail/Big Beaver Border Crossing was once operational, but it was reputed to be the least-used border crossing between Canada and the United States and was decommissioned (in 2011 on the Canadian side and 2013 for the US side; Montana, n.d.).

The Sweetgrass/Coutts border crossing—along the "Ports to Plains" corridor—is the largest border crossing in Montana and is the only twenty-four-hour crossing between Alberta and Montana. Interstate 15 and Canada's Highway 4 are both key parts of the truck route, which leads from Canada through the United States to Mexico. Additionally, this border crossing connects three large Canadian cities: Lethbridge, Calgary, and Edmonton. This POE has NEXUS lanes and a FAST lane (Montana, n.d.) and services about a million people annually (US Customs and Border Protection 2014).

Operationalizing Security

Private-sector and government officials involved with security across the Prairies were asked to define the concept of security. Individuals who participated in interviews held representative roles in the agriculture, government, advocacy, and agricultural-chemical sectors. Respondents identified two main border security concerns: risk assessment and different types of security.

Risk assessment is particularly prevalent in the Prairies. The potential threats carried by commodities such as meat and plant products require expertise that is generally unavailable at the border. Instead, safeguards to manage the risk are put in place before the product arrives at the border. If an item arrives at the border without the proper certificate or paperwork, then US Customs and Border Protection knows that there is a disproportionate risk that the product may pose harm because it has not been properly inspected. A private-sector security agent explained the importance of intent when analyzing security: "Security is about intention and intentionally trying to cause harm. [. . .] It is the intention to harm that separates safety from security."[1] While agricultural products crossing the border *cannot intend to cause harm*, the people involved in this chain could pose a security threat. However, most of the processes involving agricultural products monitor the quality of meat, seed, and food to ensure consumer safety on both sides of the border.

Interview participants also highlighted the importance of economic stability in tandem with security. Trade with the United States is crucial to the regional economy. Much of the border traffic consists of trade in food, meat, and agricultural goods. Preclearance maintains food safety and allows Canada to trade quality goods and maintain a reputation as a reliable trading partner for consumers. As one interviewee explained, "there are two kinds of security: everyone talks about security as public. We have to stop counterfeit goods and catch the bad guys. That is usually the perception when you say security. However, there is economic security. Until 9/11, US customs had a balanced approach—public and economic security [sic]."[2] The border processes in the Prairies must be tailored to the threat that agricultural goods pose while keeping them accessible to consumers.

This unique balance relies on the security processes that products encounter before being traded. If these practices were not in place, products would pose not only a security risk, but also a significant threat to consumers, who might seek other, more favorable, trading opportunities. A member of an association representing Prairie farmers outlined the importance of open markets for the prairies and the different conceptions of security: "For canola we export 90 percent of what we produce in Canada; it goes out in seed oil or meal and they have different processes. I'm not sure that we really deal with keeping Canada safe, when we use the term security; we use it in terms of security of the market and open access. We also make sure that what we export is free from plant pests, which is governed under the plant protection act in Canada—we call it biosecurity."[3]

Since the canola produced is mostly destined for foreign markets, clearing the border in a timely and efficient manner is critical to the health of the industry. An American canola-rolling mill requires the Canadian raw product, and the Canadian raw product requires the American mill to produce a product for market (United States Department of Agriculture 2012). This relationship is symbiotic, because the survival of one industry relies on the other party. This interaction is also true for chickens, cattle, pigs, wheat, and oats. Should security processes fail, the trade relationship could collapse and risk economic security. Impediments to the canola trade, for example, would be detrimental to the economy of the Prairies; so, the security process must adjust to the nature of cross-border trade. This cross-border relationship exemplifies the open-border paradox, insofar as the border is key to an open trading relationship and at the same time a security relationship that extends well beyond the physical border.

Perception of Security in the Prairies

Other regions and actors perceive the border to be a physical entity and a source of border concerns, and security is often associated with the border because many security practices take place at the border. The Prairies differ, because security at the physical border is not of primary concern. The physical border is not aligned with the regular perception of the border: most security and clearance activities take place at locations away from the physical border.

In the Prairies, most movement across the border is of agricultural products, not people (Zahniser et al. 2015). While the movement of people has generally been stagnant in recent years, agricultural cross-border trade has grown exponentially. Border biosecurity processes have had to adapt and scale accordingly. Many different actors are involved at a single stage of the preclearance process. A producer or veterinarian might be present for the slaughter of an animal, but then lose touch with the carcass. A packager, who knows that the animal was cleared for any disease before being slaughtered, receives the product. The packager has a responsibility to prevent contamination. The packager is aware of the security steps required before the product is processed, but the packager then loses contact with the product and never sees it reach the border. The only people who interact directly at the border are the respective border agents and the transport driver. By contrast, everyone engaging with the preclearance security process is aware of the steps required to secure a product. A person receiving a shipment of seed knows that a certificate and inspection were required for the item to cross the border. Products crossing the border in the Prairies usually pose threats that cannot be inspected at the border, so there is no need to keep product at the border for further inspection. Instead, questionable products are diverted to another layer of security for inspection.

Three common perceptions of security in the Prairies became evident during interviews. The combination of low mobility, preclearance, and the security culture makes the Prairies a unique border environment. Farmers across the region consider the preclearance approach to border security to be part of the border culture. Farming practices, such as shipping cattle between provinces, require a stringent inspection regime. As such, farmers are already accustomed to the preclearance requirements and layered security approach. Many farmers actually appreciate the process because it also assures the quality of their product.

Low Mobility

The Prairies are often characterized as crossings with relatively low mobility. A member of a binational transportation group noted that not enough people cross the border in the Prairies for *significant* security issues to arise. Prairie crossings are unique because they do not offer cross-border amenities. In Michigan, for example, people take advantage of closer, cheaper facilities. But without that dynamic of two close communities, the anticipated security threat is lower. In addition, the market for contraband goods is small since the population on either side of the border is small. Cities such as Toronto, Montréal, and Vancouver are more likely to see illicit goods trafficked across the border.

Preclearance and Biosecurity

While traffic volumes at the border crossings are relatively low, there are several layers of security before goods cross the border. This preclearance approach is more prominent in the Prairies due to the items that commonly cross the international border in the Prairies: livestock and plant products. These items are very difficult to inspect directly at the border because they require a licensed expert to examine the product. In addition, these goods harbor a unique threat potential. Unlike with auto parts, cars, or people, it is impossible to assess the biosecurity threat and dormant disease without expert opinion, which is often beyond the capabilities of border agents. The expertise of veterinarians and food inspectors provides a layer of security away from the border that is necessary to ensure the integrity of both the goods and the border.

Farmers Do Not See the Border as an Issue

A member of the Canola Growers Association explained that her clients ship substantial amounts of product to the United States. Few of these clients view the border as an inconvenience. Farming is a private-sector business that tends to be passed on through generations. As such, many of the farmers grew up near the border and have previous experience with the process. As a result, many do not view the border as a hindrance—the border process has become part of the farming culture. Similarly, a representative of a meat-inspection group explained that farmers embrace the inspection process and do not view the safeguards as barriers. Farmers appreciate the process of cataloging and inspecting livestock. Without the inspection process, the risk is greater that dangerous or contaminated product will pass through the border. Farmers have a vested interest in having approved livestock. The practice of inspecting livestock before trade is so commonplace that cattle must be inspected before being transported domestically. This inspection process is so engrained that it is seen as a necessary fixture in the trade environment and as an integral part of the farm security culture.

By contrast, members of the private sector who do not have goods that risk infection or require extensive inspection often see the border as a hindrance. A member of the planning branch of a coalition of municipalities noted that before September 11, 2001 (9/11), there was a movement toward making the border more porous and fluid to reduce wait times. After 9/11 the border prioritized security instead of reduced wait times. However, a member of the planning branch of an association of elected officials in the region believes that there has been significant movement toward reducing red tape surrounding border processes. Sometimes removing barriers for a more efficient border requires the implementation of FAST lanes or NEXUS. While these programs can make the border more efficient, they do require some personal contribution. A member of a binational border trade alliance explained that the hesitation to provide information required for faster programs causes delays. NEXUS allows border officers to process four cars in the time it would normally take to process a single car, which expedites crossing the border. However, to become a member of NEXUS, the applicant must be fingerprinted. According to one interviewee, fewer Canadians are enrolled in NEXUS because they perceive the act of being fingerprinted as associated with a criminal process.

Actors in the Region

Alberta

In 2009, the United States was the largest source of Alberta's international tourists, and it received two-thirds of the province's foreign direct investment and 90 percent of Alberta's exports. In addition to agricultural products, including cattle, beef, and grain, oil and gas comprise a significant percentage of the province's exports to the US (Mouafo, Morales, and Heynen 2004). Alberta has supported the Montana-Alberta bilateral advisory committee, which is usually chaired by Alberta's minister of international and intergovernmental relations and Montana's lieutenant governor. Primary concerns include agriculture, transportation, and the environment. The state and the province prioritize rail transport and recognize that both governments need to strengthen the north-south rail connection.

Alberta has several agricultural organizations that deal with cross-border issues. The Alberta Invasive Species Council is a nongovernmental entity that views security through an agricultural and ecological lens. It facilitates communication between levels of government, NGOs, and academics to prevent invasive species from having a significant impact on the environment and industries (Alberta Invasive Species Council, n.d.). The Council also works to preserve the quality of goods so they can pass the first layer of security, inspection, before reaching the border. If disease or bugs that plague goods are detected, then the goods will not be cleared and will not continue through further inspection.

Saskatchewan

Saskatchewan has a low level of cross-border cooperation with the United States. While the province's interaction with the United States is relatively low—it does not even have an office in the United States—Saskatchewan is party to many intergovernmental agreements. Saskatchewan and Montana share an intergovernmental accord, which is manifest in an annual meeting between the lieutenant governor of Montana and Saskatchewan's minister of government relations. Saskatchewan recently created the Department of Government Relations to focus on the province's international presence (Abgrall 2005). The assistant deputy minister oversees the management of intergovernmental and international agreements. The Saskatchewan Trade and Export Partnership (STEP) manages trade and export activities. This partnership extends beyond the government sphere and is public-private in nature. While exports are overseen by STEP, investment is often administered by the Department of Industry and Resources (Mouafo, Morales, and Heynen 2004).

Manitoba

Manitoba has had a cross-border agreement with Minnesota since 1988 (Abgrall 2005). While this relationship began by focusing on trade, hydropower, and tourism, it has evolved to encompass water sovereignty and bioscience. Water sovereignty is especially applicable during flooding season. The Red River, which crosses from North Dakota to Manitoba, is subject to flooding. In 1997, the Red River rose to unparalleled levels. The flood caused more than $5,000,000 in damage and was heralded as the "flood of the century" (Haque 2000). In Canada, the Manitoba Emergency Measures Organization facilitates responses to emergencies within the province. This group liaises with Canada's federal government to acquire additional funding. The Manitoba Water Stewardship Department also coordinates with locals to manage flood response (Wachira and Sinclair 2005). North Dakota has two separate agencies that prepare and respond to floods: the Division of Emergency Management and the North Dakota State Water Commission. The State Water Commission coordinates funding for emergency management and flood preparation (North Dakota State Water Commission 2015).

Transboundary Cooperation

North American Agriculture Marketing Officials

This group was created in July of 1921 and meets annually to discuss marketing strategies and approaches for agriculture. The members share ideas, techniques, and approaches to managing issues in agriculture across North America. The group is composed of agricultural ministers and private-sector stakeholders, and its approach to security threats affects the security climate of the region. In their 2015 meeting minutes, the group addressed a new Food Safety Modernization Act ruling on food safety. The group recognizes biosecurity threats, and it is in their mandate to make goods and services in agriculture appealing despite these risks. They seek to improve trade within North America, so when a risk is presented the group shares marketing ideas. In this role, the group has the ability to shape the security discourse of a region through marketing, which allows them to manipulate the public's perception of threat and the security environment across North America.

Canada–US Consultative Committee on Agriculture

In 1998, Canada and the United States signed the US–Canada Record of Understanding on Agriculture Trade. Subsequently, the Canada–US Consultative Committee on Agriculture was formed. It has worked to identify threats early and to create a forum where solutions can be found. The committee includes the US Department of Agriculture, the US Trade Representative, and the US International Trade Policy Directorate of Agriculture. These groups collaborate with Agriculture and Agri-Food Canada and Canada's Department of Trade to address cross-border trade issues in the agricultural sphere (Canada-US Consultative Committee on Agriculture 2015).

Intergovernmental Relations

Canada's New West Partnership is an intergovernmental partnership among Saskatchewan, British Columbia, and Alberta. This coalition aims to promote the Prairies as a region in the global market, to lower costs, and to attract business and people with new skills. Beyond membership and advocacy, it focuses on protecting trade corridors and reducing barriers to trade and the movement of labor. This partnership is closely tied to the Trade, Investment and Labour Mobility Agreement (New West Partnership 2015). In addition to this particular agreement, Canada's New West Partnership also promotes an international presence, innovation capacity, and purchasing power through the New West Partnership International Cooperation Agreement, New West Partnership Innovation Agreement, and the New West Partnership Procurement Agreement (New West Partnership 2015).

Environmental Scan

Infrastructure

Border infrastructure is a major issue across the Prairies. This infrastructure often extends beyond the physical border to the processes that bring goods to the border. Preclearance infrastructure involves security checks and processes to ensure that goods are safe. Goods unfit to cross the border will slow the process, which can cause congestion at the border.

A key means for hauling grain to the border for trade is the rail system and the preapproval process. Complying with the requisite security process takes time. A farmer who sells grain across the border must have it certified as secure and dispatch the confirmation packet to the border before the shipment arrives. Farmers want this process to be as streamlined as possible, because participation in the cross-border market allows for greater trading opportunities. However, the ability to participate and bring grain to the border crossing in time can often be impeded by inadequate infrastructure. The Canadian Canola Growers Association described the Prairies as "captive" since they are served by only two railways. Farmers who do not live close to the border must travel as much as a thousand miles to sell their grain if they wish to trade with the lucrative US market. Not only is the distance itself an obstacle, but the rail infrastructure can often be overwhelmed during harsh weather. Snowfall during the winter of 2014–15 was so extreme that many trains were unable to move grain. This had significant economic repercussions. Following that winter, the government set minimum thresholds for the amount of grain to be moved by train. The lack of railway lines in more peripheral parts of the Prairies and harsh weather can often interfere with the preclearance process.

The Prairies and other crossings also experience delays because of asymmetric infrastructure. Programs that expedite border crossing, such as the vicinity, Radio-Frequency Identification chips, and trusted trader programs, are not always available. A director at a regional transportation-planning agency explained that after 9/11, many travel programs were implemented before the infrastructure existed to support them. These programs required corresponding infrastructure, such as dedicated approach lanes, but the inspection agencies did not receive enough funding to it. Partners coordinated to make these investments. Still, security programs may struggle to be put to proper use, and regional actors may need to provide support to enhance security at the border. FAST program cards are administered separately by the United States and Canada: US Customs

Trade Partnership Against Terrorism administers the cards and Partners in Protection is the Canadian counterpart. A commercial shipment must be delivered by a driver with a FAST card, the trucking company must be enrolled, and the owner of the goods in the truck must also be enrolled to make the process as effective as possible. Many of the goods being shipped across the border can be time-sensitive, so enrollment in the FAST program is beneficial. Carriers have an incentive to enroll in these programs to minimize wait times at border crossings, but there is no major pressure on the supplier to enroll. Without a consistent enrollment in the FAST program, FAST lanes are underused or improperly applied. While the carriers are enrolled in FAST, they cannot use the FAST lane unless the goods are also approved by FAST. So the lane is often used when the truck is empty, because there are no goods on board but the driver and carrier have been pre-cleared.

Biosecurity

Since the agricultural sectors loom so large, biosecurity is of major concern in the Prairie region. Biosecurity can be complicated because security threats are often difficult to detect and can be impossible to inspect for directly at the border without the help of a specialist. Implementing preclearance practices and transboundary cooperation agreements can often reduce security threats, such as those associated with pesticides. Preclearance comprises several inspection "checkpoints."

A member of a Canadian plant-licensing agency cited the processes for registering seed in Canada and the United States as an illustration. In the United States, there is no overarching registration process. Instead, seeds must be registered state by state. Conversely, Canada has a stringent, robust, single body to register seeds. Due to this asymmetry, a seed used in the US may not be registered in Canada. There is also a preclearance process to ensure that seeds entering either country are approved in that country's registry. When a product enters the US, it must comply with United States Department of Agriculture requirements. Product entering Canada needs to be accompanied by a seed-import certificate. These pre-approvals require the application to be submitted two weeks in advance; consequently, preclearance necessitates a good deal of advance legwork.

However, not all farmers perform the preclearance. As expected, when one layer of security is not properly performed, then other security measures must occur, which can result in lost time and spoiled product. If seed is stopped at the border and it lacks official approval, then the product or shipment is turned away. Turning away seed for shipment can be problematic because there is a specific "seeding window" during which seed must be transferred to the buyer in time for the planting season.

Biosecurity also entails protecting goods from theft before they cross the border. Because the security process for livestock requires exposing the goods to different processes and people, the threat of theft looms large. Branding has helped to limit the amount of theft at the border, but there is always the possibility that people may cross with stolen livestock. For example, there have been recent concerns about cattle crossing the border at reserves where fencing is more porous. The theft of cows and porous fencing can be especially dangerous if the wandering or stolen cow carries a disease. This is often an issue of documentation, and if the problem persists the US Department of Agriculture intervenes.

Case Study: Pesticides and Mad Cow

Canada announced its first case of bovine spongiform encephalopathy (BSE) in May 2003. Months later, the United States confirmed that a cow in the state of Washington, which had been born in Canada, was infected with BSE. The US unilaterally imposed an export ban on live cattle from Canada. The Canadian government interpreted this as a punishment, and indeed, Canada's meat industry suffered greatly (O'Neill 2005). The repercussions of the ban were so great that some Canadian producers considered seeking a remedy under NAFTA. The BSE "mad cow" epidemic became increasingly uncertain and tensions surrounding the cattle trade heightened.

Mad cow was a biosecurity threat that disrupted the trade relationship between the Canadian Prairies and the US. The economic devastation for Canada alone was considerable: Canada's beef trade relationship with the US was worth $3.5 billion. Without US participation in the beef trade, Canada lost 40 percent of the market (O'Neill 2005). The Canadian Food Inspection Agency and the US Food and Drug Administration advocated for security strategies that resembled a "preclearance" format. The cattle feed and materials would be closely monitored. Cattle testing programs were also expanded.

The Canadian Meat Council is a trade association that has represented the interests of "federally inspected meat processors of beef, pork, poultry, horse and lamb since 1919" and advocates for secure processing of those goods. The exchange of meat at the border is the largest food industry in

Canada: seventy-eight trucks with Canadian meat cross the border into the US daily for a total of 28,150 truckloads of meat per year. Evidently, the meat industry relies heavily on the border for trade, but the issue of inspection looms large. Meat inspection requires expertise, and even with so many trucks crossing the border, goods still need to be inspected.

Beyond the Border and the Food Safety and Inspection Service joined with the Canadian Food Inspection Agency (CFIA) to create a plan to inspect meat crossing the border without creating unrealistic wait times. The goal was to implement a process that would inspect the quality of the meat to promote biosafety. In 2012 the plan was fairly narrow in scope. For one year, a small number of CFIA meat-exporting centers would participate in preclearance. The data from this pilot was reexamined in 2013. This pilot inspired several steps of preclearance to ensure that meat was safe before it crossed the border. First, an animal must be inspected before being sent to slaughter. Furthermore, quality-control officials must always be in the processing plant. Second, a veterinarian, Canadian Food Inspection agent, and inspector must be at the plant during a slaughter. Once the animal has been slaughtered, the meat is analyzed by the CFIA and inspected to meet proper safety standards. To ensure that the safety of the meat is clearly communicated, the meat is then marked with the meat inspection legend. US meat being traded to Canada is similarly marked with a legend that indicates that the meat is "US inspected and passed by the Department of Agriculture."

Another layer of security is added when meat approaches the border. Border Patrol officers screen meat shipments southbound from Canada. Trucks must then report to any one of the ten US inspection plants before reaching the buyer. US meat being traded to Canada is not subject to as stringent a process. However, there are other layers of security. Ten percent of trucks carrying meat are randomly selected to undergo further inspection away from the border at one of 125 inspection plants registered with the CFIA. By contrast, the US screens all trucks entering the US and further inspection is mandatory, yet there are only ten inspection plants.

The Canadian Meat Council contends that preclearance can be ineffective and costly. By the time the truck has reached the border and is redirected for further inspection, the meat has already been packaged and wrapped. The inspection process at the slaughtering plant is more thorough, and the meat has already been inspected and certified by several professionals. Sending the meat for further inspection results takes time, uses fuel, and produces additional wear on trucks. The Canadian Meat Council reports that being redirected to the inspection house often adds two additional hours of travel time and then a few more hours waiting for the inspector to become available. Due to this additional time, the driver often hits additional driving hours and must be paid for rest. Meat quality might also be sacrificed at the inspection house. If a truck is redirected to an inspection house, the time it takes to get back en route could cost the meat three to ten days of shelf life—meaning there will be fewer days to sell the product to consumers. This loss of shelf life may cause some buyers to reject the shipment outright. In addition, when a shipment of meat leaves the slaughterhouse, it is preserved in cold temperatures to ensure freshness. However, when the truck reaches an inspection plant, the doors are opened and the meat is often inspected in warmer temperatures. This breaks the "cold chain" and threatens the shelf life and safety of the meat.

The process of trading meat is an example of preclearance necessary in the Prairies. The security mechanisms involve the participation of the private sector, border officials, and both governments. All portions of this process work to make items crossing the border more secure, yet no inspection takes place at the actual border. While this process has been effective at reducing outbreaks of mad cow and other biohazards, it can still be inconvenient: Redirection to inspection plants can potentially spoil the meat, reduces shelf life, and is often costly for the producer. While physical security is protected by this layered approach to security, economic security is still vulnerable.

Use of Pesticides

The railway system is close to the border, which provides incentives for farmers to do business closer to the international border. Farmers closer to the border do not have to travel as far with their grain and can integrate their production into the US market. However, close proximity to the border can give rise to distinct biosecurity hazards. As farmers move closer to the border, they also bring field pesticides closer to one another. From 1973 to 1998 the use of pesticides in Canada increased by 500 percent, the vast majority of which are used on the Prairies (Goldsborough and Crumpton 1998).

Goldsborough and Crumpton (1998) describe the movement of pesticides as the "off-site transportation" of pesticide residues. When a pesticide is applied through spray—or "aerially"—particles are often caught in the wind and transported to a different region. They explain the case of a herbicide called atrazine that is usually applied in the central Great Plains. Aerial spraying of this herbicide, usually applied to corn, resulted in particles of the pesticide being transported off site as far away as the lakes in Northwestern Ontario (Goldsborough and Crumpton 1998). Pesticides are a biosecurity hazard because the chemicals do not abide by physical borders: on a windy day, pesticides are prone to drift from one farmer's field to another. If the crop that is being sprayed with pesticide is not the same as the one in the other farmer's field, it may kill the crop.

The "off-site" contamination of pesticides is not only an economic concern for farmers, but a physical security concern. Canada and the United States approve different pesticides for use. A pesticide that is legal in the US but banned in Canada may float from an American farmer's field across the border and infect a Canadian crop. While a crop advisor explained that there are few cases of farmers intentionally infecting or destroying another farmer's crops, the close proximity of farming fields at the border can be hazardous.

Biosecurity threats can only be reduced by the goodwill security environment, in which farmers act in a manner that does not harm the crop yield of other farmers, and practice a multistep process of registering a pesticide and administering it. If another farmer's field is affected by the use of pesticides at the border, a complaint is filed and investigated. Bilaterally, Canada and the United States have worked cooperatively, and many of their regulatory boards mirror each other. Pesticides must be registered and categorized premarket. Canada's Pest Control Products Act is similar to the American Federal Insecticide, Fungicide, and Rodenticide Act (Pralle 2006). However, some federal control is lost, as it is up to provinces and states to interpret the regulation and sale of pesticides. Locally, some cities may have the ability to advise against the use of pesticides, but the bulk of pesticides sold in North America are intended for agriculture. Agriculture Canada usually ensures that pesticides being imported or administered are registered and approved as safe by the minister (Ilgen 1985). Advisory committees such as the Federal Interdepartmental Committee of Pesticides ensure that federal departments communicate the status of pesticides.

Conclusion

The Prairie region illustrates the extent to which the approach to border security is layered and extends beyond the physical border. Border security practices reach back to farms, loading docks, and offices away from the international border. Traditionally, we think of security as the inspection process at the border. The Prairies require a nuanced approach to pre-clearance that reflects the combination of minimal infrastructure at border crossings and the nature of agricultural goods crossing the border, such as meat, grain, and livestock. This region further reflects the open-border paradox, whereby various levels of security, at and away from the border, are necessary to cater to economic imperatives in keeping the border open. Absent the multilevel security cooperation necessary for preclearing agriculture products, the efficiency of the border as a transit point for trade goods would be in question. The region illustrates that even in areas of low population and low border transit rates, coordination, cooperation, and collaboration can still be maintained to create the border regimes necessary for vibrant cross-border economic linkages. In all, collaboration takes place across multitier levels of government agencies and internationally and is driven by strong public-private partnerships in areas concerned with trade and environmental and health issues.

NOTES

1. Interview on June 22, 2015.
2. Interview on June 17, 2015.
3. Interview on June 23, 2015.

REFERENCES

Abgrall, Jean-François. 2005. "Working Papers: A Survey of Major Cross Border Organizations between Canada and the US." *North American Linkages*, 1–47.

Alberta Invasive Species Council (AISC). n.d. https://www.abinvasives.ca

Blank, Stephen. 2006. "North American Trade Corridors: An Initial Exploration." Centre d'etude et de recherche international. *Faculty Working Papers*, 50.

Canada–US Consultative Committee on Agriculture (CCA). 2016. "Terms of Reference." https://www.international.gc.ca/trade-agreements-accords-commerci aux/topics-domaines/goods-produits/ccamin38.aspx?lang=eng

Goldsborough, L. G., and W. G. Crumpton. 1998. "Distribution and Environmental Fate of Pesticides in Prairie Wetlands." *Great Plains Research* 8, no. 1: 73–95. http://www.jstor.org/stable/24156335

Haque, C. Emdad. 2000. "Risk Assessment, Emergency Preparedness and Response to Hazards: The Case of the 1997 Red River Valley Flood, Canada." *Natural Hazards* 21, no. 2–3: 225–45. http://resolver.scholarsportal.info/resolve/092103 0x/v21i2-3/225_raepar1rrvfc

Ilgen, Thomas L. 1985. "Between Europe and America, Ottawa and the Provinces: Regulating Toxic Substances in Canada." *Canadian Public Policy/Analyse de Politiques* 11, no. 3: 578–90. http://www.jstor.org/stable/3550511

Montana. n.d. http://www.ezbordercrossing.com/list-of-bordercrossings/montan a/#.VghU1rSdLzI

Montufar, Isolde Jeanette. 1996. "Trucking and Size and Weight Regulations in the Mid-Continent Corridor." *National Library of Canada.* http://www.collectionsca nada.gc.ca/obj/s4/f2/dsk3/ftp05/mq23428.pdf

Mouafo, Dieudonné, Nadia Poncé Morales, and Jeff Heynen. 2004. *Building Cross-Border Links: A Compendium of Canada–US Government Collaboration.* Ottawa: Canada School of the Public Service, Action Research Roundtable. https://www.npstc.org/download.jsp?tableId=37&column=217&id=3302&file=RESOUR CE_Canada_Compendium_US_Agreements.pdf

New West Partnership. 2015. http://www.international.alberta.ca/985.cfm

North Dakota. n.d. "North Dakota/Canada Border Crossings." http://www.ezbord ercrossing.com/list-of-border-crossings/north-dakota/#.VghT-7SdLzJ

North Dakota State Water Commission, and Office of the State Engineer. 2015. *State Water Management Plan.* http://www.swc.nd.gov/info_edu/state_water _plan/

O'Neill, Kate. 2005. "How Two Cows Make a Crisis: US–Canada Trade Relations and Mad Cow Disease." *American Review of Canadian Studies* 35, no. 2: 295–319. http://www.tandfonline.com/doi/abs/10.1080/02722010509481374?journalCo de=rarc20

Pralle, Sarah B. 2006. "Timing and Sequence in Agenda-Setting and Policy Change: A Comparative Study of Lawn Care Pesticide Politics in Canada and the US." *Journal of European Public Policy,* 13, no. 7: 987–1005. http://www.tandfonline .com/doi/abs/10.1080/13501760600923904#.VtElgISdJSU

United States Department of Agriculture. 2012. *Economic Research Services: Soybeans and Oil Crops.* http://www.ers.usda.gov/topics/crops/soybeans-oil-crops/canola .aspx

U.S. Customs and Border Protection. 2014, March 11. "Sweetgrass Station." https://www.cbp.gov/border-security/along-us-borders/border-patrol-sectors /havre-sector-montana/sweetgrass-station

Wachira, Jacqueline K., and John A. Sinclair. 2005. "Public Participation in the Emergency Response Phase of Flooding: A Case Study of the Red River Basin." *Canadian Water Resources Journal* 30, no. 2: 145–58. doi:10.4296/cwrj3002145.

Zahniser, Steven, Sarah Angadjivand, Thomas Hertz, Lindsay Kuberka, and Alexandra Santos. 2015. *NAFTA at 20: North America's Free-Trade Area and Its Impact on Agriculture.* Washington, DC: US Department of Agriculture, Economic Research Service, Outlook Report No. WRS-15–01. 3 February.

FIVE

Ontario and the Great Lakes

Todd Hataley and Christian Leuprecht

Ontario differs from other Canadian border regions in demographic, economic, and environmental characteristics. It also has more bilateral trade of manufactured goods with the United States than any other province. At the same time, Ontario's cross-border relationship is marked by considerable competition with some American states for locational manufacturing advantages, and also with Québec—which is both a partner for Ontario in competing with the United States and Ontario's major provincial competitor. Thus, competition is a distinct feature of Ontario's border, borderlands, and cross-border relationships. At the same time, provincial border security governance is particularly limited in Ontario because Canada's international border with the United States is governed by federal policies and maintained by federal law enforcement agencies. Ontario thus exemplifies the extent to which the regions and provinces along the border face diverse challenges and do not necessarily share Ottawa's priorities for border security.

At 14.5 million people and growing steadily, Ontario is Canada's most populous province, and it generates just under 40 percent of Canada's economic output. In absolute terms, no province makes a greater contribution to the volume of trade in goods and services between Canada and the United States. In 2019 Ontario's bilateral trade relationship with the United States was valued at CDN$397.2 billion (US$299.3 billion): CDN$201.9 billion in exports (US$152.2 billion) and CDN$195.3 billion in imports (US$147.2 billion). In 2014 Ontario's share of Canadian exports to the United States was 37.4 percent, the highest of any province or territory (Government of British Colombia 2015). By 2019, Ontario accounted for 52.8 percent of total trade in goods between Canada and the United States, which breaks down to 45.2 percent of total exports and 64.1 percent of total imports. Ontario is the top trading partner for nineteen US states, and no province is more reliant on exports for jobs: about one in five jobs in Ontario relies on trade.

The many lakes and rivers that interweave along Ontario's border with the United States necessitate extensive bridge and tunnel infrastructure for cross-border trade (Transport Canada 2016). Almost all that trade traverses six bridges or tunnels, all of which run at maximum capacity. As a result, Ontario's trade with the United States, and therefore Canada's economy, is disproportionately disrupted if any of Ontario's critical cross-border transportation infrastructure is compromised. Since that infrastructure is aging, is subject to volumes of traffic for which it was not designed, is increasingly securitized, and is deteriorating at an accelerating rate due to climate change, the risk to disruption in Ontario's cross-border trade is growing exponentially. These challenges to the Ontario–United States border region reflect the importance of the open-border paradox, whereby the economic importance of the border functions alongside the security and safety apparatus necessary to maintain open trade corridors.

This chapter provides a detailed account of the main security actors in Ontario's border region, regional approaches to security, current and emerging security threats, and vertical and horizontal governance models. It concludes with two policy case studies. Given Ontario's unique characteristics, future efforts to enhance border security in Ontario will need to mitigate risk by devoting more resources beyond the physical boundary line of the border, notably gathering intelligence and targeting transboundary crime organizations and individuals who smuggle persons and illicit goods, especially firearms, across the border.

Profile: Ontario Region

Ontario shares international borders with the US states of Minnesota, Michigan, and New York, mostly demarcated by waterways. Spanning Ontario's international border are fourteen bridge border crossings, four passenger ferries, one freight-train tunnel, one motor vehicle tunnel, and one truck ferry. The border crossings at Sarnia, Windsor, and Fort Erie/

Niagara are the busiest international crossings in Canada, measured in terms of the annual number of trucks, volume of goods, and number of passengers that cross the border (Ministry of Transportation, Ontario 2015). In 2012 the Windsor-Detroit corridor alone handled CDN$91.6 billion (or 28.2 percent) of trade between Canada and the United States; over $250 million in commodities travels through that corridor daily. By 2019, the daily equivalent trade in goods between Ontario and the United States was valued at CDN$1.1 billion (US$820.1 million): CDN$553.1 million in exports (US$416.9 million) and CDN$535.1 million in imports (US$403.3 million). In 2018, total daily equivalent visits between Ontario and the United States totaled 90,838 people: 56,444 outbound visits and 34,395 inbound visits.

Ontario's trade is concentrated in the Great Lakes–St. Lawrence Region, a historic, economic, and political entity that comprises eight US states, from Minnesota in the west to New York in the east, and the provinces of Ontario and Québec. This border region generates approximately fifty-one million jobs and represents 30 percent of binational Canada–US economic activity (Porter 2015). In the region, trade in 2019 comprised 28.6 percent (or CDN$7.8 trillion, US$5.8 trillion) of the total Canada–US economic activity of CDN$27.3 trillion (US$20.6 trillion): 32.6 percent (or CDN$245.0 billion, US$184.7 billion) of total trade in goods between Canada and the US, valued at CDN$752.0 billion (US$566.7 billion). If the region were a country, it would be the third-largest economy in the world (Council of the Great Lakes Region 2015). In 2019, Ontario's trade with the GLSLR totaled CDN$213.4 billion (US$160.8 billion), comprising 53.7 percent of the total trade in goods between Ontario and the United States.

Regional Security Actors

Federal

Federal security agencies, departments, and initiatives necessarily play a key role in all of Canada's border regions, including Ontario, notably the Canada Border Services Agency (CBSA), Royal Canadian Mounted Police (RCMP), Public Safety Canada, Department of Citizenship and Immigration Canada, Transport Canada, Health Canada, Agriculture and Agri-Food Canada, and the Canadian Food Inspection Agency. Some federal agencies and departments take a more active role in Ontario's border security than they do in other provinces because the border runs along so many waterways. The Department of Fisheries and Oceans, the Canadian Coast Guard, and the Department of National Defence assist the RCMP and CBSA in marine security programs and initiatives in the Great Lakes and St. Lawrence Seaway.

Provincial

The Ontario Ministry of Community Safety and Correctional Services (MCSCS) is the main provincial actor responsible for the physical and economic security of Ontario. The MCSCS oversees Ontario's correctional services, the Criminal Intelligence Service of Ontario, and all police services in Ontario, including the Ontario Provincial Police, fifty municipal police services, and nine self-administered First Nations[1] police services. The MCSCS also oversees Emergency Management Ontario and the Provincial Emergency Operations Centre, which alerts key policymakers to evolving situations in and outside of Ontario and mobilizes resources in an emergency.

Municipal

Local governments, communities, and law enforcement agencies make up the microlevel component of border security in Ontario. In cases such as the City of Windsor, municipal governments are directly involved in the ownership, management, and operations of border crossings. Along with provincial law enforcement agencies, municipalities along the border tend to be the first responders to border security issues. Municipal, provincial, and federal law enforcement agencies attempt to prevent and combat the security consequences of illegal goods and persons smuggled or trafficked into Ontario's border communities.

Intergovernmental Organizations (Including Public/Private)

The Great Lakes–St. Lawrence Region hosts many cross-border intergovernmental organizations that focus on different policy areas, including environmental protection and economic security. Many of the intergovernmental organizations bring together representatives from the public sector with business, nonprofit, and academic communities.

The Great Lakes Commission is one of the oldest organizations in the region. Created in 1955, it includes Illinois, Indiana, Michigan, Minnesota, New York, Ohio, Pennsylvania, and Wisconsin. In 1999 Ontario and Québec were officially included as associated members. The Commission works to protect and manage the natural resources, mostly water and land, of the Great Lakes. The Commission has also created several other initiatives and organizations on environmental protection. The International Association of Great Lakes and St. Lawrence Mayors is one example. This Association is mostly concerned with protecting and restoring the Great Lakes ecosystem, but it also focuses on issues related to governance, economics, and science. Other Great Lakes Commission initiatives include the Great Lakes Information Network and Great Lakes Cities Initiative.

Created in 1983, the Council of Great Lakes Governors now includes Michigan, Minnesota, New York, Ohio, Pennsylvania, Wisconsin, Ontario, and Québec. Initially, the primary priority of the Council was environmental issues that plagued the GLSLR. However, in the late 1980s the Council increasingly recognized the close relationship between the region's environmental and economic health. With the Economic Development Agreement in 1988, the Council broadened its scope and continues to champion environmental and economic initiatives at the Conference of Great Lakes and St. Lawrence Governors and Premiers.

Nonstate Actors

There are many nonstate actors in the GLSLR that focus on a wide range of cross-border issues and represent the interests of different business, academic, and nonprofit organizations. The Council of the Great Lakes Region (CGLR) is a key nonstate actor. The 2011 founding summit in Windsor brought together regional leaders from government, business, labor, interested groups, and academia to promote stronger collaboration in a variety of cross-border policy areas. CGLR seeks to inform policymakers on the region's long-term economic, social, and environmental goals and to connect private, public, and nonprofit actors across the region. On September 29, 2015, the CGLR announced the formation of a regional border issues work group. Similar to the Pacific North West Economic Region's Borders Issues Work Group, the CGLR's group includes private- and public-sector stakeholders and coordinates policy working groups (CGLR 2015).

The Cross-Border Institute at the University of Windsor and the Canadian American Border Trade Alliance (CAN/AM BTA; CGLR 2015) are nongovernmental actors with a particular interest in policy spanning the Ontario border region. As an academic institution, the Cross-Border Institute is committed to research and public outreach related to the movement of people, goods, and services across the Canada–US border. The CAN/AM BTA is a binational trade organization that represents the interests of more than 60,000 corporations and organizations on issues related to border trade, management, transportation, and visits. Both organizations are interested in border security insofar as it affects cross-border trade and travel.

Similarly, the Council of Great Lakes Industries and the Retail Council of Canada are also interested in the impact of border security policy on trade and travel. The Retail Council of Canada is a nonprofit association that represents the interests of 45,000 retail businesses across Canada. Canadian retailers have a vested interest in how border security practices influence the flow of goods and services because the volume of goods and services that cross the international border is so high. The Council of Great Lakes Industries is an umbrella of major US and Canadian industrial organizations that focuses on six sectors: transportation, manufacturing supply chain integration, regional energy use, the environment, land use, and regional trade.

Transboundary Cooperation and Governance Models

Although Ontario has formal agreements with other states and provinces, Ontario's transboundary interactions are mostly informal and conducted through intergovernmental organizations that include leaders from the public, private, and third sector.

Horizontal Border Governance

Ontario's proximity to the United States, large volume of bilateral trade, and shared environmental concerns have given rise to intense bilateral coordination on myriad policy issues using a variety of means. For example, premiers and governors in the GLSLR meet ad hoc to discuss border issues. The premier of Ontario typically travels to the United States two or three times a year, primarily to New York and Michigan. The premier also receives governors and premiers throughout the year. Ministers and deputy ministers also maintain contact with their US counterparts informally and through intergovernmental organizations.

Ontario enjoys an exceptionally strong relationship with Michigan, dating back to the 1965 Auto Pact Agreement (Abgrall 2005). The increase in border traffic after the introduction of NAFTA in 1994 motivated Ontario and Michigan to form the Ontario-Michigan Border Transportation Partnership (Abgrall 2005). The Partnership set out strategies to address the needs of transborder traffic. In 2002 the two provincial governments signed a memorandum of understanding to foster cooperation in trade, tourism, transportation, and border security (Abgrall 2005).

There is also extensive cooperation on binational policy issues at the municipal level. Municipalities along the border coordinate with their American counterparts on emergency management, transportation, economic development, environmental protection and ownership, and management of international border crossings. The Great Lakes and St. Lawrence Cities Initiative exemplifies binational municipal coordination. The Initiative is a coalition of more than 110 US and Canadian mayors and local officials to advance the protection and restoration of the Great Lakes and St. Lawrence River. It does so through advocacy and programs such as the Green Cities Transforming towards Sustainability program, which provides information and financial support for municipal green infrastructure projects.

Bilateral cooperation among municipalities also extends to private and nongovernmental actors. For example, the Great Lakes Metro Chambers Coalition advocates on issues related to federal transportation infrastructure funding and policy, energy development, immigration of highly qualified personnel, and water-quality protection in the Great Lakes.

Vertical Transboundary Governance

Ontario's formal relationship with the federal government is coordinated by the Ministry of Intergovernmental Affairs. Informal vertical linkages between the province and the federal government occur on an ad hoc basis through connections between provincial and federal ministries and agencies.

Ontario coordinates with provincial municipalities in a similar fashion. Formally, the province maintains its relationship with municipalities through the Association of Municipalities of Ontario, to which all municipalities in Ontario belong except the City of Toronto. Through this Association, the province consults municipalities on proposed changes to the legislation, regulations, and agreements Ontario negotiates with the federal government that will have a bearing on municipalities. Similar to the federal and provincial relationship, the province coordinates informally among provinces and municipalities as issues arise. The Niagara International Transportation Technology Coalition is an example. This Coalition coordinates with provincial and municipal actors on both sides of the border on traffic and roadway information to improve traffic flows and enhance the efficiency of emergency assistance and response. The group's partners include cities and towns in the Niagara-Buffalo region, the provincial and state departments of transportation, and provincial and state police forces.

Vertical and Horizontal Governance

The ownership, operation, and management of Ontario's international border crossings illustrate horizontal and vertical multilevel governance in the province. Different models of ownership, operation, and management in use at international border crossings in Ontario include federal, provincial, and municipal actors from both sides of the border. The Detroit-Windsor tunnel and the Buffalo and Fort Erie Public Bridge Authority reflect the differences in the ownership, operation, and management of Ontario's border crossings and the levels of government and actors involved.

The Buffalo and Fort Erie Public Bridge Authority (otherwise known as the Peace Bridge Authority) owns and operates the Peace Bridge in the Niagara region. The Authority is based on an international compact between the Government of Canada and the State of New York (McLean and Eagles 2014). It is governed by a board of ten members, composed equally of Canadians and Americans. Canadian members are appointed by the governor-in-council on the recommendation from the minister of transportation. The minister in turn receives recommendations for appointments from a local member of parliament (McLean and Eagles 2014). Two of the American members are appointed by the governor of New York, the remainder by the attorney general of New York State, the Niagara Frontier Transportation Authority chairman, and the commissioner of the Department of Transportation of New York State (McLean and Eagles 2014).

In contrast to the Peace Bridge Authority, the ownership and management structure of the Detroit-Windsor Tunnel has a lot more participation from local municipalities (McLean and Eagles 2014). The cities of Windsor and Detroit both own half the tunnel and a plaza. A private company, Detroit-Windsor Tunnel LLC, a subsidiary of American Roads LLC, operates the tunnel from plaza to plaza. The Detroit-Windsor Tunnel

LLC conducts separate business relationships with each city under different conditions (McLean and Eagles 2014).

Social Dimensions of Transborder Security

Terrorism

Conceptions of and approaches to border security in Ontario are informed by their societal context. After the events of 9/11, terrorism came to dominate American and Canadian border security concerns (Anderson 2014). The risk of terrorist attacks in Ontario is higher than in the other border regions, because the province is the home of Canada's capital city, the country's largest city, the busiest border crossings, and the busiest and largest international airport in the country (Leuprecht, Hataley, and Skillicorn 2013). Security concerns motivated the US government to close the Canada–US border after 9/11 and then re-open it with more stringent border protocols (Anderson 2014). The new border-security protocols led to extreme traffic delays and resulted in a significant decline in bilateral trade volumes between the two countries, with deleterious consequences for Canadian—and especially Ontario—exports to the United States (Anderson 2014; Globerman and Storer 2009). The decrease of Canadian exports had an adverse impact on the United States since imports from Canada promote higher real income levels in the United States in general, and in northern states that border Canada in particular (Anderson 2014; Globerman and Storer 2009). Trade flows were eventually eased with the implementation of trusted-trader and -traveler programs and have continued to improve with bilateral commitments such as the 2011 Beyond the Border action plan.

Trade

Ontario's high volume of trade with the United States makes the province an important consideration for border policymakers. Almost every province along the border has the United States in general, and a US state in particular, as its top trading partner, but no province has a greater share of Canadian exports to the US than Ontario (37.4 percent in 2014; Government of British Colombia 2015). Ontario's GDP made up 36.4 percent of Canada's nominal GDP in 2014, and in the same year 79.26 percent of Ontario's total exports went to the US (Ministry of Economic Development, Employment and Infrastructure, Ontario [MEDI], 2015). The destiny of Canada's national economy is thus largely determined by Ontario's trade with the United States.

Ontario's trade with the United States is facilitated by distinct features: the province's strategic location in the center of the GLSLR and just above the northeastern United States, where it is a distance of one trucking day from 125 million people. A dynamic workforce and large, skilled population positions Ontario as a successful competitor for exports to the United States (Brunet-Jailly 2006, 2012).

A significant portion of Ontario's trade with the US is with Michigan. Ontario imports 56.75 percent of its goods from the United States; 8.45 percent of that total comes from Michigan (MEDI 2015). Ontario's high level of economic integration with Michigan is largely due to the province's automotive sector, which comprises a large portion of the industry in southwestern Ontario, particularly in Windsor. Automotive companies such as General Motors, Ford, and Chrysler have countless supply chains moving goods across the border in southwestern Ontario. In 2014 autos, engines, and other motor vehicle parts accounted for more than 84 percent of goods exported from Ontario to Michigan (MEDI 2015). Similarly, 53 percent of Ontario's imports from Michigan in 2014 were motor vehicle parts, goods, transport vehicles, and autos (MEDI 2015)

The automotive supply chains that cross the Michigan–Ontario border facilitate just-in-time delivery for the automotive industry. A just-in-time inventory strategy means that automotive producers have low levels of inventory and rely on their supply chains to deliver the parts they need to build their products. Any delay in the transport of automotive materials at the border can hold up the entire production process and incur substantial losses for the automotive company. To prevent losses, companies in the auto industry or in another industry that relies on just-in-time delivery take into account unpredictable wait times and possible delays at the border.

Trade with Michigan in particular, and the United States in general, is not only instrumental to the Ontario's economic success, but also to the national GDP. Uncertainty and border travel delays can be detrimental to the production processes of key industries in Ontario, which border policymakers must take into consideration when discussing security.

Municipal and Subregional Actors

Municipal and subregional actors also shape border policy. Generally, North American cooperation is characterized by a highly decentralized system wherein Canadian federal, provincial, regional, and municipal actors utilize informal transborder networks to coordinate with their American counterparts to influence foreign policy (Friedman 2014). Despite the complexity and ambiguity of a system with many actors at different levels, a decentralized system has the advantage of responding to the competing demands of different municipal, provincial, nongovernmental, and regional actors (Friedman 2009).

The disagreements between the Mohawks of Akwesasne and the Canadian federal government demonstrate the influence of municipal actors on federal border security, and the flexibility of a decentralized system. Akwesasne is a First Nations territory in southeastern Ontario that not only straddles the international border between Ontario and New York and also the provincial border between Ontario and Québec. In 2009 there were community protests when the federal government granted Canada Border Services Agency (CBSA) border personnel in Akwesasne the right to carry firearms (CTV 2009). The protests resulted in the temporary closure of the border and the relocation of the CBSA checkpoint off traditional Akwesasne land on Cornwall Island (CBC 2009). After the checkpoint was moved, issues arose when some residents of Akwesasne stopped on the island before checking in with CBSA (Peerenboom 2015). By not checking in before stopping on the island, residents violated the Immigration and Refugee Protection Act and the Customs Act (Peerenboom 2015). In protest, the Mohawk Council of Akwesasne took legal action to prove that the charges laid against residents for stopping on Cornwall Island before checking in with CBSA were unconstitutional (Peerenboom 2015). The case of Akwesasne demonstrates how border security in Ontario was challenged to fit the aspirations and demands of municipal and subregional actors. Akwesasne also demonstrates that the border and border security is a multijurisdictional issue where Indigenous governments need to be treated as a separate order of government.

Environmental Scan

Organized Crime

Organized crime groups smuggle illicit goods and people between and through Ontario's ports of entry. Most contraband is smuggled in and out of Ontario via air or land points of entry (Humphreys 2013; Leuprecht and Aulthouse 2014; Campanella 2015). Findings from the RCMP's Project Spawn show that Toronto Pearson International Airport had the highest number of organized crime groups using it for criminal activity, including drug trafficking out of Canada's class one international airports (RCMP 2006). Pearson has direct routes from high-risk source and transit countries, which organized crime groups can use to smuggle contraband (RCMP 2006). On the ground level, transboundary criminal organizations capitalize on Ontario's high volume of commercial and personal traffic to smuggle illicit goods and irregular migrants. Such organizations coerce, convince, or bribe travelers, traders, or border personnel to smuggle contraband and irregular migrants over the border. Once past the point of entry, there is a good highway system to distribute illicit goods throughout the province.

In terms of commodity smuggling across the border between Ontario and its American neighbors, the region is unique in a couple of ways. The high population density between the eastern seaboard of the United States and the Greater Toronto Area drives demand and, therefore, a higher volume of contraband: firearms move north and controlled substances move in both directions (Leuprecht and Aulthouse 2014; Leuprecht, Hataley, and Skillicorn 2013). Ontario has the most police-reported drug offenses in Canada (Dauvergne 2009). In 2012 Ontario also had the most lifetime cocaine/crack abusers in Canada (Health Canada 2012). The high level of drug-related offences and drug usage in the province, combined with Ontario's large market for drug dealers, means that there is a greater demand for illegal goods, and consequently a greater cross-border flow.

Contraband tobacco is also of concern in Ontario. The contraband tobacco trade is particularly prevalent in southeastern Ontario and southwestern Québec (Leuprecht 2016). Sundry tobacco manufacturing, distribution, and retail operations on Indigenous reserves and territories located on both sides of the Canada–US border range from small ad hoc operations to industrial manufacturing plants.

By dint of geography, with several ports of entry and areas along the St. Lawrence River, where it is fairly easy to cross, human trafficking and smuggling are also prominent in the region (Perrin 2011; Leuprecht 2019). Within this region are the busiest international airports in North America, the largest market for trafficked persons, and the largest segment of the population who wish to be smuggled across the border illegally.

Environmental and Health Security

Environmental security is of growing concern to the states and provinces in the Great Lakes–St. Lawrence basin. Climate change is one of the main issues threatening the environmental security in the GLSLR. Many of the states and provinces in the GLSLR have launched climate-change programs and initiatives in recent years, but evidence is still growing that regional climate change is altering the GLSLR ecosystem. According to the Mowat Centre (2014), if future water levels in the Great Lakes and St. Lawrence River remain near the low end of the historic range for sustained periods, the long-term cost to the region could reach $18.82 billion by 2050.

The introduction and spread of more than 180 nonnative aquatic species are also compromising the ecological health and consequently the economic prosperity of the GLSLR (Great Lakes Commission [GLC] 2012). Invasive species disrupt the existing Great Lakes food web, which jeopardizes commercial and sport fishery (GLC 2012). Zebra and quagga mussel shells clog water intake pipes and take over popular swimming areas, disable industrial water users, and compromise tourism (GLC 2012). The Asian carp brought from Asia to North America in the 1960s and '70s (Government of Canada 2020) have since migrated north through US waterways toward the Great Lakes. If they proliferate in the Great Lakes, they could potentially eat the food supply on which native species depend and crowd them out of their habitat. The decline of native fish species would damage sport and commercial fishing in Ontario (Government of Canada 2020). Prevention is the most cost-effective approach to protecting the lakes from invasive species (GLC 2012). Once introduced, species are virtually impossible to eradicate and costly to control. The region continues to be threatened by potential invasions via a host of pathways, including ballast water discharges, connecting waterways, trade in live organisms, and recreational activities (GLC 2012). Effective solutions require intergovernmental coordination among states, provinces, and border municipalities in the GLSLR (GLC 2012).

Threats to water quality are another transborder issue related to environmental security. Contamination from aging municipal waste-treatment infrastructure, harmful algal blooms, industrial and nonpoint sources of pollution, atmospheric deposition of toxic substances, oil, and spills of sixteen hazardous material all threaten water quality in the GLSLR. Deteriorating water quality threatens public health and environmental security with the degradation of wildlife habitats and public drinking water supplies (GLC 2012). Threats to water quality combined with climate change and the introduction of invasive species are some of the many environmental concerns shared by Ontario and US states in the GLSLR.

Methods to Combat Current Security Threats

Border Security Technology and Trusted-Traveler Programs

The implementation of border security technologies and trusted-trader and -traveler programs has revolutionized how border security is carried out, and how traders and travelers experience the border. Canada Border Services Agency (CBSA) officials use a variety of these types of technologies at the Ontario border including X-ray imaging (fixed units, mobile units, and vans), gamma-ray imaging, vehicle and cargo inspection system (VACIS) units, and radiation detection. They also use biometrics, the automated use of physical and biological information, to verify and authenticate an individual's identity. In conjunction with the American government, CBSA offers several trusted-trader and -traveler programs to secure supply chains and facilitate legitimate cross-border trade and travel, including the trusted-traveler program NEXUS and the trusted-trade program FAST. These programs permit low-risk travelers and traders to transit the border expeditiously and allow border security agencies to concentrate their scarce resources on high-risk travelers and traders who may transit illegal goods and irregular migrants across the border. Trusted-traveler and -trader programs also attempt to align the needs of the large volume of commercial and personal traffic that transit Ontario's points of entry daily with provincial and federal security priorities. Although there are limitations to this approach, it provides an option for both the Canadian and American governments to balance the high volume of trade that transits Ontario's POEs every day with municipal, provincial, and federal security requirements.

Specialized Law Enforcement Teams and Initiatives

Other than border technologies and trusted-trader and -traveler programs, specialized law enforcement units and initiatives counter the flow of illegal goods and people into Ontario. This includes marine law enforcement initiatives such as Marine Security Enforcement Teams and Integrated Cross-border Maritime Law Enforcement Operations (Shiprider) programs, as well as various Integrated Border Enforcement Teams that have disrupted smuggling rings; confiscated illegal drugs, weapons, liquor, tobacco, and vehicles; and made numerous arrests.

Environmental and Health Security

To tackle transborder environmental issues, Ontario, Québec, American states, and many border municipalities in the GLSLR joined regional organizations and agreements that address climate change and environmental protection. The Council of Great Lakes Governors, the Council of the Great Lakes Region, the Conference of Great Lakes and St. Lawrence Governors and Premiers, the Great Lakes Commission, and the Great Lakes Commission's many initiatives and partners are examples of transborder organizations and initiatives that bring together private-sector, nonprofit, and public-sector actions on federal, provincial, and municipal levels to coordinate environmental protection and climate-change efforts. There are also transborder agreements such as the 2012 Great Lakes Water Quality Agreement that solidify American and Canadian commitments to environmental protection in the GLSLR.

Horizon Scan

Many emerging security issues in Ontario and the GLSLR stem from a lack of capacity in current border security policies and programs. Emerging security concerns could be addressed by expanding the layered approach that current border security programs utilize in Ontario.

Trusted-Trader and -Traveler Programs

Despite the availability of trusted-trader programs and facilities in Ontario, obtaining and maintaining certification can be costly for individuals and small businesses (Anderson 2014). For some programs trusted traders must not only pay a membership fee but also implement costly updates to security systems to secure their supply chain. Failure to adhere to the initial and periodic security audits can result in decertification and loss of membership benefits. This process puts small firms at a competitive disadvantage because most large firms already have a high level of supply chain security (Anderson 2014), and it increases the administrative burden on small businesses, making the processes ineffective due to the complexity of pre-assessment and the consequent cost and inconvenience. Trusted-trader programs can thus hinder the economic security of Ontario if businesses cannot afford the requirements of the programs and cannot cross the border as quickly as larger competitors.

Marine Security

Three years after 9/11, in the 2004 National Security Policy the federal government set out measures to increase marine security,. These measures included clarifying responsibilities and strengthening coordination of marine security; increasing the on-water presence of the Canadian Armed Forces, RCMP, and Canadian Coast Guard; conducting aerial surveillance by the Department of Fisheries and Oceans; establishing marine security operation centers; pursuing greater marine security cooperation with the United States; and strengthening the security of marine facilities. To achieve these objectives the federal government established one Marine Security Operation Centre, four Marine Security Enforcement Teams units, and several Shiprider operations in the Great Lakes–St. Lawrence Seaway. Although these programs enhance marine security in Ontario, their structural weaknesses limit their success.

Environmental Security

Emerging concerns in Ontario's transborder lakes and rivers that threaten the public health and environmental security of Ontario include aging water-related infrastructure. Piers, breakwaters, and other marine infrastructure enables safe marine transportation to support core industries and a large boating and sport fishing economy, and help provide tens of millions of people with drinking water (GLC 2012). However, sewage discharges, particularly from aging infrastructure, close Great Lakes beaches, threaten public health, and damage local economies. Upgrading and replacing aging infrastructure such as sewers prevents oil and hazardous material spills, but it is difficult because funding wastewater and other marine infrastructure is a costly challenge for many municipalities. Identifying the most sensitive at-risk areas and infrastructure and developing tools to assess risks and track movements of spills protects habitat, public drinking water supplies, and other water uses (GLC 2012).

Case Studies

Case Study 1: License to Smuggle?

Trusted-trader and -traveler programs also have the potential to become an emerging security issue. They can provide a "license to smuggle" for transborder crime groups. Individuals and private companies that have undergone rigorous background checks, paid their fees, upgraded their supply chain security, and received their designation as low-risk traders and travelers are ideal intermediaries for illegal goods and irregular migrants. Actors can convince, bribe, or coerce cleared trusted travelers and traders to smuggle illegal goods and irregular migrants across the border with a high probability of success. Trusted traders and travelers are less likely to be referred to secondary inspection because they have been vetted as low risk by having already gone through extensive security validation. As a criminal strategy, becoming a trusted trader and traveler is a good way to avoid discovery, confiscation, and prosecution.

Due to the clandestine nature of crime, it is difficult to determine the rate at which trusted traders and travelers transport illegal goods and people. However, there is evidence that it occurs in Ontario. In 2009 Customs and Border Protection (CBP) officers from the Fort Street Cargo Facility in Detroit caught an individual who was part of the Free and Secure Trade (FAST) program attempting to smuggle drugs into the country. On October 8, 2009, Goran Poljak, a sixty-year-old Canadian from Windsor, arrived at the cargo facility and presented a FAST card to the CBP border officer (Sootoday 2009). He told the officer at the primary booth that he had an empty trailer. The officer referred the truck to secondary inspection, where officers found two duffel bags containing 27.5 kilograms of marijuana (CBP 2009).

There have also been cases of corruption at the Ontario border (Tunney 2020; Office of the Auditor General of Canada 2017). In 2012, an unnamed CBSA officer at the Pigeon River port of entry near Thunder Bay was dismissed for affiliating with known organized crime figures in Thunder Bay who operated throughout Canada and internationally. An investigation by the Office of the Public Sector Integrity Commissions of Canada found that he failed "to take enforcement action on these individuals as his duties required" (Office of the Public Sector Integrity Commissioner of Canada 2013).

Border technologies and trusted-trader and -traveler programs indicate a shift toward a layered border security approach at the Canada–US border. A layered border security approach focuses on extending border security practices beyond the physical boundary line. Both Canada and the United States have attempted to implement a layered approach by moving customs and immigration inspection activities away from the border, using technologies and approaches that focus on prescreening travelers. For example, under the CBSA's Advance Commercial Information program, carriers and freight forwarders must submit electronic cargo and conveyance data in advance to the CBSA so that threats to Canada's health, safety, and security can be identified prior to the arrival of cargo and conveyances in Canada (CBSA 2015). The layered approach to border security rationalizes resources by identifying risks and dangers while facilitating the flow of legitimate goods, people, and transportation.

Case Study 2: Marine Security and Shiprider

Colloquially known as Shiprider, Integrated Cross-Border Maritime Law Enforcement Operations in Ontario stretch from Cornwall/Massena in the east to the Detroit-Windsor corridor in the west. Shiprider's Framework Agreement dictates that operations will provide both the Canadian and American federal governments with "additional means in shared waterways to prevent, detect, suppress, investigate, and prosecute criminal offences or violations of law including, but not limited to, illicit drug trade, migrant smuggling, trafficking of firearms, the smuggling of counterfeit goods and money, and terrorism" (Government of Canada and Government of the United States of America 2009; US Office of National Drug Control Policy, 2020). Despite these goals, in practice Shiprider is limited in its ability to enhance border security because it is restricted to acting only at the border, not beyond.

According to the Framework Agreement, Shiprider officers may only continue activities undertaken during an operation on land in urgent or exceptional situations (Government of Canada and Government of the United States of America 2009; US Office of National Drug Control Policy 2020). Urgent and exceptional circumstances occur when a Shiprider officer has reasonable grounds to suspect that the continuation of the activities undertaken in the course of integrated cross-border maritime law enforcement operations on land is necessary to prevent (1) imminent bodily harm or death to any person, (2) the immediate and unlawful flight of persons liable to detention or arrest, or (3) the imminent loss or imminent destruction of evidence (Government of Canada and Government of the United States of America 2009; US Office of National Drug Control Policy, 2020).

Thus, only in emergency situations can a Shiprider officer follow up on criminal activities beyond their marine jurisdiction.

Giving Shiprider the powers and resources to investigate and pursue transboundary criminal organizations who orchestrate the smuggling of illicit goods and people over Ontario's marine borders would enhance Canadian border security by eliminating the source of the transborder criminal activity rather than just containing its effects. Extending Shiprider's mandate would require expanding the layered border-security approach that the Canadian government currently uses, adding another layer of security that attempts to stop transboundary criminal organizations from broadening criminal activities in Ontario. Shiprider would also be uniquely equipped for this position because its formal structure allows for efficient information-sharing between American and Canadian law enforcement agencies. By leveraging its partnership with the US Coast Guard and extending its mandate beyond the border boundary line, Shiprider could partner with other federal agencies to combat transborder crime.

Conclusion

Border security in Ontario and the Great Lakes–St. Lawrence Region is shaped by the area's demographic, economic, and environmental characteristics. As in other border regions, border security in Ontario focuses on traditional threats to security: terrorist activity, organized crime, and the smuggling of goods and people. However, Ontario's shared waterways, geographic landscape, high volume of trade with the United States, and traditional Indigenous lands spanning the international border create additional priorities and concerns for border security and management.

The lakes and rivers that dominate Ontario's border with the United States are not only a resource for manufacturing, fishing, and tourism industries in the region, they also support a large ecosystem of native species and provide drinking water for Ontarians. Provincial, state, and municipal governments collaborate on environmental protections for the GLSLR.

Expanding the province's layered approach to border security will help federal, provincial, and municipal law enforcement agencies address emerging security threats, including transborder criminal organizations that smuggle illicit goods and irregular migrations through Ontario's points of entry and over transboundary lakes and rivers. A cross-border layered approach that prioritizes intelligence-gathering and law enforcement activity beyond the border would enhance both transportation and marine security by focusing on transnational criminal organizations as the source of illegal activity rather than just the individuals who get caught at the border. The investigative powers of both marine security initiatives and preventing smugglers from capitalizing on the low-risk designation of trusted traders and travelers shift border security from a reactive to a layered approach that proactively bolsters a safe and profitable Ontario.

NOTE

1. First Nations is the referent used in Canada to denote the Indigenous populations. An analogous term in the United States would be Native American.

REFERENCES

Abgrall, Jean-François. 2005. "A Survey of Major Cross-Border Organisations between Canada and the United States." Working Paper Series 009, Policy Research Initiative. Ottawa: Government of Canada.

Anderson, William. 2014. *The Border and the Ontario Economy*. Windsor, ON: University of Windsor, Cross Border Transportation Centre. http://ebtc.info/wp-content/uploads/2014/07/Anderson-Border-and-ON-economy.pdf

Brunet-Jailly, Emmanuel. 2006. "Security and Border Security Policies: Perimeter or Smart Border? A Comparison of the European Union and Canadian-American Border Security Regimes." *Journal of Borderlands Studies* 21, no. 1: 3–1.

Brunet-Jailly, Emmanuel. 2012. "A New Border? A Canadian Perspective of the Canada–US Border Post-9/11." *International Journal* 67, no. 4: 963–74.

Campanella, Emanuela. 2015. "More than Two Metric Tonnes of Cocaine Seized at Southwestern Ontario Borders from 2007 to 2013." *London Free Press*. http://www.lfpress.com/2015/08/21/more-than-two-metric-tonnes-of-cocaine-seized-at-southwestern-ontario-borders-since-2007

Canada Border Services Agency (CBSA). 2015. *Advance Commercial Information (ACI)*. CBSA. https://www.cbsa-asfc.gc.ca/prog/aci-manif-ipec/hcc-ctr-eng.html

Canada Broadcasting Corporation (CBC). 2009. "Cornwall Border Post Could Be Moved Off Mohawk Land." *CBC*. http://www.cbc.ca/news/canada/ottawa/cornwall-border-post-could-be-moved-off-mohawk-land-1.820864

Council of the Great Lakes Region (CGLR). 2015. "Council of the Great Lakes Region Establishes Border Issues Work Group." *CGLR*. http://councilgreatlakesregion.org/council-of-the-great-lakes-region-establishes-border-issues-work-group/

CTV. 2009. "Akwesasne Mohawks Protest Border Gun Plan." *CTV*. http://ottawa.ctvnews.ca/akwesasne-mohawks-protest-border-gun-plan-1.394879

Dauvergne, Mia. 2009. "Trends in Police-Reported Drug Offences in Canada." *Statistics Canada*. Statistics Canada catalogue no. 85–002-X Jusistat. http://www.statcan.gc.ca/pub/85-002-x/2009002/article/10847-eng.pdf

Friedman, Kathryn Bryk. 2009. "Through the Looking Glass: Implications of Canada-United States Transgovernmental Networks for Democratic Theory International Law, and the Future of North American Governance." *Alberta Law Review* 46, no. 4: 1081–97.

Friedman, Kathryn Bryk. 2014. "Between a Rock and a Hard Place? North American Security in the Twenty-First Century." In *Is Geography Destiny? A Primer on North American Relations*, edited by Christopher Wilson and David Biette, 41–47. Woodrow Wilson International Center for Scholars. https://www.wilsonc enter.org/sites/default/files/media/documents/publication/primer_north_ame rican_relations.pdf

Globerman, Steven, and Paul Storer. 2009. "The Effects of 9/11 on Canadian-U.S. Trade: An Update Through 2008." Brookings Institution. http://www.brookin gs.edu/~/media/research/files/papers/2009/7/13-canada-globerman/0713_can ada_globerman.pdf

Government of British Colombia. 2015. *Trade Profile-United States*. BC Stats. http://www.bcstats.gov.bc.ca/statisticsbysubject/ExportsImports/Data/Countr yTradeProfiles/TradeProfileUnitedStates.aspx

Government of Canada. 2018. *Beyond the Border: A Shared Vision for Perimeter Security and Economic Competitiveness (Action Plan)*. Ottawa: Government of Canada. https://www.publicsafety.gc.ca/cnt/brdr-strtgs/bynd-th-brdr/index-en.aspx

Government of Canada. 2020. "Asian Carp." https://www.dfo-mpo.gc.ca/species-es peces/profiles-profils/asiancarp-carpeasiatique-eng.html

Government of Canada and the Government of the United States of America. 2009. "Framework Agreement on Integrated Cross-Border Maritime Law Enforcement Operations Between the Government of the United States of America and the Government of Canada." Washington: Department of Homeland Security. http://www.dhs.gov/xlibrary/assets/shiprider_agreement.pdf

Great Lakes Commission (GLC). 2012. "Aspects of New Great Lakes Water Quality Agreement Take Shape at Great Lakes Commission Meeting." https://www .glc.org/news/2012-aspects-of-new-great-lakes-water-quality-agreement-take -shape-at-great-lakes-commission-meeting/

Hataley, Todd, and Christian Leuprecht. 2013. "Organized Crime Beyond the Border." Ottawa: Macdonald-Laurier Institute, National Security Strategy for Canada Series, no. 5.

Health Canada. 2012. *Canadian Alcohol and Drug Use Monitoring Survey (CAD-MUS)*. Ottawa: Health Canada. http://www.hc-sc.gc.ca/hc-ps/drugs-drogues /stat/_2012/summary-sommaire-eng.php#s8

Humphreys, Adrian. 2013. "Cocaine Smuggling a 'Threat,' Report Shows, as $2M Worth of Drugs Found in Toronto Airport Bathroom." *National Post*.

Leuprecht, Christian. 2016. *Smoking Gun: Strategic Containment of Contraband Tobacco*. Ottawa: Macdonald Laurier Institute. https://www.macdonaldlaurier.ca /files/pdf/MLILeuprechtContrabandPaper-03-16-WebReady.pdf

Leuprecht, Christian. 2019. *The End of the (Roxham) Road: Seeking Coherence on Canada's Border-Migration Compact*. Ottawa: Macdonald Laurier Institute. https:// macdonaldlaurier.ca/files/pdf/20191108_MLI_ROXHAM_ROAD_Leuprecht _PAPER_FWeb.pdf?mc_cid=f0bfa4676f&mc_eid=38a00fb976

Leuprecht, Christian, and Andrew Aulthouse. 2014. "Guns for Hire: North America's Intra-continental Gun Trafficking Networks." *Criminology, Criminal Justice, Law & Society* 15, no. 3: 57–74.

Leuprecht, Christian, Todd Hataley, and David B. Skillicorn. 2013. "Cross-Border Terror Networks: A Social Network Analysis of the Canada–U.S. Border." *Behavioural Sciences of Terrorism and Political Aggression* 5, no. 2: 155–75.

Mclean, Dylan S., and Monroe Eagles. 2014. "Governance Regimes for Cross-Border Infastructure: A Comparative Study of Facilities on the Canada–United States Border." *International Journal of Canadian Studies* 49: 285–313.

Ministry of Economic Development, Employment and Infrastructure, Ontario (MEDI). 2015. *Ontario Trade Fact Sheet.* MEDI. https://www.ontario.ca/page /published-plans-and-annual-reports-2015-16-ministry-economic-developme nt-employment-infrastructure

Ministry of Transportation, Ontario (MTO). 2015. *Ontario Border Crossings.* MTO. http://www.mto.gov.on.ca/english/ontario-511/ontario-border-crossings.sht ml#windsor

Mowat Centre. 2014. "Low Water Blues—Economic Fallout from Lower Future Water Levels in the Great Lakes–St. Lawrence Region Could Total More Than $18 Billion by 2050." Mowat Centre. http://mowatcentre.ca/low-water-blues -economic-fallout-from-lower-future-water-levels-in-the-great-lakes-st-lawre nce-region-could-total-more-than-18-billion-by-2050/

Office of the Auditor General of Canada (OAG). 2017. *Preventing Corruption in Immigration and Border Services.* https://www.oag-bvg.gc.ca/internet/English/pa rl_oag_201705_03_e_42225.html

Office of the Public Sector Integrity Commissioner of Canada. 2013. "Case Report: Findings of the Public Sector Integrity Commissioner in the Matter of an Investigation into a Disclosure of Wrongdoing." Office of the Public Sector Integrity Commissioner of Canada. http://www.psic-ispc.gc.ca/quicklinks_lien srapides/crmarch2013_rcmars2013-eng.aspx#Results

Peerenboom, Greg. 2015. "MCA Challenging Customs Act." *Cornwall Standard-Freeholder.*

Perrin, Benjamin. 2011. *Invisible Chains: Canada's Underground World of Human Trafficking.* Toronto: Penguin Group.

Porter, Douglas. 2015. "Great Lakes–St. Lawrence Region: North America's Economic Engine." *BMO Capital Markets Economics.* Ottawa. http://www.bmonesb ittburns.com/economics/reports/20150427/sr-great-lakes-201506-QC-en.pdf

RCMP. 2006. Project SPAWN: *A Strategic Assessment of Criminal Activity and Organized Crime Infiltration at Canada's Class 1 Airports.* https://publications.gc.ca/co llections/collection_2012/grc-rcmp/PS64-95-2007-eng.pdf

SooToday. 2009. "Trusted Trucker Arrested at Windsor Border Crossing." https:// www.sootoday.com/local-news/trusted-trucker-arrested-at-windsor-border-cr ossing-126034

Transport Canada. 2016. *Transportation in Canada.* Ottawa. https://tc.canada.ca/en /corporate-services/transparency/corporate-management-reporting/transport ation-canada-annual-reports/transportation-canada-2016#freight-transportati on-flows

Tunney, Catharine. 2020. "CBSA Warned Bill Blair that Organized Crime Groups May Be Corrupting Border Officers." *CBC News*, 4 June. https://www.cbc.ca/news/politics/cbsa-organized-crime-warning-1.5584691

US Office of National Drug Control Policy. 2020. *National Northern Border Counter Narcotics Strategy*. Washington: Government of the United States. https://www.hsdl.org/?abstract&did=834361

SIX

Québec and the Eastern Seaboard

David Morin, Stéphane Roussel, and Carolina Reyes Marquez[1]

Introduction

In Canada, the federal government has legislative authority with respect to border security. However, the provinces have a substantial role to play in this area because of their jurisdiction in the administration of justice, public safety, civil rights, and immigration. Due to the diversity of the various provinces' histories, geographical situations, economies, and demographic makeups, each province has constructed its own set of priorities and practices with respect to security issues. This is especially the case for Québec, which, for historical, linguistic, and cultural reasons, has frequently claimed a distinct international status and role with respect to the federal government, and which has progressively made security a linchpin of its government policy and of its "ability to be recognized as a credible and responsible actor in international relations (Gouvernement du Québec 2017a, 55)."

This chapter seeks to analyze Québec's role and activities in North American transborder security. Prior to the events of September 11, 2001 (9/11), security was of little concern, but the attack transformed it into an issue of increasing politicization and securitization. This evolution initially appeared to be dictated by ad hoc political and economic imperatives, rather than by security considerations *stricto sensu*, or by a particular desire on the part of Québec to play a role in transborder security. The issue was nonetheless the subject of political announcements and of some international agreements, and it was a factor in strengthening (on the technical and administrative levels) the intergovernmental relations network between certain Québec organizations, notably the police, and their foreign counterparts.

Context

Québec, territorially the largest of Canada's provinces, comprises 1,667 square kilometers and is home to 8.2 million people, the majority of whom are francophone. Québec's only international border is with the United States. That border, 813 kilometres long, stretches along four American states: Maine, New Hampshire, Vermont, and New York. Although it traverses several lakes and waterways, it is essentially a land border, unlike the one between Ontario and the United States. There are thirty-two official ports of entry along the border, in addition to US Customs and Border Protection situated at Montréal's Pierre Elliott Trudeau airport.

Québec's principal transborder concern, like that of the other provinces, has long been economic. Québec's international trade figures are similar to those of the country as a whole: they account for 30 percent of gross domestic product, with 70 percent of that deriving from trade with the US. In 2016, Québec exports amounted to $60 billion (half of Ontario's exports) and represented 14.5 percent of all Canadian exports to the United States (Gouvernement du Québec 2017a, 32; Gouvernement du Québec 2017b). Québec, which benefited greatly from the North American Free Trade Agreement (NAFTA), was principally concerned during the 1990s with maintaining the free flow across the border of this ever-increasing trade, which was essentially the domain of the federal government.

Security was not really an issue in that transborder context. This is not to say that the border space was always exempt from security problems. The fight against bootleggers during Prohibition gave rise to the first initiatives for police cooperation to fight organized crime on both sides of the border (Cormier 2012). Over the last forty years, other problems have gradually arisen, notably environmental issues. However, given the weak politicization of security issues and Québec's strong political, cultural, and economic relations with its American neighbor, the border was managed and studied above all as a space of integration and interdependence (Ackleson 2009), consistent with security being generally ranked as a secondary issue in the Québec public sphere.

The 9/11 attacks marked a turning point: the priority thereafter given to security imperatives by the American authorities changed the management of the transborder space, and demolished the dominant concept of an open border (Andreas 2003; Konrad and Nicol 2008). In this new context, according to Québec's 2017 international policy statement, "one of the main issues is to reconcile the goal of the optimal flow of people and goods with the security imperatives, including the fight against terrorism and against local and transborder crime." The terrorism concern was aggravated, during the second decade of the twenty-first century, by the appearance of domestic violent extremism, including within Québec's borders. Since 2017 Québec has been confronted with a new problem: the highly publicized arrival at the Canada–US border of an ever-growing number of migrants claiming refugee status (Leuprecht 2019). Although the security aspect of this migration is questionable and has been contested, various media outlets, as well as some political figures and members of the public, have interpreted the phenomenon through the prism of transborder security. This "resecuritization" of the border has reminded the Québécois of the existence and the importance of the border with their American neighbor.

This evolution has had two consequences. First, it has contributed to the (re)politicization of transborder security and to the securitization of certain problems, such as organized crime, immigration, and even environmental and health risks. In many cases, transborder security concerns, earlier seen as falling only within federal jurisdiction, are now conceived as involving multiple sectors and fields of constitutional responsibility. Second, the evolution directly engages the provincial powers of administration of justice, public safety, health, and natural resources. In several of these fields a form of de facto intergovernmental cooperation has developed, with Québec's participation. In this context, although all the provinces promote their interests, Québec is in general the one that most vigorously defends and seeks to occupy its fields of competence (Nossal, Roussel, and Paquin 2015, 340–46), including that of transborder security. The Québec government maintains its traditional activism in this area through multiple statements and initiatives, by formulating policies and adopting new regulations, and by discussions held in the framework of regional forums.

Concepts

On the theoretical level, the definition of "security" is, in itself, challenging. Not only has the concept evolved over the last decades, but its meaning remains what it has always been: controversial (Smith 2005). Several conceptual elements are useful to better understand this complex notion and how it functions in the context of Québec transborder security.

First, the evolution of security issues in the Québec public sphere is characterized by politicization and securitization. Politicization is the process whereby a social object that is neither politicized nor problematized in the political sphere is made political and debated such that it becomes the duty of the government to take responsibility for it and control it. Securitization, a concept popularized by Ole Weaver, is the process whereby a political object is transformed, by discursive and nondiscursive acts, into a security object, is presented by the authorities and professionals as an urgent matter, and is accepted as such by a target audience. Although both processes are eminently political, securitization can be seen as an extreme version of politicization, in that it presents an object as an existential threat and a priority requiring immediate and sometimes exceptional political decisions (Buzan, Waever, and De Wilde 1998, 23). These two concepts explain why and how transborder security, which was, if not invisible, certainly long perceived as a matter falling squarely within the routine administrative practices of the federal government, has progressively become first a political issue and then a security issue in Québec.

Second, how the Québec government defines security is of interest. Mirroring the approach of security studies, Québec has examined and enlarged the concept, accepting a broad definition that covers diverse economic, political, social, and environmental activities. Québec's 2017 international policy statement, aiming to "contribute to a more sustainable, just and secure world," reiterates this broad concept of security:

> The increased transnational flow of talent, goods and services, data and capital is a source of prosperity and economic resilience and a catalyst for innovation. But it can also reveal systemic weaknesses and help crises spread from one country, region or continent to another. Financial crisis, terrorist attacks, natural disasters, pandemics, hard-to-control migratory flows, cross-border organized crime and cybercrime are among the risks of direct concern to governments. All over the world, governments must learn to deal with greater uncertainty and implement appropriate methods of management and governance. They must also take the necessary measures to protect and reassure their populations and promote the importance of learning to live together. (Gouvernement du Québec 2017a, 10)

Although public safety (as classically understood), the fight against climate change, and sustainable development are given a predominant place in this definition, aid to victims of humanitarian catastrophes (including welcoming refugees) and the promotion of human rights are also mentioned. With respect to security issues, the policy statement observes:

> The Government of Québec takes actions and supports, where appropriate, Canadian and American government initiatives to facilitate the flow of people and goods through such means as pre-clearance systems and facilities and investments in border infrastructure while at the same time strengthening continental security in a manner respectful of the rights of citizens. Québec also aims to ensure that train stations and airports within its jurisdictions and the border it shares with four American states are given the priority that reflects their importance in the implementation of these initiatives. (Gouvernement du Québec 2017a, 56)

The Québec government thus adopts a broad definition of the concept of security within a transnational perspective. The development of transport and communications has turned the border into an area of spaces and of flows, physical and symbolic, which affect both the border and the domestic regions. Transborder security is therefore characterized by the overlapping of international, national, and local levels, and is similar to distinct sectorial "secure flows," whose relation to the border space differs according to the nature of the sector (Leuprecht, Hataley, and Nossal 2012). Former premier Philippe Couillard made a similar analysis with respect to violent extremism when he observed, "Québec is not an island separate from the rest of the world, that [international] phenomena could happen here" (quoted in *La Presse* 2014).

A last definitional field relates to the notion of cooperation between the different levels of government and the agencies on both sides of the border involved in managing transborder security. According to the 2017 international policy statement:

> The resilience of the international system to shocks and crises depends in large part on the level of cooperation between relevant actors. The global nature of issues such as the stability of the international financial system and the fight against illegal trafficking, tax evasion, terrorism and climate change calls for the adoption of

shared priorities and the implementation of formal and informal cooperation mechanisms. (Gouvernement du Québec 2017a, 11)

The concept of *multilevel governance*, which fits well here, permits the recognition of the coexistence of two distinct types of government (Hooghe and Marks 2003). The first, corresponding to Canadian federalism, is characterized by the sharing of general competencies between a limited number of government levels (provincial, federal, and municipal). This is done "from the top down," by means of Québec's intergovernmental and transgovernmental relations, as well as through policy statements and agreements between governments. The second and more flexible type of government is aimed at more specific challenges and allows the powers of multiple institutions (police, firefighters, transport, etc.) to overlap. It can be seen as arising from "the ground up" in that it is concerned more with the administrative and operational dimension (whether formal or not) of the relations between government agencies at diverse levels of the bureaucratic pyramid (Keohane and Nye 1974). These agencies are often called on to develop, more or less autonomously, interactions and structures of cooperation, joint patrol groups, or particular agreements in the course of their investigative or information-gathering work. Although these concepts do not exhaust all of the intricacies of the definitional debate, they do expose the variety of governance dynamics at play in the field of intergovernmental cooperation in transborder security.

Actors

In Québec, the Ministry of Public Security, the municipal and Indigenous police forces, and the provincial police, the Sûreté du Québec, maintain public order. The Act respecting the Ministry of Public Security gives duties and powers to the ministry relating to the maintenance of public safety, crime prevention, the police, and the correctional services, and also to civil protection and fire safety. Another important Québec actor is the Ministry of International Relations and of the Francophonie, whose mission is "to promote and defend Québec's interests internationally while ensuring respect for its authority and the consistency of government activities" (Gouvernement du Québec 2017b). This ministry is very different, if not unique, when compared with the agencies of other provinces.[2] In 2017 the ministry had a network of twenty-nine government offices (general delegations, delegations, bureaus, or trade offices) located in sixteen countries; nine of these offices are in the United States. Québec's 2006 international policy statement therefore marked a turning point in the post-9/11 context when it announced, for the first time, that priority would be given to the aim of "contributing to the security of Québec and the North American continent" (Gouvernement du Québec 2006, 67–77). This priority was subsequently reiterated, in varying degrees, in Ministry Information Bulletins (Gouvernement du Québec 2008), Action Plans (for example, Gouvernement du Québec 2009), and in the Government of Québec's *US Strategy Plan* (2010a, 27–29).

Québec participates in most North American regional forums, many of which deal with transborder security issues. It has been an associate member of the Great Lakes Commission since 1999 and in 2015 joined the Conference of Great Lakes and St. Lawrence Governors and Premiers. The annual Conference of New England Governors and Eastern Canadian Premiers, whose mandate is to establish agreements for international assistance in emergency management and civil protection, is more directly concerned with security matters. Québec, which has participated in the Conference since 1973 and is one of the ten founding members, uses this forum to discuss security issues. Over the last fifteen years, Québec has taken part in several multilateral and bilateral forums on transborder security. It is notably a member of the Northeast Regional Homeland Security Directors Consortium, which it hosted in 2008, and of the Canada–US Cross-Border Crime Forum. It participates in the annual conference for the prevention of US–Canada cross-border crime and strives in other settings to strengthen its image as a credible partner in transborder security. The main goal of these initiatives is to keep the lines of communication open. Finally, in the field of public safety, Québec participates, with the four Atlantic provinces and the six New England states, in the International Emergency Management Assistance Compact, an agreement providing for a mutual aid mechanism.

Québec has also signed agreements for the exchange of information and for cooperation in security matters with the four US states along its border (Vermont: 2003, 2010, and 2013; Maine: 2004 and 2013; New Hampshire: 2004; and New York: 2004 and 2008), as well as with Massachusetts (2007). Its agreements with other American states for the exchange of information are principally concerned with cross-border crime and the fight against terrorism.

Issues

The Securitization of the Economic Flows
at the Canadian–American Border

Trade with the United States is as important for Québec's prosperity as it is for that of Canada as a whole. In 2016, "the value of Québec merchandise exports to the United States represented 71% of Québec's total international merchandise exports [whereas] Québec's merchandise imports from the United States represented 35.2% of Québec's total merchandise imports" (Gouvernement du Québec 2017b). Québec's principal American trade partners start with the nearby New England states but include some states farther afield, such as Texas, Ohio, Tennessee, and Pennsylvania. The statistics show that trade with the United States is vital for both Québec and Canada. According to political scientist Denis Stairs (1994, 8), "there is only one imperative in Canadian foreign policy, [that] of maintaining a working relationship that is politically amicable—and therefore economically effective—with the United States."

Trade between Canada and the US grew exponentially after the signing of the 1989 and 1994 trade agreements. However, the 9/11 attacks, the difficulties to the US economy suffered due to the 2008 financial crisis, and positions taken by the Trump administration have created a new situation for Québec's external trade. Trump's 2016 election reinforced the fact that Québec's number-one priority was the difficult matter of guaranteeing the security of economic flows to the United States. The president's intention to renegotiate the Free Trade Agreement (NAFTA), even to end it, created turmoil in both Ottawa and the provincial capitals. Québec's 2017 international policy statement makes clear the government's determination to protect this agreement: "Québec will do all it can to protect access to markets and safeguard the principles that guided both FTA and NAFTA" (Gouvernement du Québec 2017a, 14). However, Québec's ability to act in this area is limited and the best means at its disposal to defend its interests—namely, contributing to Ottawa's strategy—is not something that proceeds smoothly due to the federal government's attitude (Paquin 2017).

Although trade fluctuations can be caused by multiple factors, the US authorities' prioritization of security imperatives and the temptation to return to protectionism have resulted in major changes in border management and have done away with the concept of an open border. As former Québec Minister of International Relations Monique Gagnon-Tremblay noted, the strengthening of security measures at the border has had a "significant impact on [Québec's] exports, but also on laws relating to immigration, justice, rights and freedoms, transport, and public safety" (Gouvernement du Québec 2004). In this context of heightened security and protectionism, "the multiplication of administrative formalities, of requirements and of inspections at the border, as well as the absence of mutual recognition of certain norms between the Canadian and American agencies, bog down the processes and increase unnecessarily the cost of trade for the companies of both countries" (Gouvernment du Québec 2004, 16).

In this context, for Québec to secure the border in an *intelligent* manner means above all that it must secure Québec exports to the US market and the movement of people at the border. Québec's 2010–2013 strategy regarding the United States was to "pursue collaboration and strengthen partnerships between the Canadian and American customs agencies, notably by providing expertise in the field of transport and delivery, in order to improve the customs infrastructure at the thirty-two Québec border crossings" (Gouvernement du Québec 2010b). In the transportation sector Québec has had to adapt to and participate in federal programs, initiated by the United States, that affect the passage of its citizens and its merchandise at land and maritime borders, such as the enhanced Driver's Licence Plus,[3] or the construction of rapid-access lanes at the border. It has thus become essential that Québec and Canada react in a satisfactory manner to American security imperatives to ensure the free flow of trade.

Terrorism and Violent Extremism

It is not surprising that Québec's international policy statements of 2006 and 2017 identify terrorism as one of the major threats facing the North American continent. Although this might seem an exaggerated reading of the situation in 2006, given the then slight footprint in Canada of the phenomenon, it seems less so after 2017, with the succession of terrorist events that have occurred both within and outside of Québec. The 2014 attacks in Saint-Jean-sur-Richelieu and in Ottawa confirmed that Québec was indeed not sheltered from "jihadist violence": certain Québec citizens commit, participate in, or promote violent acts in Québec and elsewhere in the name of a holy war. A wave of young Quebeckers left for Syria and other conflict zones, or were prevented from leaving—in 2015 there were estimated to be 150 Canadians participating with terrorists overseas and 80 who had returned home (Senate of Canada 2015), underscoring the fact that this threat extends beyond the North American continent. The 2017 attack on the Québec City mosque proved beyond a doubt that violent extremism, in all its forms, is a real concern.

Apart from the question of the domestic risk level, the Québec government had to correct the persistent images of laxity and of a "porous border," and to show its readiness to respond to American concerns. The province thus amended its legislation to safeguard the production of vital statistics' documents and to bring its security agencies up to date. The border is also a concern, whether real or virtual, because of the increasing use of technology, including social media networks, to propagate or perpetrate violent extremism. The fight against terrorism requires that North American actors, as well as those of other affected countries, collaborate and exchange enhanced and relevant information. However, the resources allocated to the fight against terrorism and the management of priorities are not the same on either side of the US–Canadian border; Québec, in particular, in the absence of massive investment in security and in the fight against terrorism, has supported several important initiatives in the fields of psychosocial intervention and prevention in the francophone sphere.

Transnational Organized Crime

Transnational organized crime is a long-standing public safety concern. Although crime has decreased in Québec since the 1990s, in line with the general decline in North America and the West (Dupont and Pérez 2006, 33), investigations by the Québec Permanent Anticorruption Unit and the Commission of Inquiry on the Awarding and Management of Public Contracts in the Construction Industry have shown that cross-border crime remains a concern. Border regions lend themselves well to organized crime in such fields as the trafficking of people, drugs, contraband firearms and tobacco, as well as money laundering. Trafficking in narcotics is the most lucrative form of cross-border crime between the two countries. The United States is the main point of entry for the cocaine smuggled into Canada, and the number of annual seizures has more than doubled since 2005. Marijuana produced in Canada (grown mainly in British Columbia, Ontario, and Québec) amounts for roughly 20 percent of the total American market (USCBP, CBSA, RCMP 2010). Trafficking in contraband firearms is another major border challenge for the Canadian and Québec governments. In 2010, 96 percent of the firearms seized in Canada, hundreds of which were destined for the criminal market, came from the United States.

There are other types of cross-border crime. Contraband tobacco, a particularly profitable form of smuggling, enriches criminal organizations and deprives governments of tax revenue. Cigarettes and other tobacco products, illegally produced in the United States, cross the border for the most part over the Saint Lawrence River and are sold mainly in the Mohawk territory of Akwasasne, which straddles Ontario and Québec and the state of New York, as well as in some other Indigenous territories (USCBP, CBSA, RCMP 2010). Human trafficking is a global concern. As will be seen below, this criminal activity, which is a major cross-border challenge, relates above all to the transit of irregular migrants. According to the Canadian Border Services Agency, 23,167 irregular migrants crossed the border in 2010 (Meunier, quoted in Jimenez 2013). Finally, criminal groups tend to engage in money laundering. While there are various means to move funds, large-scale bulk currency smuggling remains popular. Alternative methods are used to transfer proceeds across the US–Canada border. Many of the proceeds of crime are laundered through electronic wire transfers (USCBP, CBSA, and RCMP 2010). Although agencies on both sides of the border share the same objectives in the fight against criminal activities, the lack of harmonization of their laws and practices presents difficulties.

Irregular Migration

Irregular migration across the border between Québec and the United States has soared since 2016. The increase over a few months in the number of asylum seekers crossing the border irregularly has resulted in numerous reactions by Québec, Canadian, and American authorities. According to Immigration, Refugees and Citizenship Canada, in 2017 the Royal Canadian Mounted Police intercepted 18,836 asylum seekers who had crossed the border irregularly (Government of Canada 2017), followed by more than 9,000 others between January and May 2018 (Government of Canada 2018). The following figure shows the growth in the number of irregular border crossings into Québec, whose numbers are far greater than those of all the other provinces combined.

The absence of the issue of asylum seekers in the 2006 International Policy Statement and its inclusion in the 2017 statement under the rubric of welcoming refugees on humanitarian grounds show that Québec has not until now treated the question as a security problem and that it has, unlike the Trump administration, distanced itself from a discourse on the securitization of immigration (Boudreau 2013/14; Vigneau 2017). Nonetheless the issue has become so heavily politicized across both sides of the border that one might well ask whether it is now a political rather than a migra-

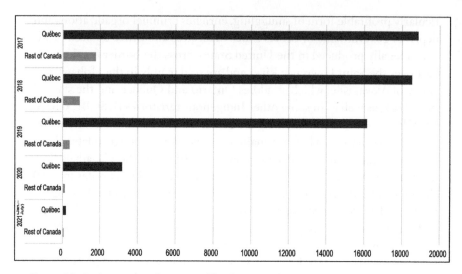

Figure 6.1. Asylum seekers intercepted by the RCMP between land ports of entry (2017–18). "The number of 'RCMP interceptions' refers to asylum seekers apprehended between the ports of entry and does not reflect other border crossings. These numbers may be included in either CBSA or IRCC processing results as the asylum seekers are turned over by the RCMP to these agencies if a claim of refugee status is made" (Immigration, Refugees and Citizenship Canada [IRCC] 2017). Compiled by Carolina Reyes Marquez.

tory crisis. On some occasions, immigration has clearly been securitized by various political figures, the media, and by a segment of public opinion (Vigneau 2017).

Case Study: Law Enforcement Cooperation on Border Intelligence

Of all the provinces, irregular migration into Canada on foot occurs most frequently in Québec, notably through the Roxham Road (north of the town of Champlain, NY, on the Canadian side. That may at least partly explain why migrant issues are more prominent in Québec than in other Canadian regions. Although border security is a matter of federal jurisdiction, in practice the local and regional repercussions of this activity engage diverse actors at various government levels. While the Canada Border Services Agency (CBSA) and the RCMP are responsible for securing the border, the Sûreté du Québec (SQ) and the municipal police forces may be called as first responders. The SQ is present throughout the province, including the municipal regions of the counties adjacent to the border. The different police forces perform such tasks as patrolling the affected districts, searching for individuals, and communicating information to their partners. Federal, provincial, and municipal agencies, as well as the various police forces, thus cooperate in managing irregular immigration.

An asylum seeker trying to evade the official ports of entry might be met in two ways by the various public safety agents present in the border area. First, the Canadian and Québec authorities could spot the migrant getting ready to cross the border. Second, the authorities—the municipal police, the SQ, or the RCMP—could intercept the migrant in Canadian territory. Although it is the RCMP's responsibility to handle both situations, other police forces sometimes intervene while carrying out the public safety mandate for their region. The CBSA or the United States Border Patrol (USBP) may thus exchange information with the RCMP, which in turn may ask the SQ or the municipal police forces for assistance. However, previous research has shown that on occasion, certain members of the SQ communicate directly with their US partners, including the USBP, to obtain information.[4]

After interception by the police, the individual is arrested and transferred to immigration officers, who begin the process of investigating and identifying the migrant. Other actors, such as Immigration, Refugees and Citizenship Canada or the Immigration and Refugee Board of Canada may also become involved. Figure 6.2 illustrates the main situations leading to interactions between the actors when a migrant transits the border irregularly.

Research concerning irregular immigration sheds light on how police cooperation functions on the ground. For example, collaboration between agencies is only as good as the collaboration between the people who make up those agencies (Reyes Marquez 2017, 122). Therefore, the personalities, values, and ways of thinking of the agents and the police, as well as their understanding of their need to cooperate and their interest in doing so, considerably affect their relations with the other law enforcement agencies. Therefore, despite the existence of initiatives and formal agreements between police forces and agencies, it is largely up to the individuals involved to make the cooperation work. For this reason, it is more difficult to broach the subject of an organization's cooperation as a whole than at a local level; the latter depends on the agents who work there, as well as the arrival and departure of team members.

The role of the individual in cooperation is very important: "it is essential that an agency not want to be king of the hill" (Reyes Marquez

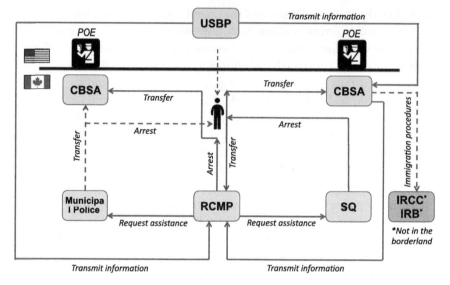

Figure 6.2. Actors and authorities involved in irregular border entry. The dotted lines are inserted for clarification. This diagram (Reyes Marquez 2017, 93) is based on information gathered in interviews with members of these organizations. It is important to note that no interviews could be conducted with members of the municipal police forces. However, their role can be included based on statements made by the other agents and police officers interviewed.

2017, 123). Cooperation does not come naturally to all members of the police. According to Giacomantonio (2015), the limits of coordinated law enforcement between police forces become apparent when the latter are uncertain about their respective mandates or activities. However, Jobard and de Maillard (2015, 54–55) argue that the agents on the front line can both define their priorities and determine how best to intervene. Given the sometimes arbitrary context in which these agents operate, the question is often whether to intervene, and, if so, how. In fact, the discretionary power of the border agents or police tends to increase as one descends the chain of command. As local bureaucrats, the agents and the police can in practice benefit from a marked autonomy because they often find themselves in situations that are too complicated to fit into predefined bureaucratic structures. This logic, which dictates the work context, confirms the importance of the individual in both maintaining cooperative relations and in understanding the tasks and duties to be performed.

Finally, aside from individual initiatives, collaborative relations can spring from carrying out similar operations. The presence of numerous actors at the border is thus a positive factor in terms of assisting partners, but it can also result in overlapping powers of intervention. However, a great deal of cooperation occurs in nonformalized contexts, where there is no desire to inhibit police coordination through the addition of bureaucratic layers (Giacomantonio 2015, 163). This ad hoc aspect that influences the study of cooperation between institutions is quite specific to each unit or individual, which makes it difficult to generalize. The flow of irregular migration across the Canada–US border may put existing methods to the test and require that the partnerships between the border agencies and police forces be reinvented in a more synchronized fashion.

Conclusion

Does security pose a transnational challenge for Québec? Although most of the issues identified here are not new and have before now had a cross-border aspect, the fact that Québec authorities now affix the label "security" to them constitutes a change in discourse. In other words, it is less the evolution of these issues in and of themselves than their politicization in security terms that makes them transnational risks and challenges. Further, the logic underpinning the Québec government's politicization of security is twofold. First, it alerts the Québec population to the impact of the transnational on Québec's security, thus justifying a certain level of concern, involvement, and collaboration (and investment). Second, it aims to reassure Québec's partners, above all the United States, that the government is taking these North American challenges seriously, at least rhetorically. In reality, taking Québec's jurisdictional claims into consideration, there is a clear desire to just talk the talk rather than to walk it. In sum, in a highly competitive environment, Québec's international agenda drives its rationale for border security policies but has not led to the implementation and formalization of cooperation.

NOTES

1. The authors thank Julien Lauzon-Chiasson (candidate for a master's degree at l'ENAP) for carrying out certain preliminary research. This article takes another look at several analyses presented in David Morin and Myriam Poliquin, "Un discours suivi d'effet? La sécurité dans les relations internationales du Québec," *Revue québécoise de droit international,* June 2016, and David Morin and Myriam Poliquin, "Governing from the Border? Quebec's Role in North American Security," *American Review of Canadian Studies* 46, no. 2: 254–72, 2016. This study was funded in

part by the Social Sciences and Humanities Research Council through its subsidy of the Borders in Globalization partnership. Translation by Susan M. Murphy.

2. Several provinces, including Ontario, also have an agency responsible for managing their international relations, but their mandate is often much broader, encompassing commerce or "intergovernmental relations." See Nossal, Roussel, and Paquin 2015, 338–40.

3. Québec participates in several programs in the transportation sector: NEXUS, for rapid crossing of Canadian and US citizens; FAST/EXPRESS, for secure and rapid crossing of deliveries; and the Customs-Trade Partnership Against Terrorism, a supply-chain security program led by US Customs and Border Protection focused on improving the security of private companies' supply chains with respect to terrorism. The Container Security Initiative and the Canada United States Cargo Security project take a similar approach to maritime transportation, including in the Port of Montréal.

4. This section draws on Reyes Marques, 2017, 88–93.

REFERENCES

Ackleson, J. 2009. "From 'Thin' to 'Thick' (and Back Again?): The Politics and Policies of Contemporary US-Canada Border." *American Review of Canadian Studies* 39, no. 4: 336–51.

Andreas, Peter. 2003. "Redrawing the Line: Borders and Security in the Twenty-First Century." *International Security* 28, no. 2 (Autumn): 78–111.

Bourbeau, Philippe. 2013/14. "Politisation et sécuritisation des migrations internationales: une relation à définir." *Critique internationale* 1: 127–45.

Buzan, Barry, Ole Weaver, and Jaap De Wilde. 1998. *Security: A New Framework for Analysis*. London: Lynne Riener Publishers.

Cormier, Yannick. 2012. "La Police des liqueurs : 1921–1961." *Les Cahiers d'histoire*, Sûreté du Québec. 3, no. 1 (May).

Dupont, Benoit, and Émile Pérez. 2006. *Les polices au Québec*. Paris: PUF.

Giacomantonio, Chris. 2015. *Policing Integration: The Sociology of Police Coordination Work*. London: Palgrave Macmillan.

Gouvernement du Québec. 2004. "Allocutions." Allocution prononcée par la vice-première ministre et ministre des Relations internationales, Madame Monique Gagnon-Tremblay, à l'occasion de la visite au Québec des membres titulaires du Weatherhead Center for International Affairs de l'Université Harvard. (September 1).

Gouvernement du Québec. 2006. *La politique internationale du Québec. La force de l'action concertée*. Québec: Ministère des Relations internationales.

Gouvernement du Québec. 2008. "Le Québec : un acteur important pour la sécurité du continent nord-américain." *L'Action internationale du Québec*. (July 3).

Gouvernement du Québec. 2009. Ministère des Relations internationales, *Politique internationale du Québec : Plan d'action 2009–2014*. Québec : Ministère des relations internationales.

Gouvernement du Québec. 2010a. *Stratégie du Québec à l'égard des Etats-Unis*. Québec : Ministère des relations internationales. (January).

Gouvernement du Québec. 2010b. Ministère des Relations internationales. Le plan d'action 2010–2013 de la stratégie du gouvernement du Québec à l'égard des États-Uni.

Gouvernement du Québec. 2017a. *Québec's International Policy. Québec on the World Stage: Involved, Engaged, Thriving.* Québec: Ministère des Relations internationales et de la Francophonie.

Gouvernement du Québec. 2017b. *Note abrégée sur le commerce Québec-États-Unis.* Québec: Ministère de l'Économie, de la Science et de l'Innovation.

Government of Canada. 2017. *Asylum Claims in 2017, Immigration, Refugees and Citizenship Canada.* https://www.canada.ca/eng/immigration-refugees-citizensh ip/services/refugees/asylumclaims-2017.html

Government of Canada. 2018. *Asylum Claims in 2018, Immigration, Refugees and Citizenship Canada.* https://www.canada.ca/fr/immigration-refugees-cititizensh ip/services/refugees/asylumclaims.html

Hooghe, Liesbet, and Gary Marks. 2003. "Unravelling the Central State, but How? Types of Multi-Level Governance." *American Political Science Review* 97, no. 2 May: 233–43.

Immigration, Refugees and Citizenship Canada. 2017. https://www.canada.ca/en /immigration-refugees-citizenship/services/refugees/asylum-claims/asylum-cl aims-2017.html

Jimenez, Estibaliz. 2013. "La criminalisation du trafic de migrants au Canada." *Criminologie* 46, no. 1 (Spring): 131–56.

Jobard, Fabien, and Jacques de Maillard. 2015. *Sociologie de la police. Politiques, organisations, réformes.* Paris: Armand Colin.

Keohane, Robert O., and Joseph S. Nye Jr. 1974. "Transgovernmental Relations and International Organizations." *World Politics* 27 (1) (October).

Konrad, Victor, and Heather Nicol. 2008. *Beyond Walls: Re-Inventing the Canada–United States Borderlands.* Burlington, VT: Ashgate.

La Presse. 2014. "Acte terroriste à Saint-Jean: Martin "Ahmad" Rouleau inspiré par l'islamisme radical." (October 20).

Leuprecht, Christian. 2019. "The End of the (Roxham) Road: Seeking Coherence on Canada's Border-Migration Compact." Ottawa: Macdonald Laurier Institute.

Leuprecht, Christian, Todd Hataley, and Kim Richard Nossal (eds.). 2012. *Evolving Transnational Threats and Border Security: A New Research Agenda.* Centre for International and Defence Policy. Kingston, ON: Queen's University.

Nossal, Kim Richard, Stéphane Roussel, and Stéphane Paquin. 2015. *The Politics of Canadian Foreign Policy.* Montréal: McGill-Queen's University Press.

Paquin, Stéphane. 2017. "Le rôle des provinces dans la renégociation de l'ALENA." *Options politiques.* http://policyoptions.irpp.org/fr/magazines/july-2017/le-role -des-provinces-dans-la-renegociation-de-lalena/

Reyes Marquez, Carolina. 2017. *La coopération interinstitutionnelle dans la gestion de l'immigration irrégulière en région frontalière au Québec.* Master's thesis, Université de Sherbrooke. http://savoirs.usherbrooke.ca/bitstream/handle/11143/113 12/Reyes_Marquez_Carolina_MA_2017.pdf?sequence=7&isAllowed=y

Senate of Canada. 2015. *Countering the Terrorist Threat in Canada: An Interim Report.* Standing Senate Committee on National Security and Defence.

Smith, Steve. 2005. "The Contested Concept of Security." In *Critical Security Stud-*

ies and World Politics, edited by Ken Booth. Boulder, CO: Lynne Rienner Publishers.

Stairs, Denis. 1994. "Choosing Multilateralism: Canada's Experience after World War II and Canada in the New International Environment." *CANCAPS Paper* no. 4. North York, ON: Canadian Consortium on Asia-Pacific Security.

US Customs and Border Protection, Canada Border Services Agency, RCMP (USCBP, CBSA, RCMP). 2010. "United States–Canada Joint Border Threat and Risk Assessment." https://www.dhs.gov/united-states-canada-joint-border-threat-and-risk-assessment

Vigneau, Elsa. 2017. Immigration et sécuritisation de l'immigration au Canada: étude de La Presse et du National Post, 1998–2015. Master's thesis, Université de Sherbrooke.

SEVEN

Atlantic Canada and New England

Kevin Quigley and Stephen Williams

Abstract

This chapter provides an overview of border security in Atlantic Canada. It examines border security as a function of the structure of the region and regional approaches to security and governance. Through a review of existing literature and interviews with practitioners in the field, the chapter considers the increasing integration of marine security forces, both nationally and internationally, and their relationships to seaports where most of the international trade occurs in the region. This chapter posits a layered approach to port security in the Atlantic region that includes the early maritime warning program, the clearance of goods, and security clearance required for port workers. We found that not all actors favor this approach: the Canadian and US governments prize efficiency of border security measures at ports. The economic prosperity of maritime communities hinges disproportionately on ports; so inefficiencies that security measures impose compromise the region's competitiveness. In addition, the chapter finds that the 2004 devolution of ports to local authorities has enhanced local agency, but communities struggle to finance updated security infrastructure, preferring instead to invest scarce resources in better physical infrastructure to maintain their ports' competitiveness.

Introduction

Atlantic Canada has experienced several securitized relationships with trade actors. The region was the traditional home of several largely independent Indigenous populations. Fisheries attracted waves of migration, and settlements grew to serve trade and commerce. As European colonies connected with colonies of the United States of America, a trade relationship evolved further.

North-south trade relationships were consolidated, as were political relationships. Nova Scotia, Prince Edward Island, and New Brunswick, originally an economic region of their own with strong links to the United States, were drawn into the east-west political and economic frame. This federation leveraged the sea trade, military, and security assets of the Atlantic region, forever altering the security landscape and level of integration among actors.

In this context, we outline the increasing integration of maritime security actors in the region, specifically since 9/11. This integration contrasts with fairly deregulated governance structures of the seaports, through which most international transit and trade in the region occurs. The analysis concludes that further efforts to enhance border security in Atlantic Canada must consider the tensions inherent in integrated control models of the security apparatus and the dis-integrated, deregulated governance models of the operators of seaports. Both integrated and dis-integrated models have strengths and weaknesses that struggle to reconcile security protection and innovative commerce in a globalized world. The global trade in goods is largely by sea way. The seacoast is the primary international border in the region; therefore, border and security issues are concentrated on the water, at the coastline, and in the ports. Without a clear understanding of how the public and private sectors overlap and interact, this international border cannot resolve existing challenges. This absence of a coordinated effort is embodied in the fractured nature of traditional resource industries. Aside from being fractured, these industries must also compete with a growth in offshore resourcing and the advent of technological growth. Nevertheless, trade remains prominent in the region, as exemplified by the endurance of ports as centers of Atlantic communities. A scan of the economic environment conveys an understanding of trade relationships, as economic challenge is often a galvanizing factor for social and policy change at all levels. This chapter seeks to understand the nature of this relationship, and how improved communication stands to help actors reap greater benefit from the border.

This chapter reviews literature and interviews with stakeholders in the field. These resources provide insight into the roles of each border actor, how marine security forces are integrated, and how decisions regarding the border are reached. Furthermore, an in-depth analysis of the infrastructure, security demands, and attitudes toward security across the region reveals how border security extends beyond the border.

The Coast as an International Border

The Atlantic region is largely defined and united by the long and varied shoreline of the Atlantic Ocean. For our purposes, the region includes the four provinces of Nova Scotia, New Brunswick, Prince Edward Island, and Newfoundland and Labrador, encompassing 550,000 km² or about 5 percent of Canada's total land area, containing 2.4 million people, or about 6.5 percent of Canada's total population in 2017 (Statistics Canada 2017). The region is separated from the rest of Canada, physically by the northern bulge of the state of Maine, and by the province of Quebec.

The main international border in the Atlantic region, the primary intersection between the sovereignty of Canada and the rest of the world, is the ocean. There are international interactions at the ports, offshore at shipping lanes and fisheries that intersect Canada's region of sovereignty, and international monitoring of ship traffic throughout the North Atlantic. Unlike many other regions that have a land border, the Atlantic region is unique. The coastal border is not a hard line that is easily defined; layers of responsibility and privilege extend into the sea as a result of international agreements such as the 1982 United Nations Convention on the Law of the Sea (UNCLOS; UNCLOS 1982).

Under UNCLOS, the rights of a coastal state diminish with distance from its coast. Territorial Seas and Contiguous Zones extend for twelve and twenty-four miles out from the coast, respectively (UNCLOS 1982). Ships of any flag have the right of innocent passage through these areas, but Canada may exercise sovereign controls to prevent infringement of its customs, fiscal, immigration, or sanitary laws and regulations. UNCLOS further defines a 200-nautical mile Exclusive Economic Zone where Canada has sovereign and jurisdictional rights over exploration and management of resources such as fisheries and oil and gas. This limit extends into the North Atlantic, interrupted south of Newfoundland to accommodate the French islands of St. Pierre and Miquelon, and intersects with the internationally mandated jurisdictional border of the United States within the Gulf of Maine, which was in dispute as late as 1984.

The Canadian Coast Guard played a role in developing Long-Range Identification and Tracking (LRIT) protocols and agreements that allow for satellite tracking of ships at sea. Under international LRIT regulations, all passenger and cargo ships and mobile offshore drilling units must report to their flag administration at least four times a day, and that information becomes available to Canadian authorities when the ship is within 1,000 nautical miles of Canada's east coast, an area that extends from the state of Georgia to the Azores to Iceland—a significant portion of the North Atlantic. The LRIT protocols highlight the importance of monitoring movement far offshore. Ergo, security standards must adapt to the nature of the sea border.

These various levels of sovereignty linked to distance from shore, as well as the multitude of governmental agencies involved in exercising that sovereignty, make the seacoast border an exceedingly complex policy environment. The scale is vast in both physical area and traffic volume. Canadian authorities and the North American Aerospace Defence Command actively monitor the eastern approaches to Atlantic Canada, which includes awareness of approximately 12,000 contacts every day over an ocean area significantly larger than the entire Mediterranean Sea (Gardham 2011).

Operationalizing Concepts

This section explains how security is operationalized in the Atlantic region. The connotations, applications, and implications of "security" are contingent on the geography, culture, and economic background of the area. Security expectations evolve as the political environment changes. For example, Atlantic Canada's security expectations were altered by the North American Free Trade Agreement, which enhanced continental trade and further integrated Mexico into Canada's trade network. This directly affected Canadian ports as it put a premium on road and rail trade through the center of the continent, making those connections even more important to the competitiveness of ports (Ircha 2001b). This had an adverse impact on the Maritimes owing to their comparatively poor rail infrastructure at the margins of the continent. As ports become the nexus between continental and global trade, maritime trade has become more dependent on foreign trade, where the Atlantic region must prevail against competition from US ports along the East Coast of North America. In the context of an increasingly continental approach to North American security, greater reliance on overseas trade and the implementation of the Canada-

European Union (EU) Comprehensive Economic and Trade Agreement means that Canadian maritime ports are now dealing with more trading partners outside of NAFTA, now called the Canada–United States–Mexico Agreement. More than 80 percent of Canada's marine trade is outside of North America, which has immediate consequences for security expectations (Council 2017). Political changes to current free trade agreements or the ratification of new trade agreements will have a corresponding impact on the security measures for ports going forward.

A concrete example of this tension is a disagreement about risk assessment expected at the border. By virtue of NAFTA, Canada became more dependent on trade with the United States, and more susceptible to changes in America's security paradigm (Avis 2003). The United States established minimal expectations for security in the form of the International Ship and Port Security (ISPS) code and initiated the Container Security Initiative (CSI). In an integrated continental trade region, Canada had little choice but to adopt these initiatives. Yet to facilitate trade and ensure the integrity of its border with the United States, Canada took further steps towards securitization with the Marine Transport Security Clearance Program (Cowen 2007).

The Marine Facilities Restricted Area Access Clearance Program employed a layered approach to security and extended the security sphere beyond the physical border. It was also modeled after airport security. The program mandated that those who had access to the restricted area required background checks, credit checks, travel history, and personal details (Cowen 2007). An additional layer of security was added when family checks of those who had access to the restricted area were also conducted (Cowen 2007). When the government faced considerable pressure from local authorities concerned about the economic competitiveness of Canadian ports, the initiative was renamed the Marine Transport Security Clearance Program and the information threshold for security clearances was lowered (Cowen 2007). The solution to this tension involved local authorities—which points to the importance of local actors in port security.

As of 2016–2017, the Canadian Border Services Agency (CBSA) has 165 offices in Atlantic Canada that oversee the movement of goods into the country. More than 95 percent of shipping containers entering the country pass through CBSA radiation portals located at the five major Canadian marine terminals (Vancouver, Prince Rupert, Saint John, Montréal, and Halifax). To detect contraband that does not emit radioactivity, CBSA authorities can refer containers for examination at a container examination facility. Full examinations involve container de-stuffs, which are conducted based on risk assessments; only containers deemed high risk are given a full examination (CBSA 2012). Some shippers, containers, and contents are less likely to pose a threat; inspecting them adds barriers, inconvenience, and delay, making Canadian ports less competitive (Romero 2003). Full-container examinations are also expensive—the cost can range from CDN$150 to CDN$7,375 to complete the inspection, an additional challenge for ports working to remain competitive and reduce costs (Collins 2018).

The CSI has also enhanced the integration of US and Canadian cooperation. The US Customs and Border Protection pre-clears containers at Canadian ports, and the Canadian Border Services Agency (CSBA) does likewise at US ports (Sands 2009). The CSI posts US custom workers at international ports beyond the contiguous United States. These officials inspect US-bound cargo to prevent terrorists from taking advantage of the primary approach to shipping-container shipping before departure (Sands 2009). Cargo assessed to be high risk is then screened through X-ray or inspection technology (Ferriere, Pysareva, and Rucinski 2005). This agreement is reciprocal, because Canada can in turn send customs officials to US ports. This exchange promotes familiarity with both systems and the exchange of information. The CSI program has been recognized as

> an advanced successful example of international cooperation in law enforcement and terrorism prevention. Proponents claim it lowers the dangers of arbitrary antiterrorist measures, while minimizing the amount of inspection and possible delays associated with Customs inspection on entering cargo through close communication between the two countries. (Romero 2003, 601)

More recently, the 2016 introduction of eManifest and the 2017 introduction of the single-window initiative aimed to increase efficiency and reduce the administrative burden on shippers (CBSA 2017). A Canadian initiative, eManifest, requires all carriers to submit advance commercial information electronically to the CBSA, which allows the CBSA to conduct a security assessment before the goods arrive at the border, thereby increasing the efficiency of the process (CBSA 2017). The Single Window Initiative (SWI) is another online tool that allows shippers to file customs documents online before their shipment arrives in Canada.

Canada and the United States are satisfied by International Ship and Port Security codes, the Container Security Initiative, and the recent implementation of online pre-arrival declarations, the SWI and eManifest. These changes address some of the Senate's 2007 Standing Committee on National Security and Defence report's findings on seaport security regarding Canada's container-screening processes. The committee agrees that the Container Security Initiative should inspect products before they enter the country, stating that it is "better to detect potential problems before they can get to Canada's ports." Furthermore, the Canadian Senate acknowledges that inspecting containers away from the physical border enhances cooperation with the United States and other major trading partners (Canadian Senate, 2007).

However, the International Ship and Port Security, Container Security Initiative, Single Window Initiative, and eManifest initiatives do not address other 2007 Senate Committee findings that favor greater security at the physical border. The Senate recommended enhanced measures to improve security at actual ports, and also enhancements to processes away from the border. The Senate deemed programs that rely on risk assessments alone, such as the Container Security Initiative, to be inadequate (Canadian Senate 2007).

The same Senate Standing Committee report specifically highlighted the lack of law enforcement at ports. According to this report, ports are understaffed:

> There is a need for specialized police in unique environments— and seaports and airports clearly qualify as unique environments. The Netherlands has about 420 police permanently stationed at the Port of Rotterdam alone. There are only twenty-four RCMP officers assigned to Canada's nineteen ports, all of which are posted to Halifax, Montréal, or Vancouver. Eight are slated to be posted to Hamilton by the end of this year. (Canadian Senate 2007, 18)

This Senate report thus equates security with a greater police presence at the physical border. It would like more containers to be inspected physically rather than relying excessively on a risk-assessment approach to port container security; the Senate Committee's report found that CBSA only inspects 7.5 percent of containers at the ports (Canadian Senate 2007, 25). The Canadian Senate noted its discontent with this rate:

> "Risk assessment" is nothing more than guesswork unless someone conducts sensitivity tests to determine what would be found employing various intensities of searching. Only if you conduct total searches will you know what you are likely to miss doing various kinds of partial searches. (Canadian Senate 2007, 25)

The percentage of containers examined was reported as even lower in 2015, when fewer than 4 percent of containers at the Port of Vancouver were examined fully (Bolan 2015b).

The Senate Committee recommends that ports adopt a model proposed by Stephen Flynn. This model requires that containers be loaded in secure areas and provided with monitors so there is a record of anyone who attempts to alter seals, or that nonintrusive vehicle and cargo inspection system (VACIS) machines be adopted. There are currently fifteen such machines in Canada, but they require sixty full-time VACIS operators (Canadian Senate 2007). In 2013, many of the country's VACIS machines were damaged or malfunctioning, and staffing shortages often prevented border security from deploying the machines, which end up sitting idle as a result (National Post 2013).

Perceptions of Security

As in many other regions, the border in Atlantic Canada is largely defined by its historical relationship with the United States. Unlike in other border regions, however, perceptions of security in Atlantic Canada are influenced by its largely abstract border, which lacks a truly concrete, physical line; by economic concerns; and by a substantial military presence. Security is also a concern at the local level, as ports influence the prosperity of local communities.

To date there have been no significant incidents of exogenous terrorism or overt piracy in the Atlantic region. Tensions and incidents between Indigenous communities and other residents recur occasionally as a result of fishing rights disputes, as exemplified by the Burnt Church conflict between Mi'kmaq and non-Indigenous fisheries in Kent County, New Brunswick, and Saulnierville, Nova Scotia, between 1999 and 2002, and the dispute in 2020 (CBC News 2001; Mercer 2020; Bilefsky 2020). Additionally, there is some known smuggling and immigration crime. The previously mentioned Canadian Senate Standing Committee report notes that seaports, including those in the Atlantic region, are afflicted by organized crime and smuggling; it recommended a major review of overall security of the ports (Canadian Senate 2007). Research into organized crime at Canadian ports found that corrupted laborers play a role in importing illegal drugs, counterfeit goods, and illegal immigrants (Public Safety Canada 2011). Since the 2007 Senate Committee's suggestions, the Canadian government seems content with the security provided by the initiatives already underway. Almost a decade after the 2007 Senate report, evidence suggested that criminal groups were still using ports to smuggle illegal drugs, including fentanyl, into Canada from China (Council 2017). One of the senators who worked on the 2007 report, Colin Kenny, noted in 2015 that the issue of organized crime at ports was still not being addressed properly (Bolan 2015a).

The federal government's "high security" priorities contrast with local "low security" ones. Atlantic Canada has struggled economically for the better part of a century and remains one of the poorest regions of Canada (Vasseur and Catto 2007). These challenges arise due to structural and global factors and are aggravated by fractured governance, given the small population of the region and the large number of jurisdictions, institutions, and identities (Conrad and Hiller 2015). Traditional resource industries such as fishing, farming, and forestry have long been in decline in the Atlantic provinces. These traditional economic drivers are being replaced by offshore oil production and knowledge industries such as ocean technology and biotechnology (Doloreux and Shearmur 2009). Yet ports remain at the center of many communities, and the competitive nature of global shipping has been exerting increased pressure on them to remain viable. Unemployment remains high, particularly in rural areas, and relative deprivation is a driving force in social and political decision-making throughout the region, both at local levels and in relation to Canada as a whole (Doloreux and Shearmur 2009).

The strained economic environment in Atlantic Canada emphasizes the importance of ports to local communities as an economic driver. Marine shipping at a national level affects virtually every region and industry; it directly contributes $3 billion to national gross domestic product and directly and indirectly creates close to 99,000 jobs across the country (Council 2017). At the local level, ports sustain sizeable portions of the communities in which they operate.

Halifax, NS, and St. John, NB, are the main international seaports in the Atlantic region, and Halifax is the closest full-service North American harbor to Europe, Brazil, and the Suez Canal. Together they handled approximately thirty million metric tons of cargo in 2014 and welcomed more than 320,000 passengers on 180 cruise ships (Sjport 2017; Halifax Port Authority, n.d.).

As economic benefits come through Canada's ports, so do security threats. Keeping ports secure and operationally efficient is a priority. Primary border issues related to the global supply chain and shipping, including potential terrorist activity, transnational crime, and environmental or health concerns, may occur either directly in ports, or during transit on the water. Security occurs both at the physical hub and beyond the border. This layered approach to security processes must occur in part because of the sheer volume of trade. Seaports are critical hubs in the global supply chain; 70 percent of the world's imports are transported by sea (Burns 2013). Security must be enforced, but not to the point where it deters trading partners due to the economic limitations that accompany regulations.

Social forces such as personal and historic connections to the military, and economic forces such as employment, are as important as any actual security threat. The security infrastructure that served the colonial states of Europe and the trade flow of North American resources outward is mirrored in the modern situation, except that the security infrastructure now serves trade flows on behalf of the Canadian federal government, and trade flows are more often inward toward the American marketplace. Market access, and the ability to exploit the maritime domain for its direct and indirect economic benefits, particularly to local communities, are key to understanding how Atlantic Canada approaches security.

Actors in the Region

Atlantic Canada: Borders and Relationships with the United States

The Atlantic region shares 400 km of land border and sixteen ports of entry with the United States. Much like the rest of Canada, however, significant portions of the border are unguarded by humans. The two major ports of entry along the land border to the United States are at St. Stephen/Calais and Woodstock/Houlton; they serve as key commercial processing centers for the region's land-based trade (Government of Canada 2010, 23). Together they register more than 90 percent of the crossings in the region. While the entire annual trade at St. Stephen Bridge is 95,000 commercial vehicles and $2.8 billion in goods, or less than 2 percent of the volume registered at the major crossing between Ontario and Michigan at Detroit/Windsor, for example, it represents 46 percent of Atlantic export to the United States (Government of Canada 2010, 22).

The border with the United States also cuts across the Gulf of Maine, an area bounded from Boston and Cape Cod in the south, to Yarmouth, Nova Scotia, in the north. The border in this region has been in some degree of ongoing dispute since the 1783 Treaty of Paris that ended the

American Revolutionary War with Great Britain. The International Court of Justice delineated a boundary through the Gulf in 1984 after no negotiated settlement could be achieved (Legault and Hankey1985; Rhee 1981).

NORAD Maritime Early Warning System

North American Aerospace Defense Command's (NORAD's) maritime early-warning mission takes a layered approach to border security. NORAD was tasked with the mission in 2006 when the United States and Canada agreed to the early-warning system, provided it did not duplicate current structures. The mission was galvanized by 9/11 and the Interim Report of 2004 and 2006 (Fergusson et al. 2015). The reports were coordinated by the Binational Planning Group and indicated that both Canada and the United States had expressed a desire for further integration and cooperation in their national security strategies. The Group recommended that these gaps be addressed through NORAD—a structure that was operational and did not require restructuring or further funding (Fergusson et al. 2015).

The early maritime warning system was thus assigned to an existing organization with a proven binational track record, with the aim of addressing significant gaps in the aerospace and maritime domains (Fergusson et al. 2015). The agreement reinforced plans for the cross-border exchange of troops in emergencies (the Mutual Assistance Pact) and minimized cost.

The creation of the early maritime warning system within NORAD was not entirely seamless. This case is an example of how cross-border cooperation agreements can struggle to integrate and involve all actors. NORAD struggled because its expertise was in the air, not on the maritime domain. Air-based threats appear quickly, require an instant response, and employ tactics that have not been planned extensively. In contrast, maritime threats are more innocuous, slow-moving, and due to geographical expanse and a greater array of potential threats and threat actors, often depend on planning and input from a collection of agencies and stakeholders. NORAD also had to adjust to new links with the civilian world. Historically a military-only organization, NORAD now had to internalize the civilian-military relationships in the maritime sector (Fergusson et al. 2015).

Initial growing pains notwithstanding, NORAD's partners were able to overcome integration concerns and now provide three services. According to the 2006 NORAD agreement, the maritime warning mission consists of processing, assessing, and disseminating intelligence and information related to the respective maritime areas and internal waterways of, and the maritime approaches to, the United States and Canada, and warning of maritime threats to, or attacks against North America utilizing mutual support arrangements with other commands and agencies, to enable identification, validation, and response by national commands and agencies responsible for maritime defense and security. Through these tasks NORAD shall develop a comprehensive shared understanding of maritime activities to better identify potential maritime threats to North American security. (Canada and the United States 2006, 2)

NORAD relies on intelligence and information from actors away from the physical border. That is, the system is designed to detect threats such as human trafficking, terrorism, or piracy long before they ever reach Canadian or American ports. This strategy is essential to the effectiveness and security of North American ports.

Cooperation Agreements

Since Confederation, the northeastern United States and the Atlantic provinces of Canada have developed the longest-standing cross-border cooperation on the continent, followed by the Pacific Northwest Economic Region. Since 1973, the New England Governors and Eastern Canadian Premiers (NEG-ECP) have met annually to advance the joint interests of the member states (Connecticut, Maine, Massachusetts, New Hampshire, Rhode Island, and Vermont) and provinces (New Brunswick, Newfoundland and Labrador, Nova Scotia, Prince Edward Island, and Quebec; Selin and VanDeever 2005). The NEG-ECP have, over the years, adopted agreements and action plans on trade relations, climate change, acid rain, and greenhouse gas emissions from the transportation sector, all of which are transboundary issues (Selin and VanDeever 2005). They have sponsored international forums on energy and environmental issues, and established agreements for international assistance in case of emergencies. For example, the NEG-ECP signed the International Emergency Management Assistance Memorandum of Understanding (IEMAMU 2000) at the 25th Annual Conference. The purpose of this memorandum was to establish a process for mutual support during emergencies, whether environmental or man-made.

Summit diplomacy aside, the administrative nature of the NEG-ECP Conference has allowed civil servants on both sides of the border to build ties and press agendas of joint interest. A former Canadian diplomat has referred to this shared para-diplomacy as "the hidden wiring" of Canada–US relations, with wide-ranging but subtle influence (Robertson 2017). The NEG-ECP relationship has advanced some environmental causes, with "three decades of environmental cooperation across the region allow[ing] civil servants to forge important professional relationships over time" (Selin and VanDeveer 2005, 355). The impact on trade and security between the two regions is less apparent. Security and border issues are more evident in formal pronouncements than actual outcomes. Formal evidence is slim, such that it's difficult to determine if the NEG-ECP relationship has had any impact on security infrastructure or action, over and above what may have occurred as a result of interaction at the federal level.

The NEG-ECP continues to meet, which helps to drive the machinery of intergovernmental relationships on both sides of the border but does not specifically bring advances in border security or trade that have not otherwise occurred at the federal levels writ large between the two states.

Changes that did transpire largely reflected federal priorities that were driven from the top down, as exemplified by transportation security, which became a priority following the events of 9/11 (Avis 2003). Since then, Canada and the United States have worked together to assess security expectations at ports, through US-led security precautions such as the Container Security Initiative (CSI), which was initiated nine days after 9/11, and the International Ship and Port Security (ISPS) code. Canada has accommodated both the CSI program and the ISPS code. Nevertheless, rumors surrounding Canada's "open border" were still prevalent in official discourse. These rumors created a good deal of tension, as suggestions that Canada's border remained undefended were worrisome to the United States, Canada's largest trading partner. Canada has taken strides to improve port security and to ease US concerns about border security (Ferriere, Pysareva, and Rucinski 2005). Luckily, the ISPS code was in line with the regulations other trading partners expected, so this move toward further securitization did not jeopardize other trade relationships. The ISPS code was implemented by the United Nation's International Marine organization in 2004, and it was readily adopted by 152 states (Cowen 2007). States may opt to meet the minimum requirements of the code, or they may opt to exceed the expectations outlined in the ISPS. Canada chose to exceed the requirements.

Environmental Scan—Government Security Actors

The Maritime Security Operations Centre (MSOC) East formally brings together five departments and agencies that share a role in Canada's marine security: the Canada Border Services Agency, Fisheries and Oceans Canada, the Department of National Defence/Canadian Armed Forces, the Royal Canadian Mounted Police, and Transport Canada (Canadian Coast Guard 2013a). Based in Halifax, MSOC (East) has daily interactions with NORAD and international military and intelligence allies (Gardham 2011). The 2011 *Beyond the Border: A Shared Vision for Perimeter Security and Economic Competitiveness* initiative articulates a shared approach to security in which both countries work together to address the shared perimeter of North America. This is an ongoing theme of US–Canada border security that has evolved through various iterations of "smart border" initiatives (Fry 2012; Jones 2012; von Hlatky and Trisko 2012). For our purposes, this initiative is part of the overall continuing integration of allied security forces.

Environmental Scan—Seaports

Canada's system governing seaports was deregulated in the 1990s with the intent of increasing efficiency and creating a more service-friendly culture (Pollitt and Bouckaert 1999). This culminated in the Canada Marine Act (1998), but in contrast to Australia, New Zealand, and the United Kingdom, which undertook more radical reforms, the Canadian government was less likely to divest publicly held resources to the private sector; politicians and senior officials preferred to keep more control than their Westminster counterparts (Aucoin 2002). Nineteen ports were designated as Canada Port Authorities (CPAs) on the basis that they were vital to domestic and international trade, financially self-sufficient, serve large and diversified markets, and have links with major rail lines or highways (Brooks 2004). Since the 1998 Marine Act designated nineteen CPAs, port authorities in Vancouver amalgamated, leaving eighteen port authorities in Canada.

CPAs such as Halifax and St. John's are considered essential infrastructure to the national ports system (Brooks 2004). Despite the reforms of the 1990s, they are subject to a wide array of regulations monitored and enforced by an equally wide array of government agencies. The Canada Marine Act (1998), the Public Safety Act, 2002 (2004), the Navigation Protection Act (1985), and the Marine Transportation Security Act (1994) are the most visible and significant. Critics of restrictions imposed on the CPAs have suggested that they are crippled from exercising the advantages that a truly deregulated, free-market-driven system would provide (Cirtwell, Crowley, and Frost 2001). The port authorities are prevented from holding a mortgage on any federal property on which the port is situated, and their ability to borrow commercially is capped (Cirtwell, Crowley, and Frost 2001; Ircha 2001a). Government appropriations may be used only for capital or security expenses, not on port operations. This makes it difficult to integrate security and commercial operations.

The British North America Act delegated shipping and navigation as under federal jurisdiction (Brooks 2007). In 1936 the National Harbours Board (NHB) disbanded local harbor commissions and replaced them with federal oversight bodies (Brooks 2004). With centralized federal control, the government was able to standardize port charges, so port charges would be consistent regardless of the local economy. National Harbours Board oversight continued well into the 1980s (Brooks 2007).

Maritime ports were eventually able to carve out space for local autonomy. Local governance was solidified in 1983 with the creation of the Canada Ports Corporation Act. According to Ircha (2001a, 6), this Act was instrumental in establishing

> a balance between national coordination through the Canada Ports Corporation (CPC) and local commercial responsiveness by incorporating major ports as subsidiary Local Port Corporations (LPC) with their own boards of directors (with the federal Minister of Transport nominating the directors for governor-in-council [Cabinet] appointment). Seven CPC ports were given LPC status: St. John's, Halifax, Saint John, Quebec, Montréal, Vancouver, and Prince Rupert.

Ports exemplify how federal governance has devolved to incorporate several levels of actors.

This movement toward deregulation continued into the early 2000s and is tailored toward local communities. In 2004, 499 ports were devolved, and at that point, 69 ports had not devolved to local authority. In these special cases, the federal government retained custody of the port if the community was too dependent to assume responsibility, or too remote to function effectively (Brooks 2007).

Devolution involves the transfer of responsibility for certain ports from a larger, more centralized authority (federal government) to other actors and agencies (Brooks 2004). Canada's devolution policy emphasized the importance of investing in smaller agencies to ensure responsiveness to local needs. Devolution was also an opportunity for the federal government to reduce expenditures. Although the policy for disposing of federal property requires the government to offer the properties to other government departments first, the Canadian federal government was able to offer the ports to private organizations before municipalities (Ircha 2001b), out of concern that municipalities might prioritize leisure over the economic functions of ports.

As a result of this process, ports are now governed by a multitude of actors. Private organizations, such as the Bayside Port Corporation, now own ports (Debrie, Gouvernal, and Slack 2007). Other private actors, such as not-for-profit corporations, also assumed responsibility for ports. Despite existing in the private sector, these organizations usually maintain a few municipal representatives on the company's board. Yet ownership of ports remains blurred. Many new port proprietors own the physical port, but the issue of contaminated seabeds has stirred apprehension about purchasing water lots. As a result, the ports are owned by private companies and municipalities, but the water lots and harbor beds are owned by the federal government (Debrie, Gouvernal, and Slack 2007). The divestiture process produced this mosaic of port ownership, and the inclusion of many public-sector representatives on company-owned port boards demonstrates not only the value these ports hold for municipalities, but also how the distinction between public and private is slightly blurred for Canadian ports (Debrie, Gouvernal, and Slack 2007).

The divestiture poses potential problems for the ability of maritime ports to upgrade security infrastructure. First, local and private actors are now responsible for the financial health of ports (Debrie, Gouvernal, and Slack 2007). Smaller ports generate limited revenue, so owners might be less inclined to invest profit to improve existing security infrastructure, instead focusing on attracting more traffic through infrastructure improvements. For example, Sydney, Nova Scotia, added an additional cruise terminal, which cost $6.5 million but attracted more traffic (Debrie, Gouvernal, and Slack 2007). Locally owned ports still struggle to collect harbor fees, because many of the water lots and harbor beds are still owned by the federal government. So, ports that want to improve infrastructure to promote traffic and secure the port struggle for want of funding (Debrie, Gouvernal, and Slack 2007).

In 2018, the federal government conducted a Ports Modernization Review with stakeholders across Canada to evolve its relationship with the country's eighteen port authorities The review, and the announced legislative priorities that emerged, were intended to make the ports safer and more competitive (Transport Canada 2022a) A parallel task force report on supply chain vulnerabilities also emphasizes stronger interactions with Indigenous communities and environmental concerns. (Transport Canada 2022b). As in past studies, these reports focus on the importance of trade, and try to reconcile efficiency with security. While efficiency concerns take pride of place in the reports, the vaccine-mandate protests in February 2022 that included blockades at the Canada–US Ambassador Bridge brought into sharp focus the continued vulnerabilities inherent in immovable infrastructure that serve as key trade routes (Rouleau 2023).

Conclusion

Globalized trade moves on salt water, and the fortunes and prosperity of Atlantic Canada have been connected to the world through the sea for centuries. The seacoast is the primary international border in the region, and border and security issues arise at sea and in the seaports. The desired globalized trade and resource development that occurs in coastal waters and at the ports is accompanied by globalized threats and issues such as smuggling, human trafficking, terrorism, and piracy. Access to markets and the ability to exploit the maritime domain for direct and indirect economic benefit continues to drive security concerns in Atlantic Canada.

The integration of maritime security such as we have examined in the implementation of the Maritime Security Operations Centres (MSOCs) in Atlantic Canada was an early adoption of a joint force operation. Layering security and maritime domain awareness is intended to identify and act on potential threats or unlawful activity while vessels are still at sea. MSOCs' partnership with allied resources and assets parallels Canada's obligations to uphold global treaties and the political commitments made between the governments of Canada and United States to integrate border enforcement.

For private-sector shippers and managers of Canadian port authorities, however, problems persist. The hierarchical and integrated control model that is working effectively for the public sector is not translating to governance and control models in the ports. Information is not shared adequately among relevant partners, and ports have limited ability to change behavior. The ports exist in a confused and multilayered reality, independent and entrepreneurial on one hand, but highly regulated, critical public infrastructure on the other. This dis-integration of the ports from the security apparatus is highly problematic for the development of security infrastructure. As early as 2007 the Senate of Canada identified this issue—but no apparent action has been taken to date.

Notwithstanding serious issues with security integration, the system continues to function and respond as expected, given the economic imperatives and operational attitudes toward security in the Atlantic region of Canada. With no publicly visible human threat on any scale, and with the integrated response of the MSOC on the ocean providing a seaward buffer, there is no sense of urgency to improve on port security. As has been true for centuries, the security apparatus supports the big picture of trade and commerce.

Future efforts to enhance border security in Atlantic Canada must consider the tensions inherent in the integrated control models of the security apparatus and the dis-integrated, deregulated governance models of seaport operators. Both models have strengths and weaknesses, intended to address the competing priorities of security protection and innovative commerce in a globalized world. Without a clear understanding and delineation of how the public and private sectors overlap and interact, neither will perform optimally in service of security and global trade.

This chapter outlined three major concerns with the maritime border. First is the lack of consensus among Canadian stakeholders regarding the degree of security at ports. The United States and Canada have reached a level of agreement with the implementation of the International Ship and Port Security code. The Canadian Senate, however, was unimpressed by port security measures in 2007, arguing that the desire for efficiency should not eclipse thorough security measures. Instead of screening high-risk containers, the Senate argued that a higher percentage of containers should be reviewed. Little has been done to follow this direction, and issues with security equipment, low rates of container inspections, and organized crime persist. The regional competitiveness of the maritime ports could decline if additional security measures are enforced. Finally, the state of port ownership and devolution should be reconciled with expectations about security infrastructure. The mix of port ownership enables different levels of government involvement, and allows local interests to be represented. The transfer of fiscal responsibility to local actors limits improvements in port infrastructure. This division of responsibility means that security infrastructure is likely to continue to be neglected for the foreseeable future.

REFERENCES

Aucoin, Peter. 2002. "Beyond the 'New' in Public Management Reform in Canada: Catching the Next Wave?" In *The Handbook of Canadian Public Administration*, edited by Christopher J. C. Dunn, 36–52. Ontario: Oxford University Press.

Avis, C. N. P. 2003. "Surveillance and Canadian Maritime Domestic Security." *Canadian Military Journal* 3, no. 1: 9–14.

Bilefsky, Dan. 2020. "In 'Lobster War,' Indigenous Canadians Face Attacks by Fishermen." *New York Times*, October 20. https://www.nytimes.com/2020/10/20/wo rld/canada/nova-scotia-lobster-war.html

Bolan, K. 2015a. "Organized Crime and the Port: Part One of My Series." *Vancouver Sun*, May 8. http://vancouversun.com/news/staff-blogs/organized-crime -and-the-port-part-one-of-my-series

Bolan, K. 2015b. "The Art of the CBSA Inspection." *Vancouver Sun*, November 5. https://vancouversun.com/news/the-art-of-the-cbsa-inspection

Brooks, Mary R. 2004. "The Governance Structure of Ports." *Review of Network Economics* 3, no. 2: 168–83.

Brooks, M. R. 2007. "Port Devolution and Governance in Canada." *Research in Transportation Economics* 17: 237–57.

Burns, Maria G. 2013. "Estimating the Impact of Maritime Security: Financial Tradeoffs between Security and Efficiency." *Journal of Transportation Security* 6, no. 4: 329–38.

Canada and the United States. 2006. "Agreement between the Government of Canada and the Government of the United States of America on the North American Aerospace Defense Command, E105060." http://www.treaty-accord .gc.ca/text-texte.aspx?id=105060

Canada Border Services Agency (CBSA). 2012. "Audit of Border Controls for Marine Ports of Entry."Ottawa.

Canada Border Services Agency (CBSA). 2017. *2016–17 Departmental Results Report*. Ottawa.

Canadian Coast Guard. 2013. "Marine Security Operation Centres." https://tc.ca nada.ca/en/marine-transportation/marine-security/marine-security-operation -centres

Canadian Senate. 2007. "Canadian Standing Senate Committee on National Security and Defence." *Canadian Security Guide Book: Seaports*. 39th Parl., 2nd sess. http://publications.gc.ca/collections/collection_2011/sen/yc33-0/YC33-0-391 -9-eng.pdf

CBC News. 2001. "Shots Fired in Burnt Church Fishing Dispute." *CBC News*, September 16. https://www.cbc.ca/news/canada/shots-fired-in-burnt-church-fishi ng-dispute-1.299558

Cirtwill, C., Brian Lee Crowley, and J. Frost. 2001. *Port Ability: A Private Sector Strategy for the Port of Halifax*. Atlantic Institute for Market Studies. https://www .aims.ca/books-papers/port-ability/

Collins, J. 2018. "Border Challenges—Atlantic Canada Ports" [PowerPoint slides]. https://biglobalization.org/events/round-table-on-ports-and-shipping-in-atla ntic-canada/

Conrad, Margaret R., and James K. Hiller. 2015. *Atlantic Canada, A History*. Oxford, UK: Oxford University Press.

Council of Canadian Academies. 2017. *The Value of Commercial Marine Shipping to Canada*. Ottawa: The Expert Panel on the Social and Economic Value of Marine Shipping to Canada, Council of Canadian Academies.

Cowen, Deborah. 2007. "Struggling with 'Security': National Security and Labour in the Ports." *Just Labour* 10: 30–44.

Debrie, J., E. Gouvernal, and B. Slack. 2007. "Port Devolution Revisited: The Case of Regional Ports and the Role of Lower Tier Governments." *Journal of Transport Geography* 15, no. 6: 455–64.

Doloreux, D., and R. Shearmur. 2009. "Maritime Clusters in Diverse Regional Contexts: The Case of Canada." *Marine Policy* 33, no. 3: 520–27.

Fergusson, J., N. Allarie, A. Charron, A. Narkovich, J. Jockel, J. Sokolsky, A. Stephenson, and M. Trudgen. 2015. *"LEFT of BANG": NORAD's Maritime Warning Mission and North American Domain Awareness*. Department of National Defense. https://umanitoba.ca/centres/media/0_NORAD_Maritime_Warning_Mission_Final_Report_8_Oct_2015.pdf

Ferriere, D., K. Pysareva, and A. Rucinski. 2005. "Using Technology to Bridge Maritime Security Gaps." National Infrastructure Institute Center for Infrastructure Expertise, University of New Hampshire.

Fry, E. 2012. "The Canada–US Relationship One Decade after 9/11." *International Journal* 67, no. 4: 879–93.

Gardham, D. 2011. "Maritime Security Co-operation—A Practitioner's View." *Maritime Security Conference 2011 Proceedings*, 33–42. http://www.coecsw.org/fileadmin/content_uploads/others/20111221_MSC2011_Proceedings_report.pdf

Government of Canada. 2010. *Atlantic Gateway and Trade Corridor Strategy*. https://publications.gc.ca/collections/collection_2011/tc/T22-181-2009-eng.pdf

Government of Canada. 2014. "Geographical Application." Office of the Administrator of the Ship-source Oil Pollution Fund. https://sopf.gc.ca/

Halifax Port Authority. n.d. *Cargo Statistics*. Port of Halifax. http://www.portofhalifax.ca/port-operations-centre/cargo-statistics/

"International Emergency Management Assistance Memorandum of Understanding" (IEMAMU). A. King, J. Hamm, J. Shaheen, and P. Binn. Resolution, 23–25. http://www.cap-cpma.ca/images/CAP/en-negecpemergencymou.pdf

Ircha, M. C. 2001a. "Serving Tomorrow's Mega-Size Containerships: The Canadian Solution." *International Journal of Maritime Economics* 3, no. 3: 318–32.

Ircha, M. C. 2001b. "North American Port Reform: The Canadian and American Experience." *International Journal of Maritime Economics* 3, no. 2: 198–220.

Jones, Riley. 2012. "Cascadian Cross Border Cooperation Challenged: The Case of the Shared Waters Alliance." *WWU Graduate School Collection*. 248. http://cedar.wwu.edu/wwuet/248

Legault, L. H., and B. Hankey. 1985. "From Sea to Seabed: The Single Maritime Boundary in the Gulf of Maine Case." *American Journal of International Law* 79, no. 4: 961–91.

Marine Transportation Security Act, Consolidated Acts. (1994, c.40, SC). Retrieved from the Justice Laws website: http://laws.justice.gc.ca/eng/acts/M-0.8/page-1.html

Mercer, G. 2020. "Two Decades after the Burnt Church Crisis, Disputes Flare Up Over Indigenous Fishing Rights in Atlantic Canada." *Globe and Mail*, September 28. https://www.theglobeandmail.com/canada/article-two-decades-after-the-burnt-church-crisis-disputes-continue-over/

National Post. 2013. "Expensive New High-Tech Border Scanners Often Break Down, Less Effective than Detection Dogs." *National Post*, August 7. http://nationalpost.com/news/canada/expensive-new-high-tech-border-scanners-often-break-down-less-effective-than-detection-dogs

Navigation Protection Act, Consolidated Acts. 1985, c. N-22, RSC. Retrieved from the Justice Laws website. http://laws.justice.gc.ca/eng/acts/N-22/

Pollitt, Christopher, and Geert Bouckaert. 1999. *Public Management Reform: A Comparative Analysis*. Oxford, UK: Oxford University Press.

Ports Saint John [Stjport]. 2017. *Marine*. Port Saint John. https://www.sjport.com/cargo/connectivity/

Public Safety Act. "Consolidated Acts." 2002, S.C. 2004, c.15 Retrieved from the Justice Laws website: http://laws.justice.gc.ca/eng/acts/P-31.5/

Public Safety Canada. 2011. "Marine Ports and Organized Crime." https://www.publicsafety.gc.ca/cnt/rsrcs/pblctns/rgnzd-crm-brf-25/rgnzd-crm-brf-25-eng.pdf

Rhee, S. 1981. "Equitable Solutions to the Maritime Boundary Dispute Between the United States and Canada in the Gulf of Maine." *American Journal of International Law* 75, no. 3: 590–628. http://doi.org/10.2307/2200687

Robertson, C. 2017, June 6. "Managing US Relations under Donald Trump." Canada. Parliament. House of Commons. *Standing Committee on Foreign Affairs and International Development*. 42nd par., 1st sess., nu. 065. http://www.colinrobertson.ca/?cat=22

Romero, J. 2003. "Prevention of Maritime Terrorism: The Container Security Initiative." *Chicago Journal of International Law* 4, no. 2: 597–605.

Rouleau, S. 2022. *Report of the Public Inquiry into the 2022 Public Order Emergency*. Ottawa. https://publicorderemergencycommission.ca/files/documents/Final-Report/Vol-1-Report-of-the-Public-Inquiry-into-the-2022-Public-Order-Emergency.pdf

Sands, C. 2009. *Toward a New Frontier: Improving the US-Canadian Border*. Metropolitan Policy Program at Brookings. https://www.brookings.edu/wp-content/uploads/2012/04/20090325_sands.pdf

Selin, H., and S. D. VanDeveer. 2005. "Canadian–US Environmental Cooperation: Climate Change Networks and Regional Action." *American Review of Canadian Studies* 35, no. 2: 353–78.

Statistics Canada. 2017. *Focus on Geography Series, Census 2016*. [Catalogue No. 98-402-X2016001]. https://www12.statcan.gc.ca/census-recensement/2016/as-sa/fogs-spg/Index-eng.cfm

Transport Canada. 2022a. *Ports Modernization Review*. Ottawa. https://www.canada.ca/en/transport-canada/news/2022/10/ports-modernization-review.html

Transport Canada. 2022b. *Action. Collaboration. Transformation. Final Report of The National Supply Chain Task Force 2022*. Ottawa. https://tc.canada.ca/sites/default/files/2022-10/supply-chain-task-force-report_2022.pdf

United Nations Convention on the Law of the Sea. 1982. A/CONF.62/122, reprinted in 21 I.L.M. 1261. http://www.un.org/depts/los/convention_agreements/texts/unclos/UNCLOS-TOC.htm

Vasseur, L., and N. Catto. 2008. "Atlantic Canada." In *From Impacts to Adaption: Canada in A Changing Climate 2007*, edited by D. S. Lemmen, F. J. Warren, J. Lacroix, and E. Bush, 119–70. Ottawa: Government of Canada.

Von Hlatky, S., and J. Trisko. 2012. "Sharing the Burden of the Border: Layered Security Co-operation and the Canada–US Frontier." *Canadian Journal of Political Science* 45, no. 1: 63–88. http://doi.org/10.1017/S0008423911000928

EIGHT

The Territorial North

Heather Nicol, Adam Lajeunesse, Whitney Lackenbauer,
and Karen Everett

Introduction

The Canadian North, which encompasses all of Canada located north of sixty degrees north latitude, includes Yukon, the Northwest Territories (NWT), Northern Québec, and Nunavut. It also includes portions of Labrador and Newfoundland. While there are extensive land and maritime boundaries in an area that represents approximately 40 percent of Canada's land mass, facilities for managing and processing traffic are limited, and there are few ports of entry for international air and maritime traffic to the region. The northern land border with the United States, situated between Yukon and Alaska, also lies in a region that is remote and sparsely populated.

Canada's northern borders are not just a boundary currently defined between three states (Canada, United States, and Denmark/Greenland); they are embedded in a larger international Arctic region and broader circumpolar connections (Keskitalo 2004). For example, Indigenous organizations and governments have created innovative regional governance structures that engage with broader international forums and often define policy and practice for the circumpolar region as a whole (Campbell 2015). Climate change complicates northern North American boundary-making as well: as environmental conditions change, new (predominantly unconventional) security threats emerge (Heininen and Nicol 2017). These include damage to critical infrastructure from melting permafrost and food insecurity caused by changes in regional biodiversity. Such developments are rapidly changing the security landscape, throwing conventional economic and environmental relationships awry. Thus, the security scenario in the Canadian North challenges the long-standing belief that regional security merely entails applying national standards of management irrespective of an area's unique needs (Everett 2017). For remote and northern regions, security can have different meanings than it does for southern, urban, or densely populated regions.

This chapter reviews border integrity and security in northern North America, specifically in northern Canada, and argues that nonconventional security threats that have emerged will warrant innovative and regional approaches in the future. Many threats are consistent with observations about the impact of climate change on human security more generally, while others are unique to the region (Greaves 2012; Gjørv Hoogensen et al. 2013). For example, as multiyear sea ice melts at the "top of the world" and opens the region to different flows of people, goods, and capital, the nature of threats and responses will change. This may affect the sustainability of state boundaries that currently divide regions, and open the door to new threats. Vulnerabilities related to climate change, heightened long-range pollution, increased migration, new economic actors, criminality, and terrorism all indicate the importance of looking at the bigger picture. This chapter looks to the present roster of emerging and nonconventional security threats while also undertaking a broad-horizon scan of security concerns about border integrity in the future. It concludes that border issues in northern Canada have become increasingly securitized in ways that prioritize nonconventional threats (Nicol and Lackenbauer 2017; Lackenbauer et al. 2020).

National Frameworks of Border Management

Northern Canada's borders range from those managed in airport foyers and those demarcated on land to those imposed on maritime domains. Here we discuss the management and capacity of each, beginning with Canada's international land boundary with Alaska. Despite the length of the Alaska-Yukon land border—some 1,210 km—there are few border posts managing the flow of people and goods. Those that do exist are found at crossing points on major roadways leading from southern Yukon and northern British Columbia to Alaska and the ports of Skagway and Haines. Two other border posts are positioned along the international border between British Columbia and the Alaskan Panhandle.

Part of the rationale for the location of border posts in the region, especially those between Yukon and Alaska, relates to the reorientation of border inspection posts built to monitor the transportation network during the Cold War. Crossings at Beaver Creek and Little Gold Creek in Canada are now linked by a system of roads and highways that connect Yukon and parts of the NWT and British Columbia, and also linked to American border posts constructed in 1971 at Poker Creek and Alcan, which replaced an inland post along the Alaska Highway at Tok. While most crossings between Yukon and Alaska take place at Beaver Creek, a small town located along the Alaska Highway, two border posts between British Columbia and Alaska (located along the Haines and the Klondike Highway) also serve as gateways for flows of Yukon goods and people to the Alaskan ports of Haines and Skagway. They service a network of roads that connect northern settlements and resources with ports for national and international shipping. The Dempster Highway and the road link heading north and east, for example, connects settlements in the NWT as far north as Tuktoyaktuk on the Beaufort Sea. There is, however, no direct point of entry between the NWT and Alaska, and there are no international land borders in the Territorial North outside of the Alaska–Yukon/BC borderlands. Highways and road networks in the Northwest Territories lead to urban centers in northern Alberta and Saskatchewan, but the vast distances between NWT settlements and Alaskan ports make northern road transportation prohibitive.

While all land border posts that process cross-border traffic between Yukon/BC and Alaska are equipped for most routine travel and commercial services, levels of flows and hours of operation differ (Everett 2017). These variations attempt to rationalize how border posts handle different types of activity and volumes of traffic. Pre-COVID, for example, most trucks loaded with exports from Yukon entering Alaska crossed directly at the Beaver Creek/Alcan crossing on the way to the Port of Haines, located west of Skagway on the Alaskan Panhandle. According to US data, in some years the Alcan border post in Alaska sees approximately ten times as much truck traffic from Yukon as the Dalton Cache Crossing with BC, and about two to three times as much traffic as the BC Fraser Skagway crossing. Alcan is the main crossing for trucks loaded with products coming from Yukon and traveling to the Port of Haines. On the other hand, the BC Fraser Skagway post, located on the Klondike Highway to both Carcross and Whitehorse, is among the busiest border crossings in terms of vehicle traffic. From here, many tourists and much local traffic follow the Klondike Highway to the Fraser/Skagway. In 2015, for example, over half of all regional land border crossings took place at the Fraser/Skagway crossing, mostly between May and September (see Yukon Government 2015, 2016, for examples).

Despite low levels of traffic, bottlenecks develop and create critical vulnerabilities for the region. For example, existing levels of cross-border traffic create diverse and seasonal demands on conventional border security services. This can make access to consistent security processing services problematic for those who operate outside certain parameters. The seasonal nature of cross-border tourism, for example, means that peak periods in border crossings are April and September. In 2015, over 250,000 travelers crossed from Yukon to Alaska using the Fraser Canada Border Services Agency (CBSA) post during these months. That year, however, the CBSA decided to reduce its hours of service. Arguing that "the infrastructure and the human resources costs are tremendous for pretty small metrics," the CBSA did not offer summer service hours between midnight and 8:00 a.m. The Skagway post on the US side followed suit. This forced Canadian travelers and tourists to clear customs in Skagway the night before for a 7:00 a.m. ferry departure for Haines or Juneau (*CBC News* 2015).

Meanwhile, despite these cutbacks, the Fraser crossing saw more commercial vehicle traffic that same year. Up to 3,000 loaded trucks cross annually from British Columbia and Yukon, and an equivalent number return back across the border for more cargo—while commercial processing closed at 4:45 p.m. on weekdays and remained closed each weekend. This restricted the hours of commercial and traveler services at Fraser more than at the Beaver Creek crossing.

Low population, and seasonal pressures on otherwise low security-demand thresholds, can complicate the situation in other ways. Nicol et al. (2019) noted, for example, that in the Yukon, there are no Free and Secure Trade (FAST) lanes, and it is not necessarily feasible to use alternative crossings to get to the port in Skagway if there are delays at the Fraser/Skagway crossing. The next-closest crossing to the port is through Pleasant Camp/Dalton Cache, and using this crossing increases the time to drive to Skagway, adding to transportation costs.

Air Borders

The dearth of road connections and the seasonal nature of ice roads that transport goods only in the winter and spring dictate that much of the region's commercial and noncommercial traffic arrive via air and sea, which makes small airports particularly important. They constitute the lifeline for many remote communities to connect to southern Canada and the United States. Still, only about 10 percent of travelers to Yukon arrive by air, mostly at the Eric Nielsen International Airport in Whitehorse. An "Airport of Entry" (AOE), it offers full services to clear all classes of scheduled and unscheduled aircraft—for both travelers and cargo. The fact that the Whitehorse AOE is the only one in Canada's Territorial North suggests that the region is underserviced compared to southern Canada. However, most flights that service the North connect with southern Canadian AOEs, and many of these flights are seasonal. There are no regularly scheduled international flights for passengers or cargo outside of Yukon, and few permanent places for processing commercial or noncommercial international flows of goods or people. In many cases, the CBSA is "on call" when unscheduled international flights and vessels arrive—creating what could be considered pop-up processing facilities.

Maritime Boundaries

In theory, security and border management in the North is more complex for Canada's Arctic Ocean maritime boundaries than its land borders because of unsettled territorial disputes between Canada and the United States and between Canada and Denmark (Huebert 2019; Nicol and Plouffe 2014; Byers 2013; Lackenbauer et al. 2020). While the Lincoln Sea dispute was settled to the satisfaction of Canada and Denmark in 2012, Hans Island remains an outstanding (albeit well-managed) issue. The line demarcating the Canadian and American Beaufort Sea remains unsettled, as does the legal status of the waters of the Northwest Passage, which Canada claims as internal waters.

Much like at other borders, entry into Canada through Arctic and sub-Arctic maritime regions is managed by federal authorities, including the CBSA, the Department of National Defence (DND), and the Canadian Coast Guard (CCG). International laws and agreements also apply to Canadian maritime jurisdictions and inform security practices, including the UN Convention on the Law of the Sea. Bilateral or multilateral agreements such as the Agreement on Cooperation on Aeronautical and Maritime Search and Rescue in the Arctic and the Agreement on Cooperation on Marine Oil Pollution Preparedness and Response in the Arctic have both been signed by the eight Arctic states. Increasing cruise ship activity in the Northwest Passage has generated discussion about the associated risk of environmental disaster (and undocumented immigration) for the small Arctic hamlets that such ships frequently visit. Since 2005, Canada has seen an increasing number of tourists and cruise vessels in the Arctic, lured by the decreasing sea ice and growing international interest. The number of these transits leveled off after 2008, however, and has remained relatively steady since (except in 2020, when COVID-related restrictions prevented cruise tourism in the region).

Lasserre and Têtu's (2013) survey of cruise ship operators in the region suggests that there is no pressing interest in expanding what are already high-end, niche operations, but Dawson et al. note "an increase in the average number of kilometers that ships have traveled in the territory as well as an increase in the number, and type vessels." They expect these developments to lead to "further increases in shipping activity," at least in Nunavut (2018, 37–38). Both reports emphasize that changing ice conditions may in the future attract larger vessels. One such example was the 1,600-person cruise ship *Crystal Serenity*, which sailed through the Northwest Passage in 2016 and 2017. This trend toward larger vessels will require new thinking and protocols for managing risks. The voyages of the *Crystal Serenity* went smoothly, despite anticipatory concerns that the venture could end badly. In this case, Canadian border and customs personnel were able to launch a special initiative to meet and clear passengers onboard the ship as it entered Canadian waters.

Further melting of the Arctic ice is likely to elicit more cruise ship operations in the future. Dawson et al. note that the influence of tourism, combined with shipping related to Arctic mining projects, had already tripled vessel traffic activity around Pond Inlet by 2017 (Dawson, Johnston, and Stewart 2014, 22), As continued reduction in the extent and age of sea ice extends the window of navigability, investments in new Arctic shipping infrastructure and continued hydrographic mapping of safe sea routes may heighten the perceived reliability and attractiveness of shipping in these waters.

At present, international maritime flows of goods and products in the Canadian Arctic remain limited, with import and export clearance facilities available only through Inuvik, Tuktoyaktuk (the only conventional port and port security management structure in the region), and Iqaluit. If traffic increases, however, Canadian Arctic maritime security institutions will face a problem of capacity. The CBSA preclearance program provides for greater oversight, and the Arctic Shipping Electronic Commercial Clearances pilot program to manage the Arctic shipping season provides an alternative to current practice. The latter allows vessels to be diverted to the nearest designated customs office on request from the regional CBSA office, or to make arrangements to clear marine vessels and cargo while they are anchored at sea on a special service basis (CBSA 2020).

Overall, the management of international land and air borders by CBSA is consistent with that in other regions of Canada. The evolving Beyond the Border framework for border management invites cooperation, but clearly aligns border practices and discourages exceptions. The potential for increased Arctic shipping in the future complicates this, however, and raises the risk of maritime disasters involving cruise and cargo ships. Existing boundary security facilities in the region are not intended or equipped to control large volumes of traffic or to monitor environmental degradation. All of these challenges have cascading effects, as we discuss below.

Defining Security, Safety, and Border Integrity

Rather than see security as either military,traditional or "human," the changing demands and practices of defense and security encourage us to differentiate conventional and nonconventional security threats, all of which have the potential to involve civilian and military actors. For example, "security-oriented" border management involves military and nonmilitary agencies with primary and supporting mandates to deal with marine disasters, search and rescue, food security and health, or economic security. In southern Canada, health security concerns are focused on pandemics, biosecurity, bioterrorism, mad cow disease, dangerous ingredients, or food tampering, and population densities mean that some of these threats can spread rapidly. In the North, on the other hand, in the face of rapid environmental change the primary biosecurity issues concern limited access to healthcare, and the ability to maintain a living and enjoy food security using country foods.

Operationalizing Security

In the following section we explore how security is perceived and then operationalized, with tasks ranging from risk assessments of conventional and nonconventional threats to other less-well-defined potential concerns. We describe the major categories of concern, including those related to legal, military, or economic issues, concerns about immigration, human mobility, and criminal and terrorist threats, and managing environmental and human security. Most of these security issues are entangled or intertwined. If Canada attempts to manage its northern border through a national legal and regulatory framework consistent with the rest of the country, it faces unique regional challenges.

Regional

As early as 1986, the US-Canada Arctic Policy Forum recognized the need for environmental cooperation in the Arctic. This high-level stakeholder meeting discerned four areas of common policymaking challenges, including the need to develop a common American and Canadian regional authority in the Beaufort Sea. Rather than focusing on the bilateral boundary dispute in the Beaufort, the forum suggested that regional authority was necessary to manage various interests, including those of Indigenous and regional actors. Today the Beaufort Partnership provides a means of managing common environmental concerns for marine protected areas and a basis for implementing the Beaufort Sea Large Ocean Management Area, one of five priority areas identified for integrated ocean management planning by the Government of Canada (beaufortseapartnership.ca). Rather than standing as a formal regional governance forum or border management authority, the Beaufort Sea Partnership is a consortium of regional stakeholders, including federal, territorial, and Indigenous agencies; municipalities; the Inuvialuit Councils and other land claim councils and committees; as well as industries with interests in the area (beaufortseapartnership.ca.; there are, as yet, no regional seas agreements in place for the Arctic Ocean, such as those developed for the Caribbean or Mediterranean under United National Environmental Program or the "Cartagena Agreement.")

Bilateral and multilateral forums also identify the need for better cross border cooperation mechanisms to support regional economic development. The Pacific Northwest Economic Region (PNWER), an influential not-for-profit organization with a dedicated Arctic caucus, supports market access and promotes Arctic transportation systems across the Canada–US border. Both Yukon and the NWT cooperate closely with Alaska through bilateral intergovernmental accords and through the PNWER Arctic caucus. The Arctic Economic Council, an independent organization that promotes Arctic business-to-business activities and responsible economic development, also has a Maritime Transportation Working Group dedicated to gathering and exchanging information on national and international Arctic maritime traffic, related regulations, and hydrographic mapping (Nicol 2018; Landriault et al. 2020; Arctic Economic Council 2021).

Legal—International Legal Issues

Various international conventions and agreements or multilateral institutions influence the management of Canada's northern borders. For example, the

UN Convention on the Law of the Sea is considered the global "constitution of the oceans," setting the basic rules of ocean governance, including maritime sovereignty and boundaries. This provides an essential international legal framework for Arctic coastal states to assert and exercise sovereignty in the maritime Arctic. Furthermore, Canada supports strong mandatory international regulations for Arctic shipping, particularly regulations to decrease the risk of pollution and the need for search and rescue missions. A prime example is the Polar Code, developed through the International Maritime Organization, which entered into force on January 1, 2017, and "covers the full range of design, construction, equipment, operational, training, search and rescue and environmental protection matters relevant to ships operating in the inhospitable waters surrounding the two poles" (Chircop 2020; Pic et al. 2021). The UN Framework Convention on Climate Change and many other global conventions regulating transboundary pollutants, biodiversity, containments, and cultural and political rights contribute to the institutional complexity of Arctic governance, which encompasses both human and environmental security dimensions. Transnational declarations such as the "UN Declaration on the Rights of Indigenous Peoples" and the Inuit Circumpolar Council's "A Circumpolar Inuit Declaration on Sovereignty in the Arctic" (2009) also contain specific provisions that relate to Arctic security (Nickels 2013; ITK 2017; Bankes 2020).

Military

Transboundary military cooperation is well developed in the Canadian North. Institutional structures such as the North American Aerospace Defense Command (NORAD) and the North Atlantic Treaty Organization (NATO) cover Canada's Arctic jurisdiction, and Canadian military personnel are posted to Alaska NORAD region headquarters in Anchorage (Charron 2015, 2019; Huebert 2019). US Coast Guard units based in that state work closely with their Canadian Coast Guard counterparts on Arctic science, search and rescue, and fisheries patrols in the North Pacific (there are currently no fisheries in the Beaufort Sea). The Canadian Armed Forces' approach to operationalizing Canada's northern strategy has downplayed conventional military threats to the region (Lackenbauer and Lajeunesse 2016, 2018). By situating the military in a supporting role to other federal and territorial departments and agencies, it deliberately avoids "militarizing" Arctic sovereignty while focusing on the most probable human and environmental security missions that they are likely to face in the next two decades. Nevertheless, Canada's 2017 defense policy statement (Department of National Defence [DND] 2017) reiterates that "the Arctic region represents an important international crossroads where issues of climate change, international trade, and global security meet." Rather than promoting a narrative of inherent competition or impending conflict, however, the narrative points out that "Arctic states have long cooperated on economic, environmental, and safety issues, particularly through the Arctic Council, the premier body for cooperation in the region. All Arctic states have an enduring interest in continuing this productive collaboration" (DND 2017, 50). Accordingly, the drivers of Arctic change emphasize the rise of security and safety challenges rather than conventional defense threats, thus confirming the line of reasoning that has become well entrenched in defense planning over the last decade (Lackenbauer 2019).

Economic

The Canadian federal government's focus on unconventional security threats is premised on the reasonable assessment of probabilities. As economic activity increases in the Arctic, and the size or number of ships passing through Canada's Arctic waters grows, responsibilities for law-enforcement, pollution control, immigration, and public safety will probably increase. Indeed, the concept of environmental security has grown apace to reflect this expectation. Although popular media intimate that Arctic shipping is primed to grow exponentially due to declining sea-ice cover and an associated increase in Arctic resource extraction, actual international transit shipping through the Northwest Passage has not materialized as dramatically as projected. Instead, overall ship traffic increased 25 percent from 2013 to 2019 (Arctic Council 2019, 2020; Anselmi 2020), and included more bulk carrier vessels and cargo ships (Arctic Council 2019). While the first successful commercial transit of the Northwest Passage by the Danish bulk carrier *Nordic Orion*, in full compliance with Canadian laws and regulations, in October 2013 ignited fears of an imminent boom in international shipping transits, surveys reveal that most commercial ships operating in the NWP have been Canadian-flagged vessels—some 72 in 2019 compared to 61 in 2013 (Arctic Council 2019). Moreover, ships operating within the NWP are comparatively small compared to ships operating elsewhere in the world (Arctic Council 2019). Accordingly, actual shipping patterns and activities in Canadian Arctic waters invite a more sober assessment of security risks associated with international transit traffic than popular literature and political rhetoric would suggest.

Security threats surrounding offshore oil and gas development and onshore mining have also been downgraded since global commodity prices collapsed in 2014. Chinese mining company MMG put its Izok Lake mine in the Northwest Territories on hold, Baffinland has scaled down its

Mary River mine in Nunavut, and three of Yukon's mines have closed in response to low prices. While this slowdown in activity may be temporary, the reduction in activity inevitably reduces the safety and security threats that government security agencies anticipated. Still, CBSA began a pilot project to enhance the management of commercial transits of Arctic waters using electronic reporting to overcome the substantial costs to the carrier of a long-distance diversion to an authorized marine port of entry for cargo and commercial vessels. The CBSA now maintains the right to require a vessel bound for the Arctic to report to a designated cargo and commercial vessels port for examination, but the Arctic Shipping Electronic Commercial Clearances Program attempts to resolve logistical problems and enhance security by providing an alternate process. Recognizing that a lack of resources and facilities in the Arctic often means limited ability to examine ships, the CBSA pilot project attempts to eliminate the risk of clearing vessels through fax or emailed documents after a vessel has arrived in the Arctic, without sufficient advance notice for a thorough risk assessment.

Environmental

The Arctic Council is the major institution managing cross-border environmental cooperation at the international level. Although the Arctic Council's mandate explicitly excludes "military security" issues, its environmental and sustainable-development pillars accommodate research and cooperation on a wide range of environmental and human security issues. The Council is a "soft law" body that has no power to enact or enforce binding treaties. Canada considers it to be the leading international body for circumpolar cooperation. It promotes environmental, social, and economic aspects of sustainable development and environmental protection in the Arctic region.

An illustrative case of the Arctic Council's engagement with "soft" security issues is the landmark Arctic Marine Shipping Assessment (AMSA), carried out by the Council's Protection of the Marine Environment Working Group, co-led by Canada, the United States, and Finland. In April 2009, the AMSA report released important findings related to maritime activities (interpreted holistically) and seventeen concrete recommendations, all of which were agreed to by the member states of the Arctic Council. In addition to remaining an authoritative text on circum-Arctic shipping activity, AMSA recommendations have provided a blueprint for subsequent activities undertaken within the Arctic Council for negotiating binding agreements, for relationship-building, and for several initiatives related to "safe shipping." Other environmental security measures that embed the kind of cross-border cooperation encouraged by the AMSA report include the 2013 Cooperation on Marine Oil Pollution Preparedness and Response in the Arctic agreement, guidelines for Arctic tourism and cruise ship operators, and the development of a risk-based, mandatory International Code for Ships Operating in Polar Waters (Polar Code).

Illegal Immigration

Compared to other nonconventional threats, illegal immigration and terrorism are considered less pressing issues in the North than in the South. However, this has given human trafficking, especially in the context of missing and murdered Indigenous women, a lower priority, and indeed the issue is understudied in northern contexts (Perry 2019; Arctic Council 2021). It is important to understand the similarities and differences in northern and southern security themes, and one of the most significant differences is that in the Canadian North the security narrative remains much more focused on the tightly linked relationship between climate change and environment, society, and security, while the concept of human security is more deeply tied to traditional military security and sovereignty than is the case in Southern Canada. Border security is complicated by a growing trend for Indigenous people's organizations to be included in land and maritime boundary management to offset the cascading effects of climate change and a growing internationalism. For example, although illegal immigration activities and entry of inadmissible foreign nationals is uncommon in the Canadian North, CBSA officers have seen increased levels of immigration related to temporary foreign worker programs in the region. This includes foreign nationals on temporary work permits from southern Canada, who relocate to take advantage of specific nomination programs. Foreign nationals wishing to relocate to Northwest Territories, for example, may apply under the Northwest Territories Provincial Nominees Program for provincial nomination, in one of four categories. This program allows immigrants with the appropriate skills and experience to receive a Northwest Territories Provincial Nomination Certificate. It allows foreign nationals to apply for Canadian Permanent Residence, with faster processing times than those for other Canadian immigration classes.

In Yukon a similar nominee program exists, and that territory also has programs to assist in the development of a regional labor force. The latter program provides most successful applicants with permanent residence within six months of verification. The security issue here is associated with inadmissible movement of foreign nationals under this provincial nominee program—particularly between companies and between provinces and territories. A controversial case of a Filipino worker deported from Yukon in 2010 for being in violation of a work permit highlights the degree to which an exclusion order is required under such circumstances (Keevil 2010).

Crime and Terrorism

Concern about foreign terrorist activity in the North is no more or less cogent than in other borderlands regions. However, opioids and human trafficking are of greater concern because of their ubiquity and significant negative consequences. Human trafficking in the context of missing and murdered Indigenous women is particularly troubling (Perry 2019).

Human Security

Human security, particularly as it is tied to insecurities associated with climate change, is highly salient in northern policy discourse (Exner-Pirot 2012; Gjørv Hoogensen et al. 2013; CIRNAC 2019). Human and environmental security dialogues emphasize the need for connectivity and cooperation, traditional knowledge, and cultural resilience. Greater attentiveness to this particular conceptualization of security would emphasize efforts to promote sustainability through transnational treaties, the establishment of marine protected areas that are jointly managed across maritime boundary lines, and codes and protocols for marine protection, cooperative management, and search and rescue. Arctic residents are virtually unanimous in their view that environmental and disaster response capacities are profoundly inadequate in the region, reflecting the limited state of infrastructure more generally (Ekos 2011, 2015; CIRNAC 2019).

The Future of Northern Security

Several evolving factors will shape Canada's future Arctic security requirements. The shipping and resource-development industries in particular are anticipated to drive activity, and as such represent the most likely vectors of illegal entry, criminal activity, and safety or security violations. An official focus on unconventional security threats is premised on a reasonable assessment of probabilities. For example, as economic and maritime activity increases in the Arctic, responsibilities surrounding law enforcement, pollution control, immigration, and public safety are likely to grow. Transportation infrastructure also plays a crucial role in timely, effective responses to security threats, including trespassing and criminal infiltration. The dearth of suitable harbors and airstrips across much of the Canadian Arctic lengthens deployment and response times, increases the cost of missions, and will create real obstacles in the future if left unresolved.

A related issue for Canada's "safety," military defense, and boundary-integrity considerations is search and rescue (SAR) capacity. SAR capabilities are limited in the North compared to southern Canada, and as maritime activity increases, SAR capabilities will need to develop apace. While much of the academic and federal political focus remains fixated on national SAR resources, Northerners highlight the importance of investing in community-level capacity to address gaps and bolster resiliency (Kikkert and Lackenbauer 2020; Kikkert, Lackenbauer, and Pedersen 2021a, 2021b, 2021c).

There are similar problems regarding the response and management capacity of shipping. Although the Arctic ice cover has shrunk dramatically over the past decade, confirming a clear trend toward less and thinner ice across the region as a whole, the process has been anything but linear, consistent, or predictable from an operator's standpoint. Scheduling a transit through specific waters of the Canadian Arctic remains both difficult and dangerous. Winds and currents shift the ice constantly, often clogging channels that had been clear the week or even the day before. Annual variability is also significant, making it impossible to predict shipping conditions for the next season. Thus, while it is almost universally agreed that Arctic waters will see more activity over the next two decades, most systematic, empirical studies project that Arctic shipping—particularly in Canadian waters—will consist of destinational shipping composed of resource carriers, service ships, resupply vessels, and cruise liners. This destinational shipping will largely be tied to the pace of mineral resource extraction, since more activity in that sector will necessitate more resupply and export capacity. While the currently depressed state of the resource industry suggests that such activity is likely to remain minimal, the long-term potential for large-scale destinational shipping remains high (Lasserre and Têtu 2013).

Canada is unlikely to have any serious difficulty exercising control over maritime boundaries related to destinational shipping. Because ships involved in this activity move in or out of Canadian ports and harbors, they are easy to track and regulate using both bilateral mechanisms (such as NORAD's maritime early warning mission) and federal partnerships (such as Maritime Security Operations Centres). Ships report to Canada's northern vessel reporting system, (Northern Canada Vessel Traffic Services Zone Regulations or NORDREG), and comply with Canadian environmental and shipping regulations—such as the Arctic Waters Pollution Prevention Act—or risk damage to their business interests in Canada.

Further melting of the Arctic ice and rising international interest in the "vanishing" Arctic environment are also likely to lead to more and larger cruise ship operations in the North American Arctic in coming decades. The continued reduction in the extent and age of sea ice will probably extend the window of navigability, enabling more reliable scheduling. Furthermore, improved Arctic shipping infrastructure (such as a planned deepwater port in Iqaluit) and the continued hydrographic mapping of safe sea routes should lower insurance premiums and allow for more diverse itineraries. The CBSA has launched a pilot project to broaden the reach of its regional offices in managing commercial shipping, while the Canadian Coast Guard and Canadian Armed Forces will address evolving search-and-rescue requirements as new domain awareness requires.

At the same time, there is growing recognition of the agency and importance of Indigenous voices in shaping broader management policies. In 2016, the Caron Report was initiated in response to the recommendation of the Standing Senate Committee on Aboriginal Peoples. Caron visited the Yukon and spoke with representatives of Teslin Tlingit Council, Little Salmon/Carmacks First Nation, Tr'ondëk Hwëch'in First Nation, the White River First Nation, and the Daylu Dena Council. His report recognized the problems experienced by Canada's First Nations communities in the Yukon/Alaska borderlands in general, and also in relation to Canada's rejection of the terms of the Jay Treaty. Caron observed, "while there was a belief on the part of some of the First Nation representatives . . . that the current issues would not exist had Canada implemented the Jay Treaty [a British–United States border agreement], there was also a view that, in order to set the path forward, what is required is a mechanism to recognise inherent and Jay Treaty rights in a modern context" (Caron 2017).

Regarding ports of entry (POEs) for Yukon, he referenced the disadvantages created by the positioning of the Yukon POE at a distance of 37 kilometers from the international borderline. It meant that members exercising traditional pursuits beyond the POE location, but still within Canadian territory, had to cross through the POE at Beaver Creek and be questioned as if they had come from the United States. They were routinely questioned about the possession of wild game and fish, even though they had not left Canadian soil. First Nations recommended relocation of the POE to avoid challenging traditional as well as current patterns of hunting and fishing in the pursuit of a traditional economy (Nicol and Chater 2021).

The Caron Report appears to have had some traction. In December 2018, Public Safety Canada announced that they would implement new border-management measures to address Canada–United States border-crossing issues for First Nations, including at the Yukon-Alaska border. CBSA officers feel that in general, the issue has been addressed, although some First Nations might not agree. Nonetheless, these measures include recognition of the cultural sensitivities surrounding border management practices and remedies to enhance the Indigenous component of CBSA staff.

Indigenous voices have been raised on other areas of border management as well. The Inuit, for example, insist that they need to be included in maritime boundary-making deliberations in the Arctic Ocean (Campbell 2015), especially in light of the delimitation of the continental shelf: "The inherent right provided by Section 35, and supporting lands claims and international agreements such as the United Nations Declaration on the Rights of Indigenous Peoples, have potentially extended the rights of Inuit to offshore areas" (Nicol and Chater 2021).

Finally, there has been some movement in recognizing the artificiality of the maritime boundary between Canada and Greenland. Greenlandic Inuit have visited and hunted in Canada for centuries, while Canadian Inuit also moved back and forth over multiyear ice to Greenland. This mobility was only actively discouraged in the 1950s when the RCMP installed a number of posts with officers. Today, however, this connection and cultural continuity is resurfacing and has led to calls for both comanagement of the North Water Polynya, or Pikialasorsuaq, and enhanced levels of mobility between Canadian and Greenlandic Inuit populations (Nicol and Chater 2021).

Movement of People: Documented and Undocumented Migration

Since the early 2000s, the popular media have raised widespread expectations that Canada is on the verge of an Arctic resource boom and that workers might soon flood into the region. The potential security dimensions of this boom include concerns about safety, increased activity at regional transportation hubs, and more crime and human trafficking. Should this boom materialize, Canada could potentially see foreign workers imported to augment local workforces—many of Canada's largest Arctic mines are already authorized to bring in foreign workers. How quickly this happens, and on what scale, will in large measure determine what challenges Canada will face in managing its border, screening foreign workers, and ensuring that development takes place safely.

While nonconventional threats from illegal immigration are important considerations, Michael Byers suggests that it is easy "to imagine a ship from a rogue nation choosing the 'under-policed' Northwest Passage over the closely watched Panama Canal to ship in missiles, weapons of mass destruction and equipment for enriching nuclear isotopes. Smugglers could transfer passengers or cargo from a vessel to a small plane on one of dozens of gravel airstrips along the waterway." Byers asserts that shifting concern from sovereignty to nonconventional security threats "could be a productive way of shifting the current emphasis from questions of sovereignty and military competition. To a large extent, Arctic states already cooperate, sharing scientific data as well as the icebreakers that nations use to map the ocean seabed and to clarify jurisdiction under international law" (Young 2010). Although cross-border criminal activity is negligible in the North, the Territories suffer from high levels of insecurity related to illegal drug trafficking and drug use, alcohol abuse, sexual assault, and domestic violence (e.g., ITK 2014; Arctic Council 2021). Given the limited policing of Canada's northern borderlands and frontiers, much depends on building trust between communities and law enforcement.

Case Studies

The following case studies were selected to highlight the anomalies, vulnerabilities, and emerging security issues faced by borderlands populations in the Canadian North.

Case Study 1: The Voyage of the Berserk II

On June 22, 2007, the Norwegian pleasure craft *Berserk II* pulled into Halifax harbor. One crew member was deemed inadmissible based on membership in a criminal organization, and another withdrew his application for entry into Canada after learning that his previous convictions for drug smuggling and assaulting a police officer (outside of Canada) made him inadmissible. Both were deported. The boat left Halifax for Hvalsey, Greenland, where it took on additional crew members—one new member (with an extensive criminal history) and one of the deported crewmen. From Greenland, the vessel proceeded west into Canadian Arctic waters.

Canada's Arctic vessel reporting system, NORDREG, does not require vessels under 500 tons to report to authorities, but foreigners coming ashore onto Canadian soil are required to report. This became an issue on August 22 when the *Berserk II* landed at Gjoa Haven, Nunavut, and failed to contact the CBSA or RCMP. The captain of the *Berserk II* later told the Gjoa Haven RCMP detachment that he thought it was unnecessary to report, claiming that he had never left Canadian waters. Before local police learned that members of the crew were inadmissible, the vessel had departed for Cambridge Bay, Nunavut. The RCMP alerted their counterparts, who prepared to meet the ship. Prior to docking at Cambridge Bay, however, the captain gave firearms to the two crew members with criminal records and put them ashore outside of town. The ship's crew was arrested promptly on arrival in the hamlet, but the two men who had disembarked earlier remained loose on sparsely populated Victoria Island. What had begun as a law enforcement and border services issue quickly became a search-and-rescue mission, given the threat posed to nonresidents by the unforgiving landscape. The RCMP did not have an air search-and-rescue capability but faced hundreds of kilometers of barren coastline around Cambridge Bay. Accordingly, they requested assistance from the coast guard vessel CCGS *Sir Wilfrid Laurier*. Its helicopter took five days before the pair of criminals, waiting by their tent for their shipmates to return, were located—with only soup and bread left as their remaining food. With wolves nearby, they seemed relieved to be arrested. Ultimately, all five crew members were removed from Canada, three of the crew under a deportation order relating to their criminality and two under exclusion orders for failing to report to the CBSA under the Immigration and Refugee Protection Act. Charges for failing to report to the CBSA were withdrawn in exchange for their immediate departure to their countries of origin.

Although this was an aberration that hardly reflects normal operations of police and border officers in the Canadian North, it nevertheless illustrates potential dangers surrounding illegal immigration or criminal infiltration into the region and the safety and security concerns inherent to an increasingly accessible Arctic. With border services so dispersed across the Territorial North, it is easier to move undetected into this region than it would be to infiltrate most southern waters. A 2010 intelligence assessment by the Integrated Threat Assessment Centre—a fusion center that includes the Canadian Security Intelligence Service (CSIS), the RCMP, and other federal agencies—raised the specter of the North as a conduit for international or domestic interlopers: "In recent years" the report noted, "vessels with links to human smuggling, drug trafficking, and organized crime have attempted to access the Canadian Arctic." Canadian security agencies are thus well aware of threats of infiltration similar to what occurred with the *Berserk II*.

In this case, the vessel was readily identified in Gjoa Haven and its crew arrested in Cambridge Bay. Had the crew attempted to escape by either land or sea, they would have had few places to go. The dearth of refueling points along the Northwest Passage would require a small vessel to stop at a Canadian settlement. Decades of Canadian Armed Forces exercises have demonstrated how difficult it is to survive and move in the region— even with extensive logistical support (Lajeunesse and Lackenbauer 2017). Criminals or illegal immigrants seeking to infiltrate Canada from the North would certainly face dangers far out of proportion to the gains of skirting Canadian customs. Accordingly, it may be appropriate for both the CBSA and RCMP to await more evidence that a serious threat along these lines has materialized before devoting significant new resources or redeploying resources from elsewhere in Canada to address it.

Case Study 2: China's Arctic Interests and the Implications for Canadian Security

The emergence of new state actors interested in the Arctic has the potential to shape the region's security. Chinese activities in Arctic waters remain a source of tension and debate, with commentators having different assessments of the types and probability of security risks (e.g., Fife and Chase 2017; Brady 2017, 2020; Lackenbauer et al. 2018; Dean and Lackenbauer 2020; Barnes et al. 2021). Historically, traffic in and out of the region has been largely confined to Canadian and select American government vessels. The reduction in sea ice opens the possibility of new users of the Northwest Passage and new political and regulatory issues. Of these new actors, China has garnered the most international attention because of its investments in polar resource development projects and its interest in transpolar sea routes. These ambitions have provoked considerable concern in some quarters. For example, Brady (2017, 1) recounts that the People's Liberation Army Navy's 2015 deployment to the Alaskan and Scandinavian Arctic was "a stunning example of China's growing maritime capacities and its ability to reach the polar regions." Huebert echoes these concerns, warning that China is now testing the use of the Canadian Arctic for regular shipping, citing the 2017 transit of the icebreaker *Xue Long* through the Northwest Passage as a precedent. Without Canadian control over its borders and internal waters, this activity would lead to "the erosion of Canadian sovereignty" (Fife and Chase 2017). Other commentators suggest that Chinese maritime activity has the potential to affirm Canada's legal position over its Arctic waters if it is undertaken in compliance with Canadian regulations and in a manner that respects Canadian jurisdiction within its maritime borders (Lackenbauer et al. 2018).

The question remains, however, of where China believes Canada's Arctic borders to be. The United States has contested the straight baselines that Canada announced in 1985 to clarify the extent of its historical internal waters. The new Chinese position is ambiguous on the issue. On the one hand, China admits that it must respect the "legislative" powers within waters "subject to [Arctic coastal state] jurisdiction." It is careful, however, not to define which waters are subject to the jurisdiction of Arctic states. Moreover, the new positioninsists that Arctic shipping must be conducted in accordance with treaties and law—without taking sides on specific legal disputes (Lackenbauer et al. 2018). China's extensive claim to the South China Sea makes it unlikely that it will echo American protests that the straight baselines that Canada has drawn to enclose its historical waters are excessively long. Like Canada, China's need to balance its interests as a coastal state and maritime nation depends on a nuanced approach to freedom of navigation that commerce and power projection requires (e.g., Tai, Pearre, and Kao 2015; Peng and Wegge 2014; Antsygina, Heininen, and Komendantova 2020; Dean and Lackenbauer 2020).

Other security concerns associated with China's Arctic interests relate to foreign influence activities, intelligence gathering, and exploitative economic practices that can go hand in hand with investments in resource development projects and sociopolitical or scientific relationships (Hamilton and Ohlberg 2020). Given China's willingness to play the "long game," some commentators worry that its real strategic intent is to set the conditions for more assertive behavior and demands in the future. For example, Robinson (2013) suggests that China is playing a "long con" in the Arctic, "lulling target states into a sense of security, commercial benefit, and complacency." The desire for northern Indigenous governments to secure funding for expensive and risky mining projects that hold out the promise of employment for local residents and revenue streams for Indigenous rights-holders make China an attractive potential partner or source of capital. Are northern governments and communities equipped to discern the nonconventional security threats associated with such partnerships? Do these risks outweigh the economic benefits of attracting Chinese capital to the Canadian North, or can they be managed to bring about the "win-win" scenarios that China's Arctic policy and Chinese investors promote?

Concerns about Chinese interests in securing access to natural resources in the Canadian Arctic made national media headlines in 2020, when Chinese state-owned Shandong Gold Mining attempted to acquire the Hope Bay mine in the Kitikmeot region of Nunavut. Shandong made a $230 million purchase offer for TMAC Resources in June 2020, expecting a deal to be finalized by February 2021. Instead, the Government of Canada ordered a national security review pursuant to the Investment Canada Act in October. In November 2020, retired Major-General David Fraser urged the federal government to reject the Chinese offer based on security concerns. "This thing has a port attached to it," he highlighted, noting that China's Arctic white paper had affirmed that country's intentions to become "a near-Arctic power." Acquiring the mine would secure "them actual Arctic access." Drawing attention to Chinese activities in the South China Sea "to extend their area of influence," he asked, "What's to stop them, once they get squatter's rights and get into this port, from doing the same thing up here?" (Fife and Chase 2020). Highlighting that Chinese companies are required by law to spy for the Chinese government when asked, Fraser stated that inviting further Chinese investment into Canada's northern and Arctic resource sector blurs the lines between economic competition and national security. Ultimately, the company reported on December 22 that the federal government had rejected Shandong's proposal on security grounds, which University of Alberta professor Gordon Houlden (Strong 2020) interpreted as sending a "strong negative signal" to China about future investments in Canada's northern mineral resources.

Conclusion

The Canadian Arctic has long been perceived as a region apart from the rest of the world, isolated by geography, climate, its vast frozen approaches, and (during the Cold War) superpower politics. As such, the region has never served as a major point of ingress: the maritime and land borders are vast and lightly guarded, and international trade has been confined to a few ports and land crossings. Controlling access has long been a question of monitoring air and maritime approaches (both surface and subsurface). In this light, the task of aerospace and maritime domain awareness has typically fallen to the Canadian military rather than to police or border services.

Nowadays, the situation is changing. This century has brought a shift toward recognition of a broad range of unconventional security threats facing the Arctic. Melting sea ice has begun to open the region to shipping (overwhelmingly destinational rather than transit shipping), and experts expect this trend to accelerate. While the ultimate consequences of this melt remain controversial and unknowable owing to the complicated, non-linear dynamics at play, commentators and government analysts generally anticipate an increase in foreign commercial and pleasure vessels entering Canada's Arctic waters—but the timeline remains uncertain. Henceforth,

Canada expects more immigration, smuggling, criminal activities, and demand for search and rescue in the Arctic, but at levels far below those of the rest of the country. Managing these risks and threats in a proportionate, efficient, and effective manner will be increasingly challenging in light of human and physical geographical realities that make Canada's Northern territories different than its southern provinces. The Canadian Arctic is a region where competition dominates, but also where specialized cooperation between the military and other agencies has been strong in areas such as search and rescue, the environment, and human security; coordination and cooperation may have to expand to policing and border services.

REFERENCES

Anselmi, Elaine. 2020. "New Report Illustrates Increase in Arctic Shipping. Arctic Council Study Shows Rise in Vessel Traffic from 2013 to 2019." *Nunatsiavut News*, April 6, 2020. https://nunatsiaq.com/stories/article/report-shows-25-per-cent-increase-in-arctic-shipping/

Antsygina, E., L. L. M. Heininen, and N. Komendantova. 2020. "A Comparative Study on the Cooperation in the Arctic Ocean and the South China Sea." In *The Arctic. Current Issues and Challenges*, edited by Oleg S. Pokrovsky, Sergey N. Kirpotin, and Alexander I. Malov, 83–107. Hauppauge, NY: Nova Science Publishers.

Arctic Council. 2019. *Arctic Shipping Status Report*. Protection of the Arctic Maritime Environment Working Group. https://pame.is/projects/arctic-marine-shipping/arctic-shipping-status-reports

Arctic Council 2020. "PAME 2020 Arctic Ship Traffic Data—ASTD." https://pame.is/index.php/projects/arctic-marine-shipping/astd

Arctic Council. 2021. "Pan Arctic Report on Gender Equality in the Arctic Sustainable Development Working Group." Phase III. https://arcticgenderequality.network/phase-3/pan-arctic-report

Arctic Economic Council. 2021. "Maritime Transportation Working Group." https://arcticeconomiccouncil.com/workinggroups/maritime-transportation-working-group/

Bankes, Nigel. 2020. "Arctic Ocean Management and Indigenous Peoples: Recent Legal Developments." *The Yearbook of Polar Law Online* 11, no. 1: 81–120.

Barnes, Justin, Heather Exner-Pirot, Lassi Heininen, and P. Whitney Lackenbauer, eds. 2021. *China's Arctic Engagement: Following the Polar Silk Road to Greenland and Russia*. Peterborough/Akureyri: North American and Arctic Defence and Security Network Engage Series/Arctic Yearbook.

Brady, Anne-Marie. 2017. *China as a Great Polar Power*. Cambridge, UK: Cambridge University Press.

Brady, Anne-Marie. 2020. *China as a Rising Polar Power: What It Means for Canada*. Ottawa: Macdonald Laurier Institute.

Byers, Michael. 2013. *International Law and the Arctic*. Cambridge: Cambridge University Press.

Campbell, Robin. 2015. "An Introduction to Inuit Rights and Arctic Sovereignty." *Law Now*, May 7. http://www.lawnow.org/introduction-inuit-rights-arctic-sov ereignty/

Canada Border Services Agency (CBSA). 2020. "Arctic Shipping Electronic Commercial Clearances Program." https://www.cbsa-asfc.gc.ca/publications/cn-ad /cn20-16-eng.html

Canadian Broadcasting Corp. (CBC) News. 2015. "Fraser Border Hours Reduced for Travellers Entering Yukon." http://www.cbc.ca/news/canada/north/fraser -border-hours-reduced-for-travellers-entering-yukon-1.3015860

Caron, Fred. 2017. "Report on First Nation Border Crossing Issues." https://www .rcaanc-cirnac.gc.ca/eng/1506622719017/1609249944512

Charron, Andrea. 2015. "Canada, the Arctic, and NORAD: Status Quo or New Ball Game?" *International Journal* 70, no. 2: 215–31.

Charron, Andrea. 2019. "Canada, the United States and Arctic Security." In *Canada's Arctic Agenda: Into the Vortex*, edited by John Higginbotham and Jennifer Spence, 93–102. Waterloo, ON: Centre for International Governance Innovation.

Chircop, Aldo. 2020. "The Polar Code and the Arctic Marine Environment: Assessing the Regulation of the Environmental Risks of Shipping." *International Journal of Marine and Coastal Law* 35, no. 3: 533–69.

Crown Indigenous Relations and Northern Affairs Canada (CIRNAC). 2019. "Canada's Arctic and Northern Policy Framework." https://www.rcaanccirnac .gc.ca/eng/1560523306861/1560523330587

Dawson, Jackie, Margaret E. Johnston, and Emma J. Stewart. 2014. "Governance of Arctic Expedition Cruise Ships in a Time of Rapid Environmental and Economic Change." *Ocean & Coastal Management* 89: 88–99.

Dean, Ryan, and P. Whitney Lackenbauer. 2020. "China's Arctic Gambit? Contemplating Possible Strategies." NAADSN. *Strategic Perspectives*, April 23. https:// www.naadsn.ca/wp-content/uploads/2020/04/20-apr-23-China-Arctic-Gamb it-RD-PWL-1.pdf

Department of National Defence (DND). 2017. *Strong Secure Engaged: Canada's Defence Policy.* http://dgpaapp.forces.gc.ca/en/canada-defence-policy/docs/cana da-defence-policy-report.pdf

Ekos. 2011. *Rethinking the Top of the World: Arctic Security Public Opinion Survey.* http://www.ekospolitics.com/articles/2011-01-25ArcticSecurityReport.pdf

Ekos. 2015. *Rethinking the Top of the World: Arctic Security Public Opinion Survey*, vol. 2. http://gordonfoundation.ca/app/uploads/2017/03/APO_PowerPoint_Volu me-2_WEB.pdf

Everett, Karen. 2017. "National Border Management Polices and Their Effect on Regional Trade: A Study of the Yukon Exporting Industry." In *The Networked North: Borders and Borderlands in the Canadian Arctic Region*, edited by Heather Nicol and P. Whitney Lackenbauer, 132–45. Waterloo, ON: Centre on Foreign Policy and Federalism. https://biglobalization.org/sites/default/files/content-at tachments/networked-north-2017_0.pdf

Exner-Pirot, Heather. 2012. *Human Security in the Arctic: The Foundation of Regional Cooperation.* Toronto: Munk School of Global Affairs–Walter & Duncan Gordon Foundation Arctic Security Programme.

Fife, Robert, and Steven Chase. 2017. "Chinese Ship Making First Voyage through Canada's Northwest Passage." *Globe and Mail,* August 31.

Fife, Robert, and Steven Chase. 2020. "Retired General Urges Rejection of Chinese Takeover of Arctic Gold Mine." *Globe and Mail,* 30 November. https://www.theglobeandmail.com/politics/article-retired-general-urges-rejection-of-chinese-takeover-of-arctic-gold/

Gjørv Hoogensen, G., D. Bazely, M. Goloviznina, and A. Tanentzap, eds. 2013. *Environmental and Human Security in the Arctic.* Abingdon, UK: Routledge.

Government of Canada. n.d. Beaufort Sea Partnership. https://www.beaufortseapartnership.ca/

Greaves, Wilfrid. 2012. "For Whom, From What? Canada's Arctic Policy and the Narrowing of Human Security." *International Journal* 67, no. 1: 219–40.

Hamilton, Clive, and Mareike Ohlberg. 2020. *Hidden Hand: Exposing How the Chinese Communist Party Is Reshaping the World.* Sydney: Hardie Grant Books.

Heininen, Lassi, and Heather N. Nicol. 2007. "Security Issues in the Circumpolar North." In *Borders, Borderlands, and Border Security: North America and the European Union in Comparative Perspective,* edited by Emmanuel Brunet-Jailly, 117–64. Ottawa: University of Ottawa Press.

Heininen, Lassi, and Heather N. Nicol. 2017. *Climate Change from a Northern Point of View.* Waterloo, ON: Centre on Foreign Policy and Federalism.

Huebert, Rob. 2019. "Canada and NATO in the Arctic: Responding to Russia?" In *Canada's Arctic Agenda: Into the Vortex,* edited by John Higginbotham and Jennifer Spence, 85–92. Waterloo, ON: Centre for International Governance Innovation.

Inuit Circumpolar Council (ICC). 2009. "A Circumpolar Inuit Declaration on Sovereignty in the North." http://iccalaska.org/wp-icc/wp-content/uploads/2016/01/Signed-Inuit-Sovereignty-Declaration-11x17.pdf

Inuit Circumpolar Council (ICC). 2014. *The Sea Ice Never Stops. Circumpolar Inuit Reflections on Sea Ice Use and Shipping in Inuit Nunaat.* https://oaarchive.arctic-council.org/bitstream/handle/11374/1478/SDWG_INUITAMSA_Doc1_Circumpolar_Inuit_Reflections_Sea_Ice_Shipping_AC_SAO_CA04.pdf?sequence=1

Inuit Tapiriit Kanatami (ITK). 2014. *Social Determinants of Inuit Health in Canada.* https://itk.ca/wp-content/uploads/2016/07/ITK_Social_Determinants_Report.pdf

Inuit Tapiriit Kanatami (ITK). 2017. "Nilliajut 2: Inuit Perspectives on the Northwest Passage Shipping and Marine Issues." Ottawa: ITK.

Johnston, M., J. Dawson, E. De Souza, and E. J. Stewart. 2017. "Management Challenges for the Fastest Growing Marine Shipping Sector in Arctic Canada: Pleasure Crafts." *Polar Record* 53, no. 1: 67–78.

Keevil, Genesee. 2010. "Illegal Yukon Worker Gets Excluded." *Yukon News,* 28 July. http://www.yukon-news.com/news/illegal-yukon-worker-gets-excluded

Keskitalo, ECH. 2004. *Negotiating the North Negotiating the Arctic: The Construction of an International Region.* London: Routledge.

Kikkert, Peter, and P. Whitney Lackenbauer. 2020. *Using Civil-Military Operations to Expand and Deepen Relationships with Northern Communities—Examples from Alaska and Australia.* NADSN. https://www.naadsn.ca/wp-content/uploads/2020/08/2020-jul-Kikkert-Lackenbauer-Civ-Mil-Northern-NAADSN.pdf

Kikkert, P., P. W. Lackenbauer, and A. Pedersen. 2020a. "Kitikmeot Roundtable on Search and Rescue: Summary Report / Qitiqmiuni Katimatjutauyuq Qiniqhiayinit Annaktinillu—Naunaitkutat." Report from a Workshop Hosted at the Canadian High Arctic Research Station (CHARS) in Cambridge Bay, Nunavut, January 31 and February 1, 2020. http://Kitikmeotsar.ca

Kikkert, P., P. W. Lackenbauer, and A. Pedersen. 2020b. "Kitikmeot Roundtable on SAR: General Report and Findings." Report from a Workshop Hosted at the Canadian High Arctic Research Station (CHARS) in Cambridge Bay, Nunavut, January 31 and February 1, 2020. http://Kitikmeotsar.ca

Kikkert, P., P. W. Lackenbauer, and A. Pedersen. 2020c. "Kitikmeot Roundtable on SAR: Mass Rescue Tabletop Exercise Report." Report from a Workshop Hosted at the Canadian High Arctic Research Station (CHARS) in Cambridge Bay, Nunavut, January 31 and February 1, 2020. http://Kitikmeotsar.ca

Lackenbauer, P. Whitney, and Adam Lajeunesse. 2016. "The Canadian Armed Forces in the Arctic: Building Appropriate Capabilities." *Journal of Military and Strategic Studies* 16, no. 4: 7–66.

Lackenbauer, P. Whitney, Adam Lajeunesse, James Manicom, and Frederic Lasserre. 2018. *China's Arctic Ambitions and What They Mean for Canada*. Calgary: University of Calgary Press.

Lackenbauer, P. Whitney, Suzanne Lalonde, and Elizabeth Riddell-Dixon. 2020. *Canada and the Maritime Arctic: Boundaries, Shelves, and Waters*. Peterborough, ON: North American and Arctic Defence and Security Network. NAADSN. https://www.naadsn.ca/wp-content/uploads/2020/03/CanadaMaritimeArctic -PWL-SL-ERD-2020.pdf

Lajeunesse, Adam, and P. Whitney Lackenbauer, eds. 2017. *Canadian Armed Forces Arctic Operations, 1945–2015: Historical and Contemporary Lessons Learned*. Fredericton, NB: Gregg Centre for the Study of War and Society.

Landriault, Mathieu, Andrew Chater, Elana Wilson Rowe, and P. Whitney Lackenbauer. 2020. *Governing Complexity in the Arctic Region*. Abingdon, UK: Routledge.

Lasserre, Frédéric, and P. L. Têtu. 2013. "The Cruise Tourism Industry in the Canadian Arctic: Analysis of Activities and Perceptions of Cruise Ship Operators." *Polar Record* 51, no. 1: 24–38.

Nickels, Scot, and Chris Furgal. 2005. *Unikkaaqatigiit: Putting the Human Face on Climate Change*. Ottawa: ITK.

Nicol, Heather N. 2018. "Rescaling Borders of Investment: The Arctic Council and the Economic Development Policies." *Journal of Borderlands Studies* 33, no. 2: 225–38.

Nicol, Heather N., and Andrew Chater. 2021. *North American Arctic Borders: A World of Change?* Ottawa: University of Ottawa Press.

Nicol, Heather, and P. Whitney Lackenbauer, eds. 2017. *The Networked North: Borders and Borderlands in the Canadian Arctic Region*. Waterloo, ON: Borders in Globalization/Centre on Foreign Policy and Federalism. http://www.biglo balization.org/sites/default/files/content-attachments/networked-north-2017 _0.pdf

Nicol, Heather N., Adam Lajeunesse, P. Whitney Lackenbauer, and Karen Everett. 2019. "Regional Border Security Management in the Territorial North." In

The North American Arctic: Themes in Regional Security, edited by Dwayne Ryan Menezes and Heather N. Nicol, 134–54. London: UCL Press.

Nicol, Heather N., and Joel Plouffe. 2014. "Canada-Denmark: The Lincoln Sea." In *Border Disputes: A Global Encyclopedia*, vol. 2: *Positional Disputes*, edited by E. Brunet-Jailly. Santa Barbara, CA: ABC-Clio.

Peng, J., and N. Wegge. 2014. "China and the Law of the Sea: Implications for Arctic Governance." *Polar Journal* 4, no. 2: 287–305.

Perry, Michael. 2019. "'That Happens Up There?' Human Trafficking and Security in the North American Arctic." In *The North American Arctic: Themes in Regional Security*, edited by Dwayne Ryan Menezes and Heather N. Nicol, 260–88. London: UCL Press.

Pic, Pauline, Julie Babin, Frédéric Lasserre, Linyan Huang, and Kristin Bartenstein. 2021. "The Polar Code and Canada's Regulations on Arctic Navigation: Shipping Companies' Perceptions of the New Legal Environment." *Polar Journal* 11, no. 1: 1–23.

Robinson, Roger W. 2013. "China's 'Long Con' in the Arctic Must Be Countered." *Ottawa Citizen*, September 14.

Strong, Walter. 2020. "Ottawa Blocks Chinese Takeover of Nunavut Gold Mine Project After National Security Review." *CBC News*, December 22. https://www.cbc.ca/news/canada/north/canada-china-tmac-1.5851305

Tai, Ray T. H., Nathaniel S. Pearre, and Shih-Ming Kao. 2015. "Analysis and Potential Alternatives for the Disputed South China Sea from Ocean Governance in the Polar Regions." *Coastal Management* 43, no. 6: 609–27.

Young, Huguette. 2010. "The Arctic: The New Eldorado." *Americas Quarterly*. http://www.americasquarterly.org/node/1684

Yukon Government. 2015. Department of Tourism and Culture. "Yukon Tourism Visitation Report December 2015." http://www.tc.gov.yk.ca/pdf/12-dec-2015-indicator-report.pdf

Yukon Government. 2016. Department of Tourism and Culture. "Yukon Tourism Visitation Report December 2016." http://www.tc.gov.yk.ca/pdf/12-Dec2016-indicator-report.pdf

Conclusion

Emmanuel Brunet-Jailly, Todd Hataley, and Christian Leuprecht

At the core of this project was the goal of understanding border security issues not just along the boundary line, but away from the border. What are the roles of culture, trade, and politics in border security arrangements? Is the governance of those security arrangements best explained in terms of center-periphery relations, or is it more a matter of varying circumstances in different contexts? The seven case studies presented in this volume address these questions, with a particular focus on understanding the shared border regions of Canada and the United States.

These seven chapters detail the nature of both intergovernmental/international and vertical/horizontal relationships across the boundary line. Our particular interests focus on the role and influence of US and Canadian federal, regional, provincial, and nongovernmental structures in matters of security; is there primacy of federal security agencies in the implementation and management of cross-border security relationships, or are other factors are at play in determining this relationship?

As suggested in the introduction, the literature led us to assume that the state-to-state power relationship and the rationality of trade and market relations had determining effects on border security. Indeed, we assumed that market rationalism would contradict the statist views and territorialist imperatives that dominate the social science literature about borders and center-periphery relationships. The implementation of free trade in the 1990s, and, as documented by Clarkson (2001), the decentralization of economic and innovation policies to the provincial and regional levels in Canada, have strengthened the role of trade in driving markets across the boundary line. Today, regional economies straddle the boundary, and so does the governance of security, following the governance scales and nested forms of those trading relationships.

The conclusions presented in this volume are contrary to those of much of the Canada–US border literature, and the work is counterintuitive in that it asserts the role of market forces in weaving networked relationships among security agencies. The scales of coordination, cooperation, and collaboration[1] are influenced, even determined, by transportation infrastructures, as well as social and cultural relations, resulting in spatially diverse and nested forms of security governance straddling the boundary. This diversity is adaptive to the economic and social distinctions of each cross-border region. Our seven local and regional cross-border regimes form specific social as well as economic relationships, which are tremendously important to borderland security. As suggested by Brunet-Jailly (2012), when looking at trade, these relationships shape and structurally influence the bottom-up governmental and nongovernmental networks that straddle the boundary line. As suggested by Chen (2005), Ohmae (1990, 1995), Brunet-Jailly (2012, 2007, 2022b), and Sohn (2020), unique economic regions straddling the Canada–United States boundary line have flourished along with cross-border, regionally specific security programs.

These are singular regional economies with particular border security governance needs and scales; government agencies have adapted and do not implement a single top-down federal border security model. In Sohn's words, they adapted because borders became "resources rather than barriers," and because relationships activate specific "regional resources." Further, driven by economic, social, and cultural interactions, each border region developed its own original security regime and scale; the ultimate result was multiscalar, nested border security.

The tensions between center and periphery and concurrent border functions and politics are particularly salient. These border functions and politics reinforce the singularity of the security of each border region. Each chapter provides significant evidence about peripheral influence in the development of regional border security governance. The top-down functionality of federally dominated security policies, insofar as they interfere with the diversity of trade flows, has adapted to regional culture and economic and social forms, resulting in different security governance at particular scales for each cross-border region. Indeed, they adapt under pressure from the bottom up, and from the horizontal nature of the politics of cross-border relations. In the end, each of our seven case studies contributes a singular lesson about the relative push and pull of culture, social interactions, and market forces on vertical/intergovernmental and horizontal/international networked relations and the resulting transboundary scale.

The following section reviews those regional cross-border security governance arrangements, beginning with the Pacific Northwest, crossing the continent to reach the Atlantic region, and concluding with a review of Canada's North (Nunavut, Northwest Territories, and the Yukon) and Alaska in the United States.

Canada's Multiscalar Borders

Each chapter reinforces how thinking about borders in conventional terms is increasingly being challenged by the nature of cross-border flows, and describes the challenges state agencies face when coming to grips with evolving transborder flows that are themselves part of broader regional, continental, and global flows.

The book shows how ideas and conversations about the border cluster by region, and how those ideas and narratives drive regional differentiation. Border concerns in the Prairie/Midwest region are preoccupied with agricultural trade and the idea that security is embedded within that trade framework. Threats to border security are quite different in the Ontario/ Great Lakes region, with movements of people and flows of goods that differ qualitatively and quantitively from cross-border flows elsewhere. These regional differences give rise to distinct regional borderlands whose attributes are locally contingent. A cooperative border, for instance, is exemplified by both institutionalized and informal cross-border mechanisms and partnerships. Different cross-border needs, values, and expectations explain why local cooperative arrangements are nuanced. They are detailed in each of the regional chapters and summarized below.

Table 9.1 summarizes the attributes of all the regions. All border regions are characterized by both cooperation and competition, and by economic imperatives, and all have some form of multilevel governance.

Table 9.1 identifies tendencies in interregional border governance models; it is a conceptual representation to make certain processes easier to understand, define, and distinguish. Without detailing the specific differences that inform these ideal types, table 9.1 highlights the nuances that emerge from each chapter, the distinguishing features of which probably inform interregional distinctions in governance models for other border dyads across the world.

TABLE 9.1. Interregional Border Governance Models

Border Region	Border Arrangement	Preponderant Attributes
British Columbia Cascadia Pacific	Collaborative: Multilevel	Structured and/or institutionalized multilevel border governance across three levels of domestic and international government. Strong public/private partnerships. Border security is defined across numerous dimensions, including but not limited to the environment, health, and economics.
Alberta Northwest	Cooperative: Multilevel public/ private	Border management includes stakeholders from various levels of government and the private sector. Borderlands and border stakeholders extend well beyond the traditional border regions and include stakeholders in other provinces.
Prairies (Saskatchewan and Manitoba) Midwest	Collaborative: Public/private	Collaboration on border functions across public and private sectors, but less structured at local governmental levels. Border functions frequently take place away from the border and are conducted by technical professionals.
Ontario Great Lakes	Collaborative/Competitive: Economic	Across the region, Ontario strives to carve out a comparative advantage, in competition with Québec and adjoining US states. Structured cross-border governance across public and private levels.
Québec Eastern Seaboard	Coordinated/Competitive: Cultural	For Québec the border demarcates a distinct linguistic and cultural space and border image that place a premium on identity and values.
Atlantic New England	Cooperative: Historic	Provinces and US states have a long history, predating the current international boundary, of extensive cooperation on both sides of the border and across the border. However, flows are light, which makes it easier to reach consensus.
Territorial North	Competitive: Emerging	Borders are not clearly delineated and are in flux due to climate change. Borders are contested. Border stakeholders are emerging, and the dominant power is not yet determined.

TABLE 9.1—*Continued*

Border Region	Border Arrangement	Preponderant Attributes
Overseas borders	Cooperative: Nonterritorial	The Arctic Council is effectively a nonterritorial mechanism to manage borders in the polar region where agreement is easier to reach due to limited flows and broad agreement on environmental protection and search and rescue.

By dint of geography, British Columbia's connections have traditionally operated north-south more so than west-east. When the province was initially settled, the North American Cordillera mountains made east-west movement difficult and encouraged north-south contacts. Connections with the United States were also encouraged by links along the continent's west coast with the Pacific Ocean, which facilitated the flow of goods and mobility of people by sea rather than by land. With most major cities in British Columbia located close to the southern border with the United States, far from other major Canadian urban centers, the north-south linkages became the source of British Columbia's prosperity. The contemporary border between British Columbia and the United States has evolved to include deeply entrenched collaborative links across multiple levels of government and civil society. Those multilevel linkages, which exist to lesser degrees in other Canadian border regions (with the exception of the Ontario/Great Lakes region), are the dominant attribute of the border in this region (Brunet-Jailly 2022a). Muller et al.'s chapter on British Columbia details well-established cross-border relationships at three levels of government, across economic and social spectrums and a broad range of issue areas.

The chapter on the border between Alberta/Northwest and corresponding provincial and international borders illustrates the impact of border policy on events that may transpire far from the actual border. The politics of pipelines and the extraction of fossil fuels, both international and domestic, have shaped the modern border as significantly as historical demographic and economic patterns. Settlement patterns dominated by a historic influx of American immigrants, oil development, and pipeline politics have shaped the cooperative development of the Alberta regional border. Like British Columbia, Alberta has carved out strong north-south ties, but they have been more limited, and they are a function historic, cultural, and economic design, not geography.

Compared to other regions, the development of the Prairie/Midwest border region has been disproportionately influenced by history. A combination of immigration patterns, strained relations with Central Canada, and what have long been perceived as unfair national policies regarding resource extraction dating back to Sir John A. Macdonald's National Policy produced a sense a western alienation and independence, which in turn fostered strong ties to American states to the south. Hataley, Leuprecht, and Green's chapter paints a picture of an isolated, sparsely populated Prairie/Midwest region where border security is closely tied historically to agricultural development, and more recently to resource exploitation. The regional border regime is characterized by strong public-private collaborative partnerships between border stakeholders, along with a border-management system that is often located away from the boundary line.

A dense array of demographic, economic, and environmental factors distinguishes the Ontario Great Lakes border region from all others along the Canada–United States boundary. The regional trade volume, the size of the regional population, and the sheer number of border stakeholders on both sides of the border create an unmatched degree of competition. Such levels of horizontal and vertical competition, both domestic and international, result in a security framework marked by collaboration across multiple sectors. To manage Canada's most important trade and security relationship effectively, border stakeholders have a vested interest in both efficiency and security. Accordingly, the number of partners and degree of complexity in border policy far exceeds that found in Canada's other regions.

For historical, linguistic, and cultural reasons, Québec has frequently claimed a distinct international status and role for itself in its relationship with the federal government. In an effort to be recognized as a credible and responsible actor in international relations, the province has progressively made security a linchpin of provincial government policy. While there is continuity across many issue areas, in recent years Québec's authorities have changed the discourses by securitizing many political issues. In other words, it's not that the issues themselves have evolved, so much as the way they have been politicized, which reflects the growing risks and challenges associated with their transnationalization across the Québec/Eastern Seaboard borderland. On the one hand, this raises awareness of the implications of transnational movement for Québec's security, which then drives and legitimates transborder cooperation and investment. On the other hand, Québec strives to affirm that it is a loyal and reliable ally to both the state and federal levels in the United States, and that it takes North American challenges to heart.

As on the west coast of Canada, in the Atlantic/New England border region geography is a major determinant of patterns. The region's economic fortunes and the viability of communities are inextricably tied to the role of Atlantic seaports as border nodes. The regional importance of seaports for the local economy has resulted in a high degree of layered and cooperative security transborder integration. Atlantic seaports compete among themselves for a finite number of goods to pass into North America. To compete, port authorities must invest in port and inland transportation infrastructure and relationships that enable transborder flows, which sometimes frustrates federal requirements.

The border in the Canadian North is only now coming into its own. Long ignored as a border region, with the opening of sea lanes and access to resources in the Arctic polar region, interest in managing emerging borders and the functions they perform is growing across the circumpolar region. This process begins with the need to agree on where the Arctic borders actually begin and end. Canada's claim on the Arctic transborder region is contested by global powers such as the United States and China, with geopolitics—rather than mere binationalism or bilateralism—superimposing itself as an arbiter on adjudicating transborder relationships across the Pole. In contrast to Canada's other border regions, nontraditional actors, notably Indigenous groups, and nontraditional threats, such as climate change and food insecurity, play an outsized role, as Nicol et al. highlight. Those factors are progressively shaping a different approach to transborder coordination policy in the North, quite unlike the way other regional borders in North America function.

The center-periphery and traditional border-studies literatures point to border policy set by central/federal governments that have the culture and power to implement uniform policy across the length of Canada's boundary with the United States. The contributions in this book show, however, that the reality is more of a dialectic. Federal policy interacts with the ideas and initiatives of local and regional stakeholders who manage local, regional, and sometimes continental movements. Power, as a variable in border policy, becomes dispersed between regional governments and private border stakeholders. As detailed in the following section, the resulting synthesis adds nuance to federal border policy with regional interpretations that reflect varied interests, values, and norms.

Regional and Multiscalar Borders in North America

Whereas early studies treated the Canada–United States border as a static and descriptive geographic phenomenon, today the border is viewed as dynamic and variable. Early scholars such as Boggs (1940), Whittlesey (1944), Jones (1945), and Fisher (1957) maintained a state-centric view of borders as rigid lines of defense, created by humans and subject to change through human interaction. These initial studies, although acknowledging the human impact on the border, were remiss in exploring the border per se and its underlying bordering processes as an object of analysis. A revival in border scholarship in the early 1980s gave way to new approaches to understanding borders, beyond the border as merely a static line (e.g., Strassoldo and Delli Zotti 1982; Sack 1986; Paasi 1996, 1999; Brunet-Jailly 2005). Scholarship on the Canada–US border during this period, however, remained firmly rooted in the view of the border as a mere component of larger issues of federal politics, such as immigration and trade.

Statist views, such as those presented by Charles Doran in *Forgotten Partnership* (1984), laid the foundations of international relations research on the diverse dynamics of cross-border relationships within international politics, by conceptually specifying the "psychological-cultural," "trade-commercial," and "political-strategic" dimensions of the Canada–US relationship. This approach has been highly influential, inspiring decades of scholarship on Canada–US relations, including very recent works by Geoffrey Hale and Monica Gattinger on the Canada–United States border (e.g., Hale 2012; Gattinger and Hale 2010). Yet *Forgotten Partnership* differs from this volume insofar as it stressed the "borderless" character of Canada–US relations, rather than the regional character of cross-border relations distinguished in this volume. Doran emphasized "Canada in the world" (Doran 1984) in the context of NAFTA and NATO. The dominant paradigms this volume uses to analyze binational and bilateral relationships differ markedly from the center-periphery, statist, and methodological nationalism approaches. The latter perspective examined international security from a vantage point where Canada and the United States were clearly on the same side, and in consequence, the border virtually disappeared. In fact, Doran's perspective purposely downplayed the border in terms of international trade; it was as if the border had disappeared so that goods and services and people could move back and forth in a fashion that was unimpeded—that is, "efficient."

This book, by contrast, describes Canada's border as reflecting a set of regionally differentiated practices and processes shaped by complex connections with the United States and other global entities and actors. It analyzes how bordering practices vary according to regional histories, geographies, and interests. Although this is the case for states across the globe, the novelty of this book is that it conveys an alternative method for maximizing the self-interest of Canada, and for maximizing the dual interests in North America of both Canada and the United States. Canada's borders are regional in character, dispersed throughout trade corridors, supply chains, seaports, food-producing communities, and international organizations. The spatiality of border functions, spanning the boundary line, makes border management and especially security functions all the more difficult and highlights the importance of nonconventional border management activities to achieve coherent policy. The book manifests the extent to which traditional notions of border security no longer reflect traditional state-to-state security considerations and power relationships, but rather are influenced by regional considerations and narratives.

With the advent of free trade and the signing of the NAFTA agreement, and the impetus of 9/11, the US–Canada relationship has morphed into a continental security community whose hallmark is the extent to which mutual coordination, cooperation, and collaboration have led to an intentional shift of the joint border away from the actual borderline. However, that shift had to reconcile an inherent tension between the imperatives of free trade and "economic globalization"; both continental and "territorial security" at the US–Canada border (Alper and Loucky 2017) frame US–Canadian border cooperation as a compromise between disparate national interests, in which Canada is primarily concerned about trade while the United States is more concerned about terrorism and irregular migration. The outcome of this bilateral cross-border cooperation reflects a compromise of ideal sovereignty and pragmatism, one that is frequently managed from a position of indifference. Instead of focusing on security at the joint border, the United States and Canada have taken a continental approach to building a comprehensive security system around common interests related to the border as manifest in policing, counterterrorism, intelligence, and defense to detect, disrupt, and deter threats.

However, borders are not necessarily located where we might expect, and our chapters on the North American borders illustrate this new counterintuitive phenomenon. Border security has been re-articulated and redefined. Globalization, security, trade, migration, and the redefining of North American space have changed transnational spaces. Borders are no longer simply territorial but are now both territorial and a-territorial

(Balibar 2002; Konrad and Brunet-Jailly 2019), with specialized functions adapting to trade flows and mobilities.

The observation that borders are multifaceted and have multiple and diverse meanings is foundational to the evolution of contemporary border theory. This led Brunet-Jailly (2005) to call for an interdisciplinary approach to developing a theory of borders. Mignolo and Tlostanova (2006) echoed this approach, arguing that borders were more than simply geographic, but also political and cultural, representing different groups of people, languages, and established relationships. Newman (2006) identified some of the problems raised by an interdisciplinary approach to understanding borders, including interdisciplinary confusion—not understanding, intentionally or otherwise, the language of other disciplines. Rumford (2006) was among the first to note the nonspatial nature of borders and the importance of moving toward a model of borders that included nonspatial as well as spatial characteristics. Rumford's approach to theorizing borders rested on an understanding of mobility and the networks surrounding borders. By contrast, Parker and Adler-Nissen (2012) suggested that borders remain the purview of states, and that any border theory had to reflect the dynamic and differentiated choices made by state actors. Cooper and Perkins (2012) posited that institutional rules set the context for border actors, be they individuals involved in "borderwork" or state actors setting border policy. Returning to the idea of borders as multifunctional, complex entities, Laine (2016) and Burkner (2019) suggested examining borders as multiscalar and dynamic phenomena, influenced by agents and structural forces.

Two consistent themes reappear in the quest to develop a theory of borders: first, borders are dynamic, insofar as bordering processes are ongoing as borders adjust to agent demands and actions and structural forces; second, borders are not geographically bound, but rather can be found in multiple locations on and away from the boundary line. The studies in this book of the Canada–US border and its constituent regional borders illustrate both themes: the bordering process is in constant movement, and processes have shifted beyond the border. On the one hand, the studies reinforce the extent to which borders are human constructs whose function is to exert control. On the other hand, the studies reify that borders are a social phenomenon, shaped by social processes, contingent on institutions, identity, and interests, but at the same time dynamic to the degree that they are subject to ideas formed both *within and beyond* those constraints; that is, they are amenable to local and regional politics.

As detailed further below, the findings in the seven chapters of this book point to the regionalization of bordering policies, the functional tensions between the unifying vertical/federal border policies, and the politics of place and ideas resulting from horizontal/regional/borderland tensions at the periphery of both states.

Multiscalar and Nested Borders

Bordering is fundamentally a social process: humans bound space "to affect, influence, or control people, phenomena and relationships, by delimiting and asserting control over a geographic area" (Sack 1986, 19). Human existence is a function of territory, which makes it possible to control access and to influence human behavior. Bounded territory is a means of creating and maintaining social order, a context that gives meaning and experience to the world. The border, then, is a differentiator that reflects and influences human attitudes and ideas, which the border encloses, dissects, and segregates. The concept of territoriality has significant explanatory power. Territories are "socially constructed forms of spatial relations and their effects depend on who is controlling whom for what purpose" (Sack 1986, 216).

That generalization, however, does not apply only at the level of the nation-state but at the substate level as well, especially in federations such as Canada, which are characterized by self-rule and shared rule. The regional borders of substate jurisdictions such as provinces and states have distinctive characteristics that reflect the interests, values, and norms of the local communities. Local ideas are manifest in local bordering practices, which reflect the communities they bound. At the periphery of states, at the international boundary, regional and national borders coincide to generate a synthesis of interests, values, and norms, which expand, with preclearance, beyond the territoriality of the state.

At all levels, the ideas that inform the border are dynamic because, as discussed in the introduction, center-periphery relationships are also dynamic and in flux; they concurrently account for the changing nature of politics and functions in peripheral regions and in borderlands, resulting in multiscalar and nested border policies. The boundary line remains, but its meaning and relevance to bordering are in flux as it extends beyond the territoriality of the state. A theory of borders is premised on an explanation of change (Rumford 2006), and one approach to explaining why borders change is to study how national borders differ across regions while nonetheless holding together to bound an entire state.

Ideas influence the development of policy across both local and national policy groups (Carstensen and Schmidt 2016; Schmidt 2011; Beland and

Cox 2016). Actors influence one another, including border stakeholders from both the public and private sectors that give rise to multilevel border governance. Ideas assert themselves through persuasion, inducement, or imposition. Stakeholders decide how acceptable an idea is. At some point, someone proposed that cattle being transported between Saskatchewan and Montana be inspected away from the border, to make their movement across the border more efficient. Customs and border officials in both Canada and the United States, truck drivers, feedlot owners, cattle producers, and veterinarians all have some stake in that decision, albeit not an equal stake. At a local level, this idea would resonate in ranch country, but not in areas where no cattle are being produced. In short, the idea is significant for a subset of border actors, and the implementation becomes a regional project.

Local policy choices tend to be driven by the subset of pertinent local border stakeholders. However, some policy choices and ideas also matter across all subsets of border stakeholders. Local choices are necessarily constrained by and contingent on federal ones, since the parameters for border management fall under the remit of the federal government. Local actors thus have to assert their ideas within multilevel governance systems. As their power and influence vary, so does their ability to shape policy outcomes. The common denominator among regional borders that is also reflected in state border thus consists of policy outcomes and ideas with the greatest uptake across all subsets of border stakeholders. As illustrated in this book, Canada shares a border with the United States along with a subset of regional border areas whose policies are strongly influenced by local provincial jurisdictions and organizations and result from their cultural, social, and economic interactions—that is, the particulars of their own singular mobile individuals and flows of trade. The result is a series of nested borders of various scales that link local identity, politics, and political clout to local and regional territoriality, and link national identity to national territoriality, mobilities, and market flows.

Sack's theory, however, pertains only to geographic boundaries that are linked to territory. But with aterritorial borders on the rise, such as cargo and passenger preclearance locations outside of the bounded territory, geography is a significant limitation. Functionally, instead, the border can be explained as a zone for sorting, a location for control of mobility, independent of territory (Rumford 2006; Konrad and Brunet-Jailly 2019). Such aterritorial border functions can be performed in multiple locations, well inside or beyond the actual territory of the states. Contra Sack, this book shows that territoriality is not—or at least, is no longer—restricted to geography. Rather, it has become a function of ideas and policy choices that are acceptable to the subsets of border stakeholders who have been able to assert themselves. Territory and sovereignty are "decoupling" as a result (Longo 2017): more than ever, sovereignty is a construct, an idea manifest in the ability of a society, through institutions of government at the national or substate levels, to sort and control mobility and flows across national or regional boundary lines. The quality and quantity of sorting and control are ultimately a function of cooperative agreements among border stakeholders pertaining to regional or national conceptions of border policies. Regional border policies and ideas, then, are nested inside higher-order ideas, such as national sovereignty, which are articulated in laws and regulations mandating bordering agencies.

In sum, the contemporary literature on border studies posits change in borders as predominately a bottom-up process driven by local border stakeholders (Brunet-Jailly 2005; Kolossov 2005; Mignolo and Tlostanova 2006; Rumford 2006; Parker and Adler-Nissen 2012; Laine 2016; Burkner 2019). This proposition is confirmed by the findings in this book about the borders between the United States and Canada. Far from being limited to national governments or stakeholders, the bordering process consists of particular local stakeholders who formulate and articulate ideas that inform coordinating, cooperative, and collaborative policy processes and concurrent regulations and/or legislation.

The governance mechanisms and scales that inform such processes are both horizontal and vertical; it is a multilevel process, where some policy ideas carry more weight than others, either because they are accepted among border stakeholders, or because a privileged border stakeholder has sufficient power to impose certain preferences over groups that are more marginal in the border processes, such as Indigenous communities. As illustrated by our chapter on Canada's North, traditional Indigenous lands have been divided by modern, colonial borders, which has consequences for movement, settlement, and the use of resources such as water, fossil fuels, and forests. Considerations of Indigenous sovereignty thus have important implications for borders and call into question established concepts and approaches to security: the chapter on the Canadian North in particular highlights how prioritizing certain border and security interests makes Indigenous communities that span the colonial border less secure.

The Canada–United States border, then, is actually based on heterogeneous regional nested borderland policies operating at multiple scales and intensities that share a common denominator: high-level national border policies often have deleterious consequences for local border stakeholders. This complex system of multilevel transborder governance prevails because it provides border stakeholders—public, private, nonprofit, and international—with a higher-level framework of ideas about what the border represents, the functions it should perform, and how and where to perform those functions. Regional bordering processes are nested within and frequently contest this overarching framework, adapting the framework to singular local/regional needs. These processes reflect the power relationship between border stakeholders and the federal government, insofar as power is dispersed across horizontal and vertical axes in disparate ways. It is not always clear why federal-level policymaking may be dominant over regional/local subject-matter expertise or rational demand, or why regional and local concerns may dominate. Why some local solutions to border security issues take hold while others do not is a fruitful area for further research.

In terms of border policymaking, two observations in particular are consequential. First, the process is dialectical. Policy ideas are generated across a hierarchical spectrum, from the highest levels of government to street-level, nongovernmental actors. While it is unremarkable to see the hand of government actors in the making of border policy, this volume documents the extent of substate and nongovernmental actors' contribution to border policy. Second, through their expertise, substate and nongovernmental actors play a hitherto underappreciated role in implementing international agreements, and their local/regional implementation as functional arrangements makes the border more conducive to local stakeholder communities' needs, values, and expectations.

Local input into border policy is hardly unique to the Canada and the United States, but this border lends itself particularly well to the study of the disaggregated dynamics of local stakeholders at the regional level. Secure borders depend on some degree of cross-border cooperation that takes into account regionally and locally differentiated ideas, values, and interests. Since differentiated dynamics characterize border dyads elsewhere, the methodical approach taken in this volume is applicable and replicable elsewhere. If the quality and quantity of cross-border coordination, cooperation, and collaboration have a direct bearing on how open and secure a border is, then the framework that informs this study should lend itself to validating the open-border paradox: that borders are open and secure precisely when they are well-governed, insofar as they account for regional nuances, stakeholders, and power dynamics.

Note

1. The scales of coordination, cooperation, and collaboration are described as follows: coordination is characterized by shared information and communication and shared border goals. Cooperation builds on this through common behaviors and policy parallelism. Collaborative relationships are mature relationships with deep cross-border networks that help each partner achieve their respective border goals (Leuprecht et al. 2021).

REFERENCES

Alper, Don K., and James Loucky. 2017. "Canada-US Border Securitization: Implications for Binational Cooperation." *Canadian-American Public Policy* 72.

Balibar, Etienne. 2002. *Politics and the Other Scene*. London: Verso.

Beland, Daniel, and Robert Henry Cox. 2016. "Ideas as Coalition Magnets: Coalition Building, Policy Entrepreneurs and Power Relations." *Journal of European Public Policy* 23, no. 3: 428–45.

Boggs, S. Whitmore. 1940. *International Boundaries: A Study of Boundary Functions and Problems*. New York: Columbia University Press.

Brunet-Jailly, Emmanuel. 2005. "Theorizing Borders: An Interdisciplinary Approach." *Geopolitics* 10, no. 4: 633–49.

Brunet-Jailly, Emmanuel. 2007. *Borderlands, Comparing Border Security in North America and Europe*. Ottawa: University of Ottawa Press.

Brunet-Jailly, Emmanuel. 2012. "In the Increasingly Global Economy, Are Borderland Regions Public Management Instruments?" *International Journal of Public Sector Management* 25, no. 6/7: 483–91. https://doi.org/10.1108/09513551211 260685

Brunet-Jailly, Emmanuel. 2022a. "US-Canada Border Cities and Territorial Development Trends." In *Border Cities and Territorial Development*, edited by Eduardo Medeiros, 209–27. London: Routledge.

Brunet-Jailly, Emmanuel. 2022b. "Cross-Border Cooperation: A Global Overview." *Alternatives, Global, Local, Political* 47, no. 1: 3–17. https://doi.org/10.11 77/03043754211073463

Burkner, Hans-Joachim. 2019. "Scaling and Bordering: An Elusive Relationship?" *Journal of Borderlands Studies* 34, no. 1: 71–87.

Carstensen, Martin B., and Vivien A. Schmidt. 2016. "Power Through, Over and In Ideas: Conceptualizing Ideational Power in Discursive Institutionalism." *Journal of European Public Policy* 23, no. 3: 318–37.

Chen, Xiangming. 2005. *As Borders Bend: Transnational Spaces on the Pacific Rim*. Lanham, MD: Rowman & Littlefield.

Clarkson, Stephen. 2001. "The Multilevel State: Canada in the Semi-Periphery of Both Continentalism and Globalization." *Review of International Political Economy* 8, no. 3: 501–27. https://doi.org/10.1080/09692290110055858

Cooper, Anthony, and Chris Perkins. 2012. "Borders and Status-Functions: An Institutional Approach to the Study of Borders." *European Journal of Social Theory* 15, no. 1: 55–71.

Fischer, Eric. 1957. "The Spatial Factor in Political Geography." In *Principles of Political Geography*, edited by Hans W. Weigert, Henry Brodie, Edward W. Doherty, John R. Fernstrom, Eric Fischer, and Dudley Kirk. New York: Appleton-Century-Crofts.

Gattinger, Monica, and Geoffrey Hale. 2010. *Borders and Bridges: Canada's Policy Relations in North America*. Oxford: Oxford University Press.

Jones, Stephen B. 1945. *Boundary Making: A Handbook for Statesmen, Treaty Editors and Boundary Commissioners*. Washington, DC: Carnegie Endowment for International Peace.

Kent, Jonathan D. 2011. "Border Bargains and the 'New' Sovereignty: Canada-US Border Policies from 2001 to 2005 in Perspective." *Geopolitics* 16, no. 4: 793–818.

Kolossov, Vladimir. 2005. "Border Studies: Changing Perspectives and Theoretical Approaches." *Geopolitics* 10, no. 4: 606–32.

Konrad, Victor, and Emmanuel Brunet-Jailly. 2019. "Approaching Borders, Creating Borderland Spaces, and Exploring the Evolving Borders between Canada and the United States." *Canadian Geographer* 63, no. 1: 4–10.

Laine, Jussi P. 2016. "The Multiscalar Production of Borders." *Geopolitics* 21, no. 3: 465–82.

Leuprecht, Christian, Emmanuel Brunet-Jailly, Todd Hataley, and Tim Legrand. 2021. "Patterns of Nascent, Ascendant and Mature Border Security: Regional Comparisons in Transgovernmental Coordination, Cooperation and Collaboration." *Commonwealth and Comparative Politics* 59, no. 4: 349–75.

Longo, Matthew. 2017. "From Sovereignty to Imperium: Borders, Frontiers and the Specter of Neo-Imperialism." *Geopolitics* 22, no. 4: 757–71.

Mignolo, Walter D., and Madina V. Tlostanova. 2006. "Theorizing from the Borders: Shifting to Geo- and Body-Politics of Knowledge." *European Journal of Social Theory* 9, no. 2: 205–21.

Newman, David. 2006. "Borders and Bordering: Towards an Interdisciplinary Dialogue." *European Journal of Social Theory* 9, no. 2: 171–86.

Ohmae, K. 1990. *The Borderless World*. New York: Harper Collins.

Ohmae, Kenichi. 1995. *The End of the Nation State: The Rise of Regional Economies*. New York: Free Press.

Paasi, Anssi. 1996. *Territories, Boundaries and Consciousness: The Changing Geographies of the Finish-Russian Border*. New York: John Wiley and Sons.

Paasi, Anssi. 1999. "Boundaries as Social Practice and Discourse: The Finnish-Russian Border." *Regional Studies* 33, no. 7: 669–81.

Parker, Noel, and Rebecca Adler-Nissen. 2012. "Picking and Choosing the Sovereign Border: A Theory of Changing State Border Practices." *Geopolitics* 17, no. 4: 773–96.

Rumford, Chris. 2006. "Introduction: Theorizing Borders." *European Journal of Social Theory* 9, no. 2: 155–69.

Sack, Robert David. 1986. *Human Territoriality: Its Theory and History*. Cambridge, UK: Cambridge University Press.

Schmidt, Vivien A. 2011. "Speaking of Change: Why Discourse Is Key to the Dynamics of Policy Transformation." *Critical Policy Studies* 5, no. 2: 106–26.

Sohn, Christophe. 2020. "Border Regions." In *Handbook on the Geographies of Regions and Territories,* edited by Anssi Paasi, 298–310. Cheltenham, UK: Edward Elgard Publishing.

Strassoldo, Raimondo, and Giovanni Delli Zotti, eds. 1982. *Cooperation and Conflict in Border Areas.* Milan, Italy: Franco Angeli Editore.

Whittlesey, Derwent. 1944. *The Earth and the State: A Study of Political Geography.* New York: Henry Holt and Company.

Contributors

Bates-Eamer, Nicole, *University of Victoria*. Nicole Bates-Eamer has a PhD in political science from the University of Victoria. Her recent research examines narratives and policies related to the intersections of climate change and human mobility within Canada and beyond. Nicole managed the Borders in Globalization research program and conducted research on British Columbia's borders and border policies in the Pacific Northwest.

Brunet-Jailly, Emmanuel, *University of Victoria*. Emmanuel Brunet-Jailly is a Professor and Jean Monnet Chair, School of Public Administration/ co-appointed Department of Political Science; he is Director of *BIG_Lab* a Research Laboratory of the Centre for Global Studies, University of Victoria, British Columbia, Canada. He is principal investigator on *21st Century Borders*, a Social Science and Humanities Research Council of Canada partnership grant, and of several European Erasmus+ grants. Emmanuel has published on comparative urban governance, governance and theorization of cross-border regions in fifteen books and special issues of academic journals, and over one hundred book chapters and articles. He is editor of *Borders In Globalization_Review*, and the director of the *BIG_Lab Data Base* project that documents worldwide dyads.

Everett, Karen, *Laval University*. Karen Everett is a senior research associate with the Canada Research Chair on Comparative Aboriginal Condition at Université Laval (Québec City, Canada). Prior to this, she was a postdoctoral fellow at Université Laval and a research scholar with the Arctic Futures

Initiative at the International Institute for Applied Systems Analysis (Lax-enburg, Austria). She completed her PhD at the Frost Centre for Canadian Studies and Indigenous Studies at Trent University (Peterborough, Canada), where she studied border management in the Canadian North.

Ferrill, Jamie, *Charles Sturt University,* is the discipline lead and lecturer in financial crime studies and lecturer at the Australian Graduate School of Policing and Security, Charles Sturt University. She has nearly a decade of law enforcement experience, having worked for the Canada Border Services Agency before her academic career.

Green, Alexandra, *Royal Military College.* Alexandra Green is pursuing a PhD in war studies at the Royal Military College of Canada. Her antici-pated thesis topic is cyberterrorism. Alexandra is a graduate of Carleton University's Masters of Infrastructure Protection and International Secu-rity program, where she was awarded a Social Sciences and Humani-ties Research Council grant to fund her research in target selection and extremism. During her undergraduate studies at Queen's University she was awarded an undergraduate fellowship, the John Rae Award, the Women in Defence and Security Scholarship, and the Chancellor's Schol-arship, and she was placed on the Dean's List with Distinction. She has engaged in research projects about border security, terrorist resourcing, countering violent extremism, policing, and critical infrastructure. She has been published in the *Journal of Money Laundering Control,* the *Serene-risc Digest,* and in books such as *Top Secret Canada: Understanding the Canadian Intelligence and National Security Community,* and *"Criminology at the Edge":
Big Data in Criminology.*

Hale, Geoffrey, *University of Lethbridge.* Geoffrey Hale is professor emeri-tus of political science at the University of Lethbridge.

Hataley, Todd, *Fleming College.* Dr. Todd Hataley is a professor in the School of Justice and Community Development at Fleming College. He is a retired member of the Royal Canadian Mounted Police. During his ten-ure as a federal police officer, he investigated the cross-border smuggling of drugs, weapons, and humans; money laundering; organized crime; national security; and extra-territorial torture. Dr. Hataley is also an adjunct associ-ate professor at the Royal Military College of Canada. His research cur-rently focuses on managing international boundaries, money laundering, Indigenous policing, and transnational crime.

Lackenbauer, Whitney, *Trent University.* P. Whitney Lackenbauer, PhD., is Canada Research Chair (Tier 1) in the Study of the Canadian North and professor in the School for the Study of Canada at Trent University. He is the author or editor of more than fifty books.

Lajeunesse, Adam, *St. Francis Xavier University,* PhD, is an associate professor teaching in the Public Policy and Governance program at St. Francis Xavier University.

Leuprecht, Christian, *Royal Military College,* and *Queen's University.* Christian Leuprecht is Class of 1965 Professor at the Royal Military College of Canada and editor-in-chief of the *Canadian Military Journal.* He also directs the Institute of Intergovernmental Relations in the School of Policy Studies and is an adjunct research professor in the Australian Graduate School of Policing and Security at Charles Sturt University. A former Bicentennial Professor in Canadian Studies at Yale University, Eisenhower Fellow at the NATO Defence College, and Fulbright Research Chair in Canada–US Relations at John Hopkins University's School for Advanced International Studies, he is an elected member of the College of New Scholars of the Royal Society of Canada and recipient of the Cowan Prize for Excellence in Research at the Royal Military College of Canada.

Morin, David, *University of Sherbrooke.* David Morin is full professor at the School of Applied Politics of the University of Sherbrooke. He is also cochair of the UNESCO Chair on Prevention of Radicalisation and Violent Extremism. His expertise and professional experience address national and international security.

Muller, Benjamin, *Western University.* Benjamin J. Muller (PhD, Queen's Belfast, 2005) is program coordinator and associate professor in migration and border studies at King's University College at Western University. Over the past two decades, Dr. Muller has published extensively on the political and sociocultural impact of surveillance and identification technologies on migration, borders, and borderlands, including his pioneering monograph *Security, Risk and the Biometric State* (Routledge 2009). Collaborating on and codirecting numerous funded research projects, Dr. Muller has given dozens of guest lectures to academic and nonacademic audiences, and served as an invited expert on biometrics and borders to the government of Canada, the European Union, NATO, and INTERPOL. He has also been an invited research fellow at several universities in Canada and the United States.

Nicol, Heather, *Trent University.* Heather Nicol is the director of the School for the Study of Canada Studies, director of the Frost Centre for Canadian Studies and Indigenous Studies, and a professor of geography in the School of the Environment at Trent University. Her research is focused on exploring the dynamics that structure the political geography of the circumpolar North, with a specific focus on the North American Arctic and Canada–US relations. Her recent work is focused on cross-border relations, tensions, geopolitical narratives, and mappings of power and sovereignty. She is currently exploring circumpolar geopolitics in relation to globalization, security, the environment, and governance. Nicol is a Fulbright Scholar and was the 2015–16 Visiting Fulbright Chair to the University of Washington, at the Centre for Canadian Studies and the Henry M. Jackson School of International Studies.

Quigley, Kevin, *Dalhousie University.* Kevin Quigley is Scholarly Director of the MacEachen Institute for Public Policy and Governance and professor at the School of Public Administration, Dalhousie University, Halifax, Nova Scotia.

Reyes Marquez, Carolina, *University of Sherbrooke.* Carolina Reyes Marquez specializes in immigration issues in Canada and Québec. She is a PhD student in political science at the University of Toronto and a lecturer on Canadian foreign policy at L' Université de Sherbrooke (UdS). She holds an MSc in international migration and public policy from the London School of Economics as well as a bachelor's and master's in political science from UdS. In addition, Carolina has worked in federal and provincial public service, for Employment and Social Development Canada, and for the ministère des Relations internationales et de la Francophonie du Québec.

Roussel, Stéphane, *École nationale d'administration publique.* Stéphane Roussel is professor of political science at École nationale d'Administration publique. From 2002 to 2012, he was professor at the Université du Québec à Montréal. He held the Canada Research Chair in Canadian Foreign and Defence Policy. He graduated from Université de Montréal (PhD, 1999). Dr. Roussel was president of the ISA Canada section in 2004–5 and the Québec Association of Political Science in 2010–11. He worked regularly with Canadian forces, including at the Canadian Forces College (Toronto), the Second Division of Canada, and the Régiment de Maisonneuve. His research interests relate to Canadian foreign and defense policy, with particular emphasis on relations with the United States and European countries. He has also developed expertise in related fields, such as international relations theory and military history. Dr. Roussel has published several articles and books related to these themes, including *The Politics of Canadian Foreign Policy* (with Kim Richard Nossal and Stéphane Paquin; Pearson Canada, 2015). He currently directs two research programs, Competing Views of Emerging Challenges in the Arctic, and Québec's Strategic Culture.

Sundberg, Kelly, *Mount Royal University*. Kelly Sundberg is an associate professor in the Department of Economics, Justice, and Policy Studies at Mount Royal University. He holds a PhD in criminology from Monash University, an MA in leadership and training from Royal Roads University, and a BA in political science from the University of Victoria. Prior to his academic career, Kelly served for more than fifteen years with the government of Canada in various immigration and border-security, investigations, and policy-advising positions.

Trautman, Laurie, *Western Washington University*. Dr. Laurie Trautman is the director of the Border Policy Research Institute at Western Washington University, where she engages in a range of research on the Canada–US border space, and the Washington State–British Columbia region. In addition to working with faculty, scholars, and students, she collaborates with the private sector and government agencies to inform policy solutions and advance cross-border collaboration, both regionally and globally. Laurie is a Global Fellow with the Woodrow Wilson Center for International Scholars and a Fellow with the Canadian Global Affairs Institute.

Williams, Stephen, *Dalhousie University*. Stephen Williams is the director of policy, planning, and performance at the Edmonton Arts Council. He holds a master's degree in public administration from Dalhousie University (2015) and was a research assistant at the MacEachen Institute for Public Policy and Governance for this project. He is currently developing courses for the Arts and Cultural Management program at MacEwan University, in Edmonton.

Index

Abbotsford, 30
Aboriginal people: government of, 17, 34; standing senate committee, 175. *See also* First Nations people
Africa, 6
Alaska, 26–27, 33–34, 41–42, 82, 179, 189; Alaskan Panhandle, 163; border with Yukon, 161–169, 175–176; oil spill in, 37
Alberta, 17–20, 26, 31–34, 37, 81–82, 87, 89, 163; oil and gas production, 55–59; pipelines in, 61, 67; policing, 69–70
Amtrak, 44
Arctic (Canadian), 20, 161, 165; Ocean, 165, 168; security of, 170–182
Arctic Economic Council, 168
asylum, 28; seekers of, 131–133
Atlantic (Canada), 17, 19–20, 56, 127, 139–150, 155–156, 189
Australia, 152
automotive industry, 19, 85, 107
Azores, the, 142

Beaver Creek, 163–164, 175
Belgium, 5
Bellingham, 34
Beyond the Border initiative, 38, 41, 152
Biden, Joe: administration of, 63

biosecurity, 81–81, 84–85, 89–95, 167
Brazil, 147
British Columbia, 17–18, 20–21, 25–43, 50–59, 65–71, 89, 130, 174, 191
Bush, George W., 14
Byers, Michael, 176–177

Calgary, city of, 51–54, 71–72, 82; International Airport, 67–68; Police Service, 65, 68, 70
Cambodia, 6
Canada Border Services Agency (CBSA), 35, 52, 100–101, 108, 111, 114–115, 130–133; Alberta 65, 71–72; North, 171–172, 176–179; RCMP cooperation, 29–30, 42–43, 68–69; reduced hours, 164–165; shipping, 143–145
Canada Energy Regulator (CER), 67–68
Canada Post, 42–43
Canadian Armed Forces, 113, 152, 169, 175, 179
Canadian Coast Guard, 30, 101, 113, 142, 165, 169, 175, 178
Canadian Meat Council, 82
Canadian National Railway, 54, 68
Canadian Pacific Railway, 68
Canadian Passenger Accelerated Service System (CANPASS), 18, 40

Toronto, city of, 85, 104; Pearson International Airport, 109
trade volume, 98–100, 103, 106, 111, 116, 148, 192
Trans Mountain, 59, 68
transnational, 5, 11, 37–38, 124–125, 135, 169, 173, 192, 195; crime, 117, 130–131, 147
Trudeau, Justin: government of, 63
Trudeau, Pierre Elliott, (airport), 122
Trump, Donald: administration of, 128, 131; Trumpian, 28
Tuktoyaktuk, 163, 166
Turner Road, 82

Uighur Muslims, 4
unconventional security threats, 170, 173, 181
United Kingdom, 5, 152
United Nations, 58, 141, 176
United States Border Patrol (USBP), 133
United States Coast Guard, 116, 169
United States Customs and Border Protection (CBP), 68, 114
United States Western Hemisphere Travel Initiative (WHTI), 29, 32, 41

University of Alberta, 181
University of Windsor, 102

Vancouver, city of, 26, 34–36, 43, 52, 54, 59, 85, 143, 145, 152–153; International Airport, 66; Island, 26, 44; Port of, 146
Venezuela, 54
Vermont, 122, 127, 150
Victoria, city of, 26, 39, Island, 178
Vietnam, 6

Washington (State), 25–36, 41–44, 66, 92
Washington, DC, 11, 22
Western Washington University, 34
Whatcom Council of Governments, 33, 42
Whitehorse, 163, 165
Windsor, 99–102, 107, 114. *See also* Detroit
Wisconsin, 58, 61, 102
World War II, 9

Yukon Territory, 26, 33–34, 42, 161–165, 168, 171–176, 189